The Good Study Guide

Ann

This publication is a set book on the Open University courses K100 *Understanding Health and Social Care,* and *Living in a Changing Society* (see inside front cover). Details of these and other Open University courses can be obtained from the Course Reservations Centre, PO Box 724, The Open University, Milton Keynes MK7 6ZS, United Kingdom: tel. +44 (0)1908 653231; e-mail ces-gen@open.ac.uk

Alternatively, you may visit the Open University website at http://www.open.ac.uk where you can learn more about the wide range of courses and packs offered at all levels by The Open University.

To purchase this publication or other components of Open University courses, contact Open University Worldwide Ltd, The Berrill Building, Walton Hall, Milton Keynes MK7 6AA, United Kingdom: tel. +44 (0)1908 858785; fax +44 (0)1908 858787; e-mail ouwenq@open.ac.uk; website http://www.ouw.co.uk

Acknowledgements

Grateful acknowledgement is made to *New Statesman and Society* for permission to use the following material in this book:

The article 'Spend, spend, spend', by Carl Gardner, from *New Statesman and Society,* 16 December 1988.

The table (Ownership of communications and information facilities among households in selected income groups) from the article 'Pulling the plugs on democracy', by Peter Gidding and Graham Murdoch, in *New Statesman and Society,* 30 June 1989.

The Open University
Walton Hall, Milton Keynes
MK7 6AA

First published 1990, reprinted 1991 (twice), 1992, 1993, 1994, 1995 (twice), 1997, 1999, 2000, 2001

Edited and designed by The Open University.

Typeset by Medcalf Type Ltd, Bicester

Printed in Great Britain by The Bath Press, Bath

ISBN 0 7492 0044 8

C O N T E N T S

Preface

This book sets out to help you improve your study skills, whether you are just starting to study, or have been studying for some time. If you are a 'beginner' you may not be sure how well you will cope with serious reading. You may have difficulty concentrating and wonder whether anything is 'going in'. You may wonder how and when to take notes. You may feel unsure about writing essays. This book will help you to confront such issues and find new ways forward.

On the other hand, if you are a more experienced student, you may be getting on reasonably well but want to develop further some particular aspect of studying, such as structuring essays, or planning your strategy for an exam. This book is organized in such a way as to make it easy to look up specific topics which are relevant to you, whatever the stage of studying you have reached. It is designed to be a reference book which you can return to regularly over many years as you continue courses of study and meet new challenges.

The book has a strong practical focus derived from many years of discussing study processes with students and working out ways of developing new skills. It draws most on the experience of students of Open University social science courses. Because of this it is especially relevant to anyone who is returning to study as an adult after a long 'lay off' and anyone who is studying part-time. On the other hand, the book is not *only* for people who are starting studies at degree level, or for people studying social sciences. It is for anyone studying a course which involves reading texts and writing essays and it is deliberately written to be useful even if you are a long way off thinking about studying at degree level. In fact, it was specifically intended for use by students taking Community Education courses with the Open University, as well as for use by students of the Social Sciences Foundation Course. It will also be useful for students of many arts and humanities courses.

It is not a book of quick, 'off-the-shelf' remedies for study problems. This is because it is written in the belief that becoming a good student is a long-term process of changing habits of working and ways of thinking about what you are trying to achieve; in the belief indeed that learning to study effectively is one of the most challenging and satisfying undertakings open to us, and is therefore deserving of serious thought and effort. However, it is not a book full of dry, formal instruction and rules. Instead, it is based on practical exercises and carefully discussed real examples, so that you can think for yourself about the processes of studying and work out new approaches which will suit *your* learning style and *your* circumstances.

Personal acknowledgements

Any book which emerges from an Open University team is inevitably the product of many minds. This book has benefited enormously from the comments and ideas of many Open University tutors and students who worked with earlier publications of study skills exercises and advice. More immediately, I must thank all the members of the D103 Foundation Course Team, who read drafts and gave detailed advice; in particular Marilyn Ricci, James Anderson, David Coates and Elaine Storkey. Then there were the members of the 'tutor panels', Lyn Brennan, Alan Brown, Ian Crosher, Donna Dickinson, Norma Sherratt, Jan Vance, Mona Clark, Phil Markey, and Brian Graham, who undertook heroic assignments of rapid reading and commentary; my thanks to them. Also to Ellie Chambers of the Institute of Educational Technology, who read and appraised every word of every draft and to Chris Wooldridge, who as editor gave painstaking attention to the all-important details.

I am also indebted to the students of the Tower Hamlets Institute who undertook reading and writing tasks and then permitted me to use their work in this book and to Peter Chester their tutor, who made that possible. Finally, I am grateful to Carl Gardner for permission to use his article as a basis for study exercises.

Andrew Northedge

Note to readers

To get the most out of the practical exercises in this book you will find it very useful to have photocopies of certain pages of the book. You should be able to get access to a photocopier at your local library, or at your local stationery shop, or photographers. The items you should photocopy are as follows:

1 The article by Carl Gardner on pages 240–43. Make two copies of this.

2 The essays by Sam and Ann on pages 115–17.

3 The revised versions of Sam's and Ann's essays on pages 119–20 and 138–40.

CHAPTER **1**

Getting started

1 How to use this book

This is not a book you sit down with and read from cover to cover. It is a book to dip into and select what you need; to begin now and come back to many times.

The skills of studying are not something you can read about once and instantly understand for all time. You learn them gradually through trial and error, through repeated practice, and through stopping to reflect on your experience. If this book is any use, you will need to return several times to the sections which are relevant to *your* particular study concerns. The way you understand and approach challenging study activities, such as note taking, or essay writing, will change as your abilities as a student develop. Passages discussing these skills will take on new meanings as you come back to them over a period of years.

Indeed, the topic of study skills is not one for beginners only. A pianist does not stop practising and seeking expert advice because he or she has 'finished' learning how to play. Whatever stage you reach in an area of skill there is always something to gain from going back over your technique and attempting to refine it. Moreover, you do not necessarily need very *different* advice when you are more expert at something. There are often basic truths about performance which you need to return to periodically and understand again at a new level. For this reason it is not easy to grade the various sections of the book as 'beginners' material', 'intermediate', or 'advanced'. You will find some ideas relevant right away because of the particular study tasks in which you are engaged. But you may find them just as relevant again in a year or two's time.

This book is therefore intended for students of all levels from absolute beginners to the comparatively experienced. This chapter starts with the assumption that you have not studied for a long time, but the following chapters include *both* introductory level discussion *and* more advanced ideas. It is up to you to pick out from them what is useful to *you* at the stage you have reached.

To help you find your way to what you need, the contents list is fairly detailed, and there is also an index at the end of the book. In

1

addition, the text has been organized with the main points picked out in boxes, the idea being that you can skim through, reading just the boxes if that is all you need. The briefest summaries are in 'key points' boxes like this:

> ## KEY POINTS
>
> This is a 'key points' box.

There are also 'discussion boxes' like this:

Discussion boxes

Discussion boxes contain short discussions of specific topics, which you can read without going into the main body of the text.

However, if you are looking for a fuller explanation you can settle down to read the main body of the text. In many places this includes closely worked examples to show exactly what is meant. To get the most out of these examples you will sometimes need to stop reading and carry out an activity.

ACTIVITY BREAK This is the first 'activity'. Make sure you have got yourself properly sorted out for studying this book.

▶ Where are you reading this book? Will you be able to concentrate without disturbance?

▶ Have you enough space to work in?

▶ Do you have pen and paper handy in case you need to carry out a writing task?

If not, sort yourself out.

These boxes and breaks allow you to read the book at different levels of detail, depending on what you currently need. In fact, each chapter goes into a fair amount of detail and this is another reason why you shouldn't try to take everything in at one attempt. In any case, you need to mix *reading* about studying with *practising* it. If you sat down to read through a manual on all the skills of perception and muscle control used in skateboarding before you even tried it, you would probably become too confused ever to start. You would have far too many abstract things to think about. Similarly, there is a real danger, if you wade too quickly into a lot of detailed discussion of study principles, that you will freeze up when you try out the real thing. As with skateboarding, the best way to start studying is to pitch in and have a go and not worry too much if you fall over. Then pick up any advice you need as you go along. Use this book as a resource when you are not making progress and feel ready for some fresh ideas.

The ideal way to use the book is as part of a course, where you have a teacher and other students, rather than working at it all on your own. You can then come to its various sections bit by bit, as suggested within the course. It was specifically written for use with the Open University Foundation Course in Social Sciences and with shorter courses produced by the Department of Community Education at the Open University.

On the other hand, the book will work perfectly well on its own if that is what you need. You will, however, need to work out a plan of attack. I would suggest that you work either by the skimming and dipping method, or by reading about ten to twenty pages at a time and then leaving the book for a while.

KEY POINTS

▶ If you are starting to study for the first time in many years, you will probably find that this book goes into a lot more detail than you need at first.

▶ Don't be put off. Take a little at a time. Skim through and find the bits which relate to what you are currently working on.

▶ Expect to take two or three months to work your way through the book.

2   Why read about study skills?

Why should you need a book on studying anyway? Isn't it a fairly straightforward activity? You read textbooks, or you listen to lectures, and then you write your essays. What could be simpler than that?

But perhaps it isn't so simple . . .

Michael looked up again and saw it was now 7.20 p.m. — nearly an hour since he'd started and still he was on page two. Only another hour and he'd have to go and collect Fran from her class — and would he ever get started again after that?

'Early start tomorrow morning — can't afford to be too late tonight. And there's the spy thriller from 9 till 10 o'clock — only two more episodes to go — can't miss this one. I wonder what that East German agent was doing in Mexico? . . . No! I must get back to the sociology — or perhaps a cup of coffee would help the old concentration a bit — the last one didn't though — and that was only 20 minutes ago anyway.'

He looked at his note-pad. The title of the book and the chapter heading were neatly written across the top. The rest was blank. They said you should make notes as you read — but notes of what?

'No point copying out the book. "Sum up what you have read." How? . . . What is there to sum up? Is it totally obvious, or have I missed the point? . . . apart from those ridiculously long words, which don't make sense even when you read the definition in the dictionary. Why am I bored? I was expecting to be stimulated. The cover of the book looked quite attractive. Now I can't get through it. Every sentence has you switched off before you can find your way to the end of it. Is it just a joke? . . . A great big con? . . . Perhaps I should sort out my desk before going any further . . .'

The phone rang. It was Robbie . . .

He brought back another cup of coffee and sat down again.

'Only half an hour left now. Must concentrate. Let's go back to the top of page two — on second thoughts, I may as well go right back to the start and try to get some notes down, since I can't remember a word of it. . . . Good grief! It still seems like garbage. Oh forget it! . . . It's too late to get anywhere now. Let's slip down the old pub for a quick half before getting Fran. I can always give it another go later on, after the serial . . .'

Meanwhile, in another room a few streets away . . .

Sandy dropped another crumpled ball in the wastepaper-basket and stared blankly at the pad. What now? She had made half a dozen starts and hadn't once reached the middle of a page before rolling it up in disgust.

'How can I be stuck when I've hardly started? How long is this whole thing going to take? Will it ever be done? Not at this rate! . . . "It is the retailers rather than the manufacturers who shape society in the 1990s: discuss." How do you start on a subject like that? How am I supposed to know what shapes society? Even the textbook doesn't seem to be able to make up its mind. What shape is it anyway? What if I wrote, "Yes and no, depending on your

point of view" . . . *or perhaps I could just take a few sentences from here and there in the textbook and change the words round a bit — at least they couldn't say I'd got it wrong. But then the tutor said to write in your own words . . .'*

As her mind slipped back to the classroom she winced. Why hadn't she kept quiet, as she'd meant to? She knew she didn't really understand what all those articulate types were spouting about — but the tutor seemed so keen for everyone to speak. When she'd finally wound herself up to say something it had been ages before there was a gap in the discussion — by then the subject had moved on. But the tutor had looked straight at her, so she'd blurted her point out — so fast that no one knew what she was talking about. They had pretended to 'use' what she'd said as they carried on the discussion, but she knew she'd made a right idiot of herself. How could she face going back again?

'Anyway — I didn't come away with that much — no notes. In fact I can scarcely remember a thing that was said. Why not give it a miss this week? Or would the tutor be offended? . . . Oh well — think about it later. Must get back to this miserable essay. I could try unrolling some of those balls and see what I wrote. No, I couldn't bear to read a single word. How about looking up "society" in the dictionary and starting from there? . . . Why am I doing this to myself? . . .'

Is it really as bad as that? Surely not; at least not *all* the time. On the other hand there *are* occasions when things *do* look pretty bleak. Although Michael and Sandy are fictitious, their problems are real enough — and they are not ones faced only by *new* students, or *'weak'* students. They are *general* problems which we all face when we study — problems of *struggling to understand*, of *managing time*, of *completing a task*, and of keeping up one's *morale*.

One of Michael's problems is *finding* enough time for study between his social commitments, his work commitments, and his leisure interests. And both of them have problems *using* what time they have effectively. Both are concerned about *what* they should be doing and *how long* it should be taking them. Both are *stuck* and cannot see a way forward. Michael is repeatedly distracted — by a phone call, by his own thoughts, by making coffee, by tidying his desk, and most of all by the 'boredom' he experiences when he reads the text. Sandy is distracted by her revulsion when she reads her own words and by her general feelings of inadequacy as a student. She sees herself as a very weak student and feels overawed by the tutor and the other students. Because of this she is approaching the essay in a very tentative way, which makes it difficult for her to get a good grip on the subject and 'express' her ideas. Instead, she is sitting almost hypnotized by the essay title, casting around in desperation for almost any way of getting shot of the essay. Both are feeling fed up and have lost the enthusiasm they had when they started their studies. They are in danger of giving up and wasting all those good intentions. They need some help!

On the other hand, they may both be doing better than they think. Studying *often* feels like a struggle — and it is in the process of struggling that important learning starts to happen. We have been spying on them at a particularly low moment, but since they are fictitious we can easily join them again when things are looking up . . .

Michael shunted the beer mat across the beads of moisture on the glossy table as he waited for Gina to finish her speech . . . 'so the point *is* that the whole fashion world is simply a way of making us buy more, so that businesses can make more profits.'

He rapped the edge of the mat on the table. 'But we *need* businesses to make profits, or the whole process of production would grind to a halt. And anyway, fashion can be enjoyable. Don't you *like* products to keep changing? Look at what you're wearing now!'

'That's on account of the way the media have distorted her value system,' Sandy chipped in with a smirk. 'Underneath that oh-so-sophisticated exterior, Gina is pining to be in a crofter's cottage weaving her own clothes. Aren't you Gina?'

'No — the point is that I don't *need* to be always seeing myself in terms of those glossy images of the "perfect woman" who lives a mythical life, flitting between moments of exotic romance. What has all that got to do with real life?'

Michael broke the mat in half. 'But you *enjoy* all those images — otherwise you'd ignore them. They enrich your ability to experience life. Where's the harm in it?'

'Don't look now,' Ali said to Sandy, 'But I think there's a *retail revolutionary* sitting next to you.' Michael grinned . . .

Later as they stood at the bus-stop Michael said, 'Nice bunch of people.'

'Amazing mixture,' replied Sandy. 'I thought they were all school-teachers and civil servants the first week. I didn't want to open my mouth in case I dropped a clanger.'

'Never thought I'd be sitting in a pub talking about social science. I didn't even think I'd ever make it through a whole chapter of the book, I was that long on the first. I still don't know how I stuck it to the end. And I *never* thought I'd be using all that jargon. Now it keeps coming out when I'm just having a chat. In fact the problem is how to *stop* it coming out when I chat to my mates.'

'Yes — makes you see everything differently doesn't it? I can't pick up a newspaper now without thinking, "Oh yes — there's so and so's theory — well, what about the opposite view?" '

'Yes — well you seem to pick it all up pretty easily.'

'Oh yes? Well you should have seen me struggling with that first essay. Nearly drove everyone in the house to a nervous breakdown — not just me. I still find the writing the worst. Still at least I seem to be improving . . . don't fancy the look of that next piece of reading though, do you?'

'Oh, I don't know — it could be quite interesting. Look out, here's your bus — see you next week — take care! . . .'

And so they both disappear into a rosy sunset and we see that studying can be wonderful after all — well I just wanted it to be clear that although studying is frustrating and tough it is also very rewarding and satisfying. It's like climbing mountains — you have a lot of hard slog on the way, and sometimes when conditions are poor you wonder why you bother, but when you reach the peaks it is also very fulfilling. Many students say that studying not only gives them greater knowledge and understanding of the subjects they study but also more *confidence, broader interests*, and more *purpose* in life. It helps them to achieve more in walks of life not necessarily connected with study at all. This is another reason why it is very well worth your while to study this book. If you develop a wide range of study techniques and strategies you will not only help yourself to succeed as a student but you will strengthen your capacities all round.

3 Getting yourself organized

When you first start studying it is difficult simply because it has no 'shape' for you. Until you have developed some kind of *system* for studying — until you can get a general feel for *what* needs to be done and *when* — you spend a lot of time dithering about, starting one thing and then another and wondering whether you are getting anywhere. Michael was clearly suffering from the lack of a thought-out purpose and plan. One of his main problems was how to *manage* his study time.

3.1 Managing time

In fact, he had *two* kinds of problems with time: *finding* enough of it, and *using* it effectively.

Finding time

He had *social* commitments (picking up Fran, talking to Robbie on the phone), *work* commitments (an early start the next day), and *leisure* interests (watching the spy thriller). *All* of these things are important. Is there enough space in between for studying? Adult students always have to make very difficult choices between calls on their time. When studying comes into your life it generally means that something else has to go out. And yet we all know what 'all work and no play' does. Even students have to have some fun. So this is one of the first problems you have to face — the juggling act you have to develop in order to keep an extra ball in play in your life. Effective studying often requires quite a *lot* of time and in fairly good-sized *chunks*. So you have to become an expert at *creating* time. One way to set about this is to draw up a chart of your 'typical' week and see where there is room for manoeuvre.

	Sunday	Monday	Tuesday	Wednesday	Thursday	Friday	Saturday
morning							
afternoon							
evening							

Figure 1.1 *Sample chart for indicating a 'typical' week's activities*

ACTIVITY BREAK   Draw yourself a chart of the kind shown in Figure 1.1. Work out the total study time you can reasonably expect to set aside and where in the week it falls. Try to identify where clashes are likely to occur and where you may have to cut back on some other things.

Don't be alarmed if you found this activity almost impossible. It is. Life is usually extremely messy. What is more, having made a plan, it is even harder to stick to it. But sticking to it is not necessarily the point. Even if you find that you are constantly having to change your plans it is *still* worth making the effort, because the decisions you make in changing your plans force you to think about *what* you are doing and *why*. Planning makes you think *strategically* instead of just drifting.

Using time

Michael was experiencing difficulty not only with finding *enough* time but also with *making effective use* of time. He could not decide what tasks to take on in the two-hour period available to him. By flitting about rather inconclusively he ended up finishing the session early, without really having achieved very much. To avoid this you need to develop ideas about *how much time* you need for *particular types of task* and how long to stick at them when you are running into overtime. You will find you can do some tasks (such as reading a difficult passage or writing a section of an essay) only when you are reasonably *fresh* and have a *good sized chunk of time* ahead of you, while others (such as organizing your notes, or reading through a draft of an essay) you can squeeze into odd moments, or manage when you are more tired. *People vary a lot in their patterns of working, so these suggestions may not be the right ones for you.* The point is that, to get the best out of yourself in the time you have available, you need to stop occasionally to *reflect* on whether you could parcel out your study time in different ways to get better results. Don't just plod on vaguely hoping for the best. You need to *manage* yourself more actively than that.

3.2 Completing a task

So far I have talked as though studying came neatly bundled into clear-cut tasks. Unfortunately, as Michael found, a lot of what you have to do as a student is extremely *weakly defined*. Indeed, it is a crucial part of your job to *create* the shape and size of the tasks you have to do. As an adult student *you* have to *define* tasks for yourself.

Defining tasks

The first thing is to have an *overall idea* of what you are hoping to accomplish in a given week. But you also need to define *smaller tasks*, such as 'reading the next ten pages of the chapter', so that you can decide how much *time* to give to each and so that you can *manage* yourself, i.e.:
– get yourself started,
– keep yourself going, and
– decide when to stop and move on to another task.

When you have set yourself a defined task, it is easier to focus your attention on it and to keep yourself working your way through it, resisting some of the distractions Michael found himself prey to. Moreover, as Sandy was finding, it is particularly important with a big task, such as writing an essay, to be able to break it down into a series of smaller tasks.

Why is it so easy to be distracted when you are studying?

It is the feeling of drifting in a sea of meaninglessness which makes you so ready to grasp at any straws of distraction you can find. When you don't really understand the text and don't really know what you are trying to do, it makes you feel restless and uneasy. Distractions offer you the chance to focus your attention on familiar and meaningful parts of your life and so escape from the uncertainties which studying often brings. The urge to avoid uncertainty is very strong. That is why it is so important to define clear-cut tasks for yourself to create a shape and a meaning for your work.

If you find that you keep stopping as you work, try setting yourself a smaller and more tightly defined task, particularly one with an *active* component in it. For example, if you keep drifting off as you read, get a highlighting pen and search for a key word or phrase in the first sentence of each paragraph. This will give you a more concrete task to focus on.

Typical study tasks you can define for yourself are:

▶ read the next two sections of the text you are studying

▶ make notes on an article you have read recently

▶ sort out and file the notes you have made over the past couple of weeks

▶ plan your next essay

▶ browse in the library, looking for useful articles and books

▶ gather together notes and ideas for your essay

▶ write a first draft of the main section of the essay

▶ make contact with other students

▶ attend class

▶ go over your study plans for the coming week.

You will get a fuller picture of the range of tasks you can define for yourself as you work through the rest of the book.

Having given some shape to your studies by identifying a number of tasks to be done, you then need to divide the time you have available between these tasks. I doubt whether you could ever do this in a precise way and then stick exactly to your plans. Studying is too unpredictable for that. But you can *set broad targets* which will help you to decide when it is time to stop doing one thing and start on the next.

Time versus task

Time management and *task management* are closely bound up with each other. You need to balance one against the other. If you become too obsessed with *time* (as Michael was), then you tend to think in terms of the 'hours put in' rather than what you have achieved. You may find that you start 'filling up' the time with relatively unimportant tasks, just to while it away until you can finish your session feeling virtuous. To avoid this, you need to set out to get a certain task, or tasks, finished (even if you don't always succeed). On the other hand, if you focus *too* much on the task you may let it drag on for much too long. That is why you need to switch your attention between both *task* management and *time* management to get a reasonable balance.

3.3 Practical arrangements

Setting up a place to study

Many people find it important to establish a place where they regularly sit down to do their studying. Ideally you need to be able to work undisturbed, with space to spread your books and papers out, easy access to your files, and good lighting and heating. You may not be able to arrange all these, but it is important to try to get as close as you can, if you are to give yourself a reasonable chance.

Figure 1.2 *A typical study 'kit'*

11

If you cannot set up a regular study spot where you can get on without frequent distractions, you will find studying rather frustrating.

Equipment

You need to set yourself up with a good supply of pens; A4 note-pads; a box of index cards; cardboard pocket files; filing boxes; labels; shelf space; and a good dictionary.

Where to keep things

If you study for any length of time, you will soon begin to accumulate large amounts of printed material, handouts, your own notes, old essays, and so on. It is important to start being systematic about how you store all this material at an early stage in your studying. As one student put it, 'It is essential to develop a good piling system.' Better still, use folders, boxes and labels. In the end you will find that, as a student, it is not so much what you can *remember* that counts, as what you can *lay your hands on* when you need it.

Bookshops and libraries

As you begin your studies it is worth making investigations as to where the best bookshops and libraries in your area are and what they have available on the subject you are studying. It can seem rather off-putting to walk into a big library or book shop and try to locate the particular section you need, especially if you are not sure what it is called. But assistants can usually give you a lot of help if you take the plunge and ask them. You may be surprised at how much relevant material there is. On the other hand, you could be disappointed and find that you need to learn how to order books through the library or how to join in book-exchanging schemes with other students.

Social arrangements

Other people often don't realize just how hard you need to concentrate when you are studying; or else they simply cannot resist the delights of your conversation. Unless you can arrange to be left alone while you study, you are in for a very hard time. It is difficult enough to think with the intensity required for making sense of subjects which are new to you. If you are going to be interrupted frequently you will require the patience of a saint. In other words, make sure the people around you understand your study plans and know when to leave you alone.

KEY POINTS

As you start on your studies you need to think carefully about the following things:

▶ *Managing your time*, which involves:
  – *finding* time by planning out your week
  – *using* time effectively by doing work of different kinds in the most suitable time slots.

▶ *Defining tasks* for yourself, then:
  – *allocating time* to them, and
  – *monitoring your progress* as you attempt to complete them.

▶ Setting up a *place* to study.

▶ *Equipping* yourself.

▶ *Organizing* things so that you can find them.

▶ Exploring *bookshops* and *libraries*.

▶ Sorting out arrangements with *family* and *friends*.

4   What is studying all about?

4.1   Learning

The purpose of studying is to *learn* and learning consists of three things:

▶ *Taking in new ideas* (and by taking in I mean *making sense* of new ideas, not simply 'hearing' and 'memorizing' them).

▶ *Thinking through new ideas* and fitting them alongside your existing ideas so that you build up a better general *understanding* of the subject you are studying.

▶ *Expressing newly formed ideas* by talking and writing about them.

Taking in ideas

Although the first aspect of learning looks rather obvious, it is easy to overlook the *making sense* element and assume that learning is simply a matter of 'cramming' lots of facts into your head — as though you could do it by reciting lists of words over and over, or repeatedly re-reading notes. Learning in this 'memorizing' sense is a very restricted form of learning. It may come in useful for learning the vocabulary of another language, or for remembering all the Wimbledon finalists for a sports quiz, but its place in most courses of adult study is very small indeed. It is rather misleading that TV shows like *Mastermind* and *University Challenge* give us the impression that being clever simply involves knowing lots and lots of facts. It *may* be the case that clever people often *do* know lots of facts — but the reason they can get at the facts quickly during a quiz is to do with how well they have the facts *organized* in their minds. What really distinguishes people who know a lot about a subject is the *understanding* they bring to bear on it; the *ideas* they have available for discussing it. Getting new ideas into your head is what Chapters 2, 3 and 4 are about.

Thinking

Thinking is not a thing you would normally sit down to do in its own right. It happens while you are busy doing other things. In fact, you think a *lot* when you are getting on with *writing notes* on a chapter of a book, *discussing* with other students, *jotting down ideas* for an essay, or *'boiling down' your course notes* into a concentrated form for exam revision. These kinds of activities may seem like extras which are tagged on to 'bigtime' activities such as *reading* and *writing*. But they are *not* 'small-time' or marginal aspects of studying. The odd moments when you are jotting down bits and pieces to yourself, for one reason or another, are often times when you are doing a lot of *thinking*, and you should not undervalue them. There is no chapter specially devoted to these thinking activities, because they tend to be meshed in with the other more obvious ones, but we shall come across them many times scattered through the book.

Expressing ideas

The third aspect of learning ideas is to be able to *use* them to say things about the world. You can learn how to do this both through speaking and through writing. Chapter 3 discusses the speaking side and then Chapters 5 and 6 take a detailed look at writing. Speaking and writing are not just things you have to do to *show* what you have learned. Expressing ideas is *part* of the learning. Until you can *use* ideas to *say* things for yourself, you have not really *mastered* them. The time you spend speaking and writing is just as crucial to your progress in learning as the time you spend listening and reading.

One thing these three aspects of learning have in common is that they are all *active* processes. They are not things which 'happen' to you while your mind quietly dozes, or while you plod routinely through a set of exercises. They require purposeful action on your part.

4.2 Being an adult student

As an adult student *you* have to take responsibility for your *own* studies. In our years as schoolchildren our teachers were prepared to take a lot of the responsibility for *what* we learned and *how* we learned it. At school level there is a general understanding that if pupils do badly in an exam their *teacher* is also open to criticism. By contrast, as an adult student it is up to *you* to *choose* a subject you want to study and to decide how much *effort* to put into studying it. Your teachers do *not* assume responsibility for telling you *what* to learn, nor *how* to learn it, nor do they put pressure on you to *make* you learn it. You have to 'manage' these things for yourself. You have to decide your own priorities, set your own targets, and work out your own strategies for achieving them.

What is more, you also have to take on responsibility for deciding *what views to hold*. As school pupils, much of what we were given to study was presented as *facts*. We gained marks for the *accuracy* with which we could repeat to the teacher what we had been told. Adult students find that the 'truth' about things is taken to be *uncertain*. Teachers expect *you* to form your *own judgements* about the strengths and weaknesses of various ideas. Your studies are an enquiry into the nature of the world which *you* are undertaking. You have to be able to *weigh-up* ideas, not just *learn* them. You have to be able to *argue* for one idea against another, not just *repeat* both. The whole emphasis changes from your being a passive *receiver* of 'knowledge' to your being an active *seeker* for 'understanding'.

This does not happen all at once. If you are returning to study after a long lay off, it is likely to take quite a long time to adjust. Nevertheless, your target is eventually to become an *independent* student: to be able to find your way round a subject for yourself, even when there is no teacher available to assist you. Instead of jumping through hoops held up by other people and then waiting to find out whether you have 'passed', you set your own agenda and study to find out whatever it is that *you* want to know. When you can take control of your own studying you are in a position to make knowledge and understanding really do some *work* for you.

4.3 What *are* study skills?

There are many different aspects to learning how to study, all of which tend to be gathered under the general heading of 'study skills'. This is a slightly misleading term because it suggests that they are all the same *kind* of thing. It also implies that they are learned in the way you might learn the 'physical' skills of catching a ball or controlling the clutch of a car. As you know, if you want to learn a physical skill, you have to practise it over and over again. You don't need to *think* much about it; you just keep doing it until you get the results you want. In fact, if you *do* think a lot about what you are doing, it tends to put you off. You miss the ball or crunch the gears. With this kind of learning you cannot take shortcuts. You just have to put in the hours, repeating and repeating the activity. However, many of the capabilities you need to develop as a student are *not* skills of that kind.

Habits

Some of the capabilities you need for studying are *habits* of work, such as how you set out your study table, where you sit, and when you take your breaks. You do not need to become 'skilled' at these kinds of things — you just need to establish certain routines, because they help you to get on with the job quickly and avoid distractions.

Techniques

Other capabilities you need for studying are *techniques* for accomplishing particular tasks — such as the way you set out your notes on a page, what abbreviations you use, how you file your notes, how you use paragraphs to structure an essay, and so on. You need *experience* in using a technique, to see how it works and how to modify it to suit your needs. So your 'performance' *does* gradually improve, as you refine your technique. But this is as a result of *thinking* about what you are doing and experimenting with different approaches. Techniques are not things you learn simply by mindless repetition.

Strategies

Another set of capabilities you need are better understood as *strategies*. These include such things as 'the way you allocate your time to study', 'the approach you take to preparing an essay', or 'the way you draw on the support of other students to help you along with your studies'. You develop these strategies by:

▶ *reflecting* on your past experience

▶ trying to *predict* future events and needs, and

▶ *analysing* the resources available to you and working out how they can best be used.

Capabilities are not produced by routine practice but by thinking, imagining and planning.

Understanding

Finally, to enable you to be effective in *reflecting, predicting* and *analysing*, you need some *understanding* of the processes of study. This is learning in the realm of *ideas* rather than *skills*.

Where the concept of skill comes in useful is in connection with the larger scale study activities; such as writing an essay, giving a presentation to the class, finding relevant articles in the library, or preparing for an exam. These are complicated activities which require you to give attention to several things at the same time. The first few times you do them you can easily give too much attention to some aspects while overlooking others, whereas a 'skilled' person would be able to 'orchestrate' a collection of habits, techniques and strategies into a successful overall performance. In the same way, a skilled job interviewee or a skilled TV presenter is someone who can orchestrate a wide range of activities, judgements, words, images, etc. into a successful ensemble.

Different kinds of 'study skills'

A good illustration of the differences between types of learning which tend to get lumped under the heading 'skill' would be the skills you have to learn to be able to use a desktop computer for word processing.

Physical skills

If you are not able to type and you set out to learn touch typing, then you have ahead of you a very long period of practising and practising. This is a true *skill* of the conventional 'physical skill' type. It will be several months at least before your typing speed is really satisfactory. Nothing your 'mind' can do will speed up the process of learning. You simply have to put in the hours.

Techniques

When it comes to using the word processor itself, however, there are many simple *techniques* to be learned, such as how to 'save' a document, how to underline words, and how to cut a section of text and 'paste' it elsewhere. These can be learned by working through a few exercises. After a short period of trial and error you soon have the hang of them.

Strategies

Then there are more general *strategic* things to learn, like how to use the storing and filing capabilities of the computer, how to

---

get it to help you with structuring your documents and so on. These take more thinking through and you can get very helpful general principles from textbooks on the subject.

Understanding

And finally you may want to develop a more general knowledge of how the word processor works within the operating system of your computer, so that you can, for instance, set the computer up to produce special effects for you. To do this you would need to develop 'ideas' or 'models' in your mind of how a computer works. This requires reading manuals and other books and hours of 'playing around', seeing what happens if . . . This kind of learning is *very* different from learning to touch type. So when people talk about 'computing skills', or even 'word processing skills', they are in fact referring to a wide range of very different capabilities.

The point of drawing out these distinctions between different uses of the word 'skill' is that this book is *not* setting out to present you with a range of very specific activities to practise over and over mindlessly, such that when you have mastered the whole set you will have become, once and for all, a 'skilled' student. Instead, it offers exercises to help you to *think* about different aspects of studying and to develop a range of *strategies* for approaching your studies. It also suggests various *techniques* you can try and *habits* you might need to develop. 'Study skills' is a convenient and widely used term and it will not cause any problems, so long as you remember that the skills referred to are not like simple 'physical' skills such as spinning a top. They are like 'craft' skills — like, say, the broad knowledge of principles, the understanding of materials, and the methodical, co-ordinated approach of an old-fashioned, 'skilled' furniture maker.

In the next chapter we begin to look at some of these skills in more detail.

KEY POINTS

▶ When you study you have to:
  – take in ideas
  – sort out the ideas in your mind
  – express ideas.
  (This book is about these three processes.)

▶ As an adult student you have to:
  – decide your own priorities
  – set your own targets
  – work out your own strategies, and
  – make up your own mind about ideas.

▶ The term 'study skills' covers a range of capabilities, some of which you can develop quickly, while others take a long time.

▶ Many study skills involve *thinking* about how you learn and *reflecting* on the usefulness of your study habits.

CHAPTER **2**

Reading and note taking

1 Introduction

Reading is one of the core activities of studying. Obviously you can *already* read in the technical sense, or you would not be following this sentence, so we are not talking about reading at *that* level. What we are concerned with is:

▶ having to do a *lot* of reading

▶ reading *difficult* material, and

▶ trying to *remember* what you have read;

the kinds of challenges Michael was facing in the last chapter.

The easiest way to start finding out about coping with these challenges is to *have a go*. You will find a short piece to read on pages 240–43 at the end of the book. It is an article taken from the weekly magazine *New Statesman and Society*, of 16 December 1988. *It is important that you read this article because a lot of the discussion in this chapter and in later chapters will assume that you have.* (Please note that paragraph numbers have been added for ease of reference.)

Note:

Before you read the Carl Gardner article, try to make copies of it. Your local library, stationery shop, or photographer might have a photocopier which you can use. You will find it very useful indeed to have *two* spare copies of the article; one to use now and one for use with Chapter 6. If you make photocopies, you can have this chapter and a copy of the article in front of you at the same time. You will also be free to write and make marks on the article without worrying.

On page viii of the Preface, I suggest that you will find it useful to have photocopies of certain other pages of this book, for use in connection with Chapter 5. You may find it convenient to do all the photocopying at the same time.

ACTIVITY BREAK   Read the article 'Spend, spend, spend' by Carl Gardner now (see pages 240–43). Then write down your thoughts on the following questions. Don't spend long — just a few quick reactions are all you need. You will find it useful to have a written record, so don't skip the writing.

1   What were your *feelings* as you read the article?

2   Did you experience any *difficulties* or *problems* as you read?

3   Were there parts of it you found *unclear*?

4   Did you find the article *useful*, or *interesting*?

5   How *long* did it take you?

6   *Where* and at *what time of day* did you do the reading?

7   In a sentence, *what was the article about*? (Don't look back — work from memory.)

8   What can you *remember*? What two or three points stuck in your mind as worth noting? Do you think you would find it easy to remember what was in the article in a few days time?

9   Did you *mark* words as you read (using a highlighting pen or underlining with a ball-point)?

10 Did you make any *notes*?

Here are the answers one student, Bob, gave.

(1) The long and technical words were frightening and I wondered whether they were actually necessary. It seemed cold and futuristic and not designed to be read by me.

(2) I decided to read slowly in order to digest what I was reading but the words became laborious. I found myself reading fast and missing key issues; places and dates just became a jumble of statistics that I thought was left to me to put in some kind of order. The long words and sentences destroyed any chance of there being a narrative.

(3) There were many parts I found difficult to decode on the first reading, particularly paragraph 8. The retailisation of Britain, I felt could have been explained better. Carl Gardner has tried to cram too much information in short paragraphs.

(4) After the second reading I found the article quite interesting. It had a political and economical flavour to it, highlighting some big multinational companies and what they have in mind for potential customers. I found some analogies quite humorous.

(5) A long time.

(6) (no answer)

*(7) The article was about the changing face of shopping centres —
how they affect us and the way we see them.*

(8) Points which stuck in my mind:

*– Shopping is a form of disease with shoppers reduced to mere
helpless victims.*

*– It's a vantage-point from which they can see and be seen, an
essential element of the voyeuristic shopping centre culture.*

*I can remember quite a bit of the article, but in a muddled order.
The central theme of shops and shopping sticks but the statistics and
names of architectural jargon would probably make me explain what
I have read in a haphazard way.*

(9) I underlined a few words which I meant to look up.

*(10) I made a few points to guide me but this was really to help me
put things in some kind of order.*

How do these compare with your answers?

To throw more light on these answers and your own, we shall
consider the questions more closely.

2 Reactions to reading

The first four questions are to do with the impact the reading task
made upon you. Perhaps it seems strange to begin by asking about
your *feelings* as you were reading. But how you *feel* about what you
are doing has a big effect on *how well* you do it.

2.1 Feelings about reading

As we have seen, Bob was intimidated by some of the long technical
words and doubted that they were necessary. He felt the article was
not written with him in mind; that it was addressed to a more formal
audience. He found the reading became heavy going and he felt
muddled by some of the more detailed information. He felt too much
was being crammed into a short space. However, by the time he had
read the article again he found it quite interesting.

I too had mixed feelings as I read the article. In fact I was not even
sure at first that I *wanted* to read about shopping centres. Then I
was put off by the second sentence because I didn't know what
exactly was meant by 'raw tech' and 'neo-constructivist', and I had
never heard of 'Crighton Design'.

Difficult words

Should you stop and look up difficult words in the dictionary?

It depends. Obviously it slows you up if you have to stop a lot.

You have to decide whether a word seems important. Does it keep coming up regularly? Do you seem to be missing something?

In this case I doubted that I would find the words anyway and I decided I could just guess and carry on rather than be held up so soon. If I had kept coming across them later in the article, I might have tried looking them up.

I started reading quickly and lightly — more 'skimming' than really reading carefully. I *underlined* 'clutch of new' and 'shopping centres' as I passed — because that seemed to capture the theme of the first paragraph. I floated over the names of the five places without really attempting to register where they were; just taking in the impression of a wide geographical spread. However, when I reached the last sentence of paragraph 1, I began to take more notice. I began to realize that I was reading about a large scale trend. Mammoth shopping centres were not a subject I had thought much about for some years — but apparently something quite significant was going on here. 'What kind of places is he referring to?', I asked myself.

Luckily the next paragraph tells us. So *with this question in my mind* I read on, underlining key words as I went. By now I was becoming absorbed in the article. I found paragraph 3 interesting because it shifted from the shopping centres themselves to the underlying trend in the economy. Paragraphs 4 and 5 then showed how wide-ranging and sophisticated these rapidly developing retail activities are, and paragraphs 6 and 7 described how their influence is seeping into our lives. All this I found easy and engaging reading.

In paragraph 8 the style of the article seemed to shift. Instead of fairly light and easy *descriptions* of changes, it started to be harder to read. I had to think quite a lot more from here to the end of the article. Suddenly we are discussing 'socialist *theory*' and its problems. (And what did the bit about the last 150 years mean — 150 years of what?) In fact, I found that paragraphs 8, 9 and 10 required particularly careful reading and thinking.

Coping with the hard bits

Did you manage to make sense out of paragraphs 8, 9 and 10? It isn't easy. In fact, the first sentence of paragraph 10 won't have made *any* sense unless you already know a bit about socialist theory.

This poses an important problem. What do you do when you cannot make sense of what you are reading? Should you go off and try to find out about 'post-Frankfurt left analysis of popular consumption'?

At this stage it isn't worth it. Instead, it would be better to start a list (or a set of concept cards; see Figure 2.1), where you jot down names or words which seem important and might be worth following up sometime. Just write down 'post-Frankfurt?' On the other hand, you might simply decide to ignore this hard bit for now, and see how you get along without knowing.

If you found paragraphs 8 to 10 too difficult to handle, don't worry too much. You will often find yourself in a position where you have had a fair try but just cannot work out the meaning. The important thing is that, even when you hit something you don't understand, you *can* move on and *still* get a lot of the main argument from the article.

Don't let the tough bits beat you! They may make more sense when you come back another time and from another angle.

Paragraph 11 felt easier to me. Worpole's basic points as set out in the last few lines seemed fairly straightforward. And paragraph 12 was interesting in its criticism of Worpole's views. But perhaps paragraphs 13 and 14 were the most compelling up to this point, because they stood the earlier arguments on their heads. These and paragraphs 17 and 18 seemed to offer a very challenging interpretation of the new shopping centres and gave me a lot to think about in terms of my own experience of them. By now I felt I had definitely gained some useful ideas. This carried me through to the end of the article and left me glad I had read it.

Notice that both Bob and I changed the *way* we were reading in response to how we felt as we read. Bob had *meant* to read slowly but found it was getting 'laborious', so he speeded up, even at the expense of 'missing key issues'. That was probably a good decision, in that it enabled him to keep going to the end. Then he read the article again and enjoyed it more the second time. By contrast, I started off reading fast and then slowed down because I began to be more interested and 'engaged' with the subject and I wanted time to think. Both of us 'succeeded' in that we got to the end of the article and found it interesting. There is no 'right' way to read. The important thing is to be able to be flexible in your approach; to be able to judge how well you are progressing and how you are feeling and to adjust your approach accordingly.

2.2 Your attitude towards the *topic* you are reading about

The first thing that affects your work is your level of enthusiasm for the topic you are reading about. In your leisure reading you can be selective and spend your time reading what you *like*. But one of the characteristics of studying on a course is that you are *set* subjects to read about, some of which may not appeal to you at first sight. This is potentially a big problem.

KEY POINTS

You cannot *learn* effectively unless you can *become interested* in the subject matter at *some* level.

Any subject can be interesting if looked at in the right way. *Whether* you are interested depends on what is currently on your mind. If you are starting on a subject you are *not* initially interested in, the first thing to do is pitch in and hope that the writer is able to *show* you some interesting angles. If you are unlucky and the writer does not grab your attention, then you need to shift your strategy and work out a way to *create* an interest in it. One way is to try to figure out *why other people have found the topic interesting*. What *questions* were they concerned with? Try to pose similar questions to yourself which *make* the subject more interesting to you.

Setting yourself questions

It is *questions* which make reading interesting. Unless you are reading with a question or two in the back of your mind (such as 'Are huge shopping centres here to stay?' and 'Do I mind?') you cannot *engage* with the words on the page in front of you.

When you can't get involved with the text you are reading it is either because you cannot see what *question* is being addressed, or because you cannot see the *point* of the question being addressed. You may need to stop reading and look at the preface to the book, or the conclusion, or skim a few other chapters — anything which helps you to form questions relevant to the subject you are reading about.

In this article I found that Gardner himself began to pose questions which engaged my interest (e.g. why so much is being invested in new shopping centres), and that was when my reading began to shift from 'skimming' to 'being absorbed' in the discussion.

Another approach is to try to connect the subject with *your own experience*. In this case, for instance, you could recall occasions when *you* have gone to shopping centres, and compare *your* experience with what the author says.

If that doesn't work, then just work out a strategy for 'getting through' the reading — such as searching for information on a specific aspect of the topic. In other words, if you cannot see a way of finding an 'intrinsic' purpose for yourself in the text, then *create* a purpose by actively seeking out something in the text.

If all else fails, just cut your way through the task by skipping large sections. You are not doing yourself, or anyone else, any favours if you just sit and wallow in a topic which is not engaging your thought-processes.

KEY POINTS

You are the person who has to *do* the learning and *you* are the person the learning is *for*. So *you* have to take charge and find a way to construct a *positive* approach to what you are studying.

2.3 Irritation with the language

Apart from the topic itself, you may react to the *way* the text is written. In particular, it is easy to be 'put off' by the words used, if some of them are new to you, or are used in unfamiliar ways. As I said, *I* was put off by some of the words in the first paragraph of the Gardner article. It makes you feel excluded from the 'in-crowd' of people who bandy all those terms around. And it also makes you feel frustrated by the struggle required to squeeze meaning out of the text. In fact, Bob found the words 'frightening' and he wondered whether they were really necessary.

One way to tackle the problem of difficult or technical language is to buy either a *specialist* dictionary for the subject you are studying (though these are sometimes rather difficult and technical themselves) or a good *general* dictionary (such as the *Concise Oxford Dictionary*) and keep it close at hand when you are studying.

Technical language

Everyone finds unfamiliar, specialist language off-putting and frustrating.

However, specialists always develop their own 'language', because it gives them extra power in analysing their subject in a detailed and systematic way. Indeed, as you study a subject and become more of a 'specialist' yourself, you will gradually find yourself using the same technical language without noticing.

Using technical language is not done deliberately to annoy students. Developing new ideas and fitting new words to them is part of the process of producing new knowledge about a subject. At times the technical language may be overdone, so that texts are unnecessarily obscure to the outsider. On the other hand, you cannot hope to enter a new subject area without having to learn a 'specialist' language.

Be forewarned. Try not to let irritation and confusion hinder your progress. Instead work out ways of tackling the problem.

Dictionaries

A dictionary is a very useful resource to have handy, but don't expect too much from it or treat it as infallible. Some specialist words will not appear in a general dictionary, and words that do may not be defined in the same way as they are used in your subject. If you try using a dictionary definition at the start of an essay, for instance, it will often lead you in the wrong direction, because the nuances of meaning are not right for your area of study. A dictionary is a useful guide when you are lost, but generally you will get a better insight into the meaning of key terms in your subject from the texts themselves.

Another approach is to have a system for writing down the difficult words you come across, so that you can add new clues to the meaning as you see the word used in different places. You could start a 'concept card' system, for instance, using a card index box, where you start a new card for each new word you think is important. You file the cards alphabetically so that you can find them easily and add new bits of information as you come across them. Why not try starting one and see whether it suits your style of studying. It is probably worth buying a small card index box. You can then try out various ways of using it in organizing your studies.

Retailization

Gardner: NS&S. 16 Dec. '89 — seems to be about the economy being run by the retailers. Growth of the new 'high-tech' shopping centres. Expansion of the retail design business etc.

Figure 2.1 Sample of a 'concept card'

Use of 'quotation' marks

While we are on the topic of words, why does Gardner keep putting words in quotation marks?

Are they all quotations? Not strictly — so what is he signalling?

Look again at the first eight paragraphs of the article and see whether you can work out what he is doing with the quotation marks.

My answers are as follows:

"drawbridge" "Mediterranean village"	The quotation marks are to signal that these are not a *real* drawbridge, or Mediterranean village — but 'mock-ups'.
"food courts" "eating experiences" "pleasure parks"	These in a sense *are* quotations from the vocabulary of the retail trade. When he uses " " he is saying, 'This is *their* language not mine'.
"alienated" "progressive" "raw tech"	These are specialist terms from social science and architectural debates.
"retailization"	I would guess this is a word made up on the spot by the author.
"spend, spend, spend"	This is a genuine quotation from a woman who won the pools in the early 1960s.

2.4 Frustration with the style

Some people are also put off by the 'academic' style of writing. What you read in everyday life usually *starts* from a well-defined point of view. It is often trying to *persuade* you of something, or it is proposing a particular *solution* to a problem. Academic textbooks, on the other hand, are generally much less committed to reaching a quick answer. You find that, instead of directly attacking a specific 'real-life' problem, broad abstract questions are raised. You may feel that the author is wilfully taking the long route all around the houses, instead of coming straight out with a view. Then he or she may offer a conclusion couched in very guarded language: 'It would seem therefore that . . .', or 'We may encapsulate the thrust of this argument as follows . . .'.

Elaborately cautious language

Everything said in academic texts tends to be cushioned in very cautious language.

In fact, this is a *necessary* part of academic writing. The writers are trying to be as *exact* as they can in their analysis, so they are careful to say *only* what they think can be justified. In everyday life we cheerfully use language as a blunt instrument for cudgelling our way through the cut and thrust of events around us. However, in academic writing language is meant to be used more like a scalpel, cutting precisely between closely related arguments, so that they can be prised apart and analysed in detail. An academic writer aims to say exactly what he or she means to say, even if it takes quite a lot of extra words.

To take an example, at one point in his article we find Gardner saying, 'One recent estimate of the value of the burgeoning British design business posited a figure of £1.7 billion . . .', instead of coming straight out and saying, 'The British design business is worth around £1.7 billion'. Here he is alerting us to the fact that it is *very difficult* to assess the size of something like the British design business. One person has tried and 'posited' (i.e. estimated) £1.7 billion, but it is quite possible that someone else would attempt the calculation in a different way and produce a very different figure. This uncertainty is deliberately reflected in the way Gardner presents the figure to us.

Bob noted that Gardner (like any academic writer) tends at times to use long and complicated sentences, which made it hard to read the text as a 'narrative'. In fact, the text is not simply a 'narrative' in the sense of telling a story. It is an argument (see Chapter 5, page 118). It requires you to pay careful attention and to stop and think.

> **KEY POINTS**
>
> An academic text is not a *narrative* — it is an *argument*.

Bob also made the interesting comment that the article was 'cold' and 'not designed to be read by me'. Academic writers aim their words at an 'academic audience'. They assume a cool, detached and very critical reader. They take for granted that you will be interested *only* in the logic of their arguments; that you would be suspicious if they wrote in a friendly style and that you would think they were trying to cover up weaknesses. They write to try to convince you of the strength of their arguments, not to make friends with you.

> **KEY POINTS**
>
> An academic text aims to be unemotional, detached and logical.

2.5 Disagreeing with the author

You can feel very frustrated simply because you do not agree with the point of view of the writer. You might, for example, be strongly opposed to the 'spending culture' of modern society, and find the whole approach that Gardner takes, in 'celebrating' shopping, very irritating. When you are reading, it is rather like a conversation with a very talkative person who goes on and on without any breaks for you to speak. It can feel very oppressive if you disagree at a fundamental level and want to raise an objection. It is very hard to carry on 'driving' yourself forward through the text.

On the other hand, *many* ideas seem implausible when you *first* come across them. If you were only to read what you already agreed with, you would not learn very much. Part of studying is learning to *cope* with not feeling too happy with what the author is saying — *distancing yourself* from your hostile feelings and reading on to see what arguments are put forward. Eventually, you may or you may not decide that the author has a point, but you need to give yourself the chance to find out what is on offer.

A detached stance

Logic is supposed to work best when it isn't distorted by passions. Thus when you are reading academic texts you are supposed to 'detach' your thoughts from your feelings. You are expected to put your own biases to one side and judge arguments by their strength and their soundness.

However, as a reader you cannot be entirely 'detached', or you wouldn't have a position from which to think about, to judge and to criticize what you read, so perhaps 'semi-detached' would be a better way of putting it.

Detachment is, of course, an ideal rather than something you can stick to all the time. You are bound to have feelings, especially when you disagree with what you read. Indeed you can use these feelings constructively. When you disagree with a text, try to write down your criticisms and your counter-arguments point by point, instead of just feeling irritated. You can learn a lot by reacting *against* what you read, if it helps you to sort out your own ideas.

2.6 Feelings and motivation

KEY POINTS

Managing your feelings

It is very important as a student to be able to *manage* your feelings towards your work. You need to be able to find ways of:

▶ building upon your enthusiasms, and

▶ avoiding sinking into despair when you hit hard times.

Specifically you need:

▶ to be able to make the topic interesting to yourself

▶ to accept specialist language and take it in your stride

▶ to accustom yourself to the style in which academic texts are written

▶ to learn how to read arguments you disagree with — making constructive use of your reactions by writing your criticisms down.

Managing your feelings involves:

▶ *recognizing* what your feelings are

▶ *reflecting* on the effect they are having on you, and then

▶ *working out* what to do about it.

You have made a beginning with the first of these simply by noting down how you felt about the reading task in this chapter; and with the second by reading the above paragraphs about reactions to reading. The third you will have to explore as you proceed, by trying out different patterns of study, drawing on support from teachers and fellow students, and switching activities when you begin to be weighed down. It is vital to make studying enjoyable and interesting if you are to learn and to keep on studying over a long period.*

3 Your reading strategy

We shall now think about the *way* you set about the reading task which you were given at the beginning of this chapter — the *strategy* you adopted.

3.1 Context

Where and when did you do this reading? Were you lying in bed, sitting at a desk, having a bath, on the bus or what? Any of these *might* be a good time and place — but it is worth pausing to think about how well they work for you. Were you able to maintain a period of steady concentration? Did you have the necessary materials to hand; for example, pen, paper and dictionary? Do you need a surface to write on as you read? Do you need to keep moving to different places to read, or are you best off establishing a regular spot? Decisions on these questions may make a significant impact on how effectively you read.

3.2 Speed

How quickly did you read the article? The issue of *reading speed* is one of the most persistent worries of students. *There always seems to be much more to read than you have time for,* so you will feel a tremendous pressure to read more quickly. In fact, it is surprising how much you *can* pick up by pushing yourself through a few pages quickly.

---

* Incidentally, if you enjoyed reading the Gardner article and are interested in finding out more about Carl Gardner's views on the subject, they have subsequently appeared in book form: Gardner, C. and Sheppard, J. (1989) *Consuming Passion: The Rise of Retail Culture*, Unwin Hyman.

Scanning first sentences

It can be very useful to read quickly through the first sentence (or two) of each paragraph to find a key word or phrase in each.

Doing this for the first nine paragraphs of the Gardner article, I came up with:

shopping centre
basic features
investment
refurbishment
marketing and design
rise in sales
leisure
socialist theory
cultural, social and psychic shifts.

I would say this list gives me a pretty good general picture of what this section of text deals with. It tells me what *topics* it is about. But it doesn't save me the job of *reading the arguments* in the article. I couldn't find out what Gardner is trying to *say* by looking at this list, though it *is* useful to have a quick guide to the contents of this part of the article.

The list would:

▶ help me to decide whether I want to go on and read the article properly

▶ put me in the right frame of mind for understanding the article

▶ remind me afterwards of what the article dealt with (i.e. this is one way of taking notes).

There will be many times in your studies when you need to move even faster than this, scanning very quickly through a lot of pages to get the gist of the topics and issues dealt with, or to find specific information. However, it is important to be clear that this is not *reading*. It is *skimming*. Skimming can tell you *about* a text, but it will not enable you to *learn* what is *in* the text. For that *you need to follow the argument*. If you are trying to grasp the core argument of a major text, then *you need to slow right down* and take it bit by bit, making plenty of notes as you go.

The purpose of reading

The underlying purpose of reading is to *develop your thoughts*; to weave *new ideas* and *information* into the understanding you already have and to give *new angles* to your thinking.

If you try to bypass this *thinking* process, you are not really *learning* as you read. Learning is to do with changing your ideas, combining them together in new ways and extending them to cover new ground. Reading a text is one way in which you trigger off these changes.

The purpose of reading is *not* to have a lot of words pass in front of your eyes, nor to add a few new items to a long 'list' of information in your mind. It is to engage your ideas and make you *rethink* them.

You cannot afford just to read at whatever speed comes 'naturally'. If you are trying to keep abreast of a course of study, you often have to push yourself to do a lot more reading than you would achieve at a 'natural' rate. However, there is a wide range of reading speeds, from a lightning skim through a whole book to the intensive study of a difficult paragraph. You need to become accustomed to working at different points on that scale depending on the circumstances. *How* fast you should go will depend on:

▶ *what you already know about the subject* you are studying
▶ how *difficult the text is*, and
▶ *how thoroughly you need to understand it.*

So how long did you spend on the Gardner article and how long *should* you have spent?

If you spent fifteen minutes on it you may have picked up all the points you needed. On the other hand, if it made you stop and think a lot, it could easily have taken more than half an hour. If you were also taking notes it might have taken an hour. If you read it more than once it could have been an hour and a half.

Because of my own special interest in the article (for the purposes of this book), I have now spent *several hours* on it. The longer I worked on it the more interesting I found it and the more clearly I grasped the issues it deals with. You would have no reason to spend nearly so long, but it shows that there is no 'right' amount of time to spend. It depends entirely on what you are trying to achieve.

Time investment

By taking up study you are *investing* your own *time* in developing your intellectual powers.

Sometimes you will get a good return by investing in a very detailed reading of a small section of a text which is central to your current interests.

At other times you will get a good return by dipping into several texts here and there and skimming in order to broaden your ideas.

Basically *you* have to decide what your current *needs* are and what *opportunities* are open to you and then *distribute your time investment* across these options in a way which gives you a good overall return.

This is easier said than done, of course. But a key test is to ask yourself, 'Is this making me *think*?', 'Am I getting a better *grasp* of the subject?' If the answer is no, the time you are investing is being wasted and you need to switch to a new activity.

As a very rough rule-of-thumb you might want to think in these terms:

Easy text; fairly familiar material   *100 plus words per minute*

Moderately hard text which you
want to follow reasonably closely   *70 words per minute*

Difficult text; unfamiliar subject
matter which you want to
understand in depth   *40 words per minute*

These speeds would give you reading times for the Gardner article of approximately 19 minutes, 27 minutes, and 48 minutes respectively.

KEY POINTS

You need to adjust your reading speed according to:

▶ the kind of text it is

▶ your purposes in reading.

3.3   Time chunks

Apart from sheer speed, there is the question of how you divide up your study time. With a two-page article you would assume a single study session, but a chapter of a book might be spread over several sessions, depending on the chapter (how long it is and how difficult) and on your own time constraints. But it is important to recognize that your span of concentration is limited and that you cannot expect to learn intensively for hour upon hour. It is wiser to divide up your reading time into several sessions during a week rather than attempt a single long session.

If your reading sessions are *too* short you will not have time to get properly into the frame of thinking required by the text before you break off. You might, perhaps, find two hours a reasonable span for a session, particularly if you are studying after a day of work. On the other hand, after an hour of intensive concentration you might need to take a short break or switch to another task. Take some time to *'observe' yourself* and your reading habits. Think about what works best for you within the general contours of your life.

3.4   Targets

All this brings us back to the point made in Chapter 1, that *as well as* being a student, you also have to act as your own *manager*, deciding:

▶ what your *overall goals* are

▶ what your *immediate priorities* are, and

▶ whether the *results* you are getting are as good as you could reasonably *expect*.

It is easy to slip into just plodding forward, hoping for the best and losing sight of the overall purpose of the exercise; but once you cease to study in a purposeful, 'managed' way your efficiency as a learner will drop sharply.

KEY POINTS

To 'manage' your reading effectively you have to keep:

▶ *defining reading tasks* and setting yourself *targets* (e.g. number of pages to read this evening)

▶ *monitoring* your progress on the reading task, and then

▶ *re-setting* your targets in the light of this.

3.5   What if you get stuck?

Sometimes as you read you will get stuck. When this happens, don't just sit staring at the page, or going over and over the same few sentences. Find an active way of tackling the problem.

Reading requires you to 'project' meaning into the words in front of you. When you are stuck it means that you have lost track of the argument and can no longer see the way it points ahead. So you have to find ways of reconstructing the argument in your mind. One way is to *cast around for clues* by looking elsewhere in the text. You can look *back* to the earlier parts — checking the title, the contents list and the introduction to remind yourself what the writer claimed to be setting out to discuss, and re-reading some of what you have covered, to firm up the arguments again. Or you can look *ahead* a few pages or more, to see what is going to be coming up; or turn to the conclusion to see where the argument eventually leads. If you are still stuck, you might look for clues in other books on the same subject, or in lecture notes, or you could phone other students to ask for help.

Another tactic is to try to use your pen. Try to write down the main questions you think the text is addressing. Try to summarize what you have read so far, particularly the part just before the point where you are stuck. Try underlining words that seem important in the section you don't understand and then see if you can summarize what those words are saying. The notes you make may not be very 'sound', but the process of writing them will help you to 'get into' the text. Writing makes you 'take hold' of ideas and put them in your own terms. It helps you to force makeshift meanings on to the subject matter, from which you can construct a base for launching your next assault on the text.

If you are still stuck, just skip ahead and see if you can pick up the thread again somewhere else in the text. Or just leave the text altogether and start on another piece of work. Perhaps it will seem clearer when you return to it. In any case, there is no point in sitting achieving nothing.

KEY POINTS

When you are stuck:
▶ Make an active attack on the problem.
▶ Look for clues in the earlier parts of the text, or later on.
▶ Make detailed notes on the preceding section and on the bit you are stuck on.

4 Memory

Were you able to write down the main points of Gardner's article immediately after you had read it? How much will you *remember* in a week or two? How much *should* you be able to remember?

When Bob answered the quiz at the beginning of the chapter he said:

I can remember quite a bit of the article, but in a muddled order. The central theme of shops and shopping sticks but the statistics and names of architectural jargon would probably make me explain what I have read in a haphazard way.

I don't think Bob needs to worry about remembering things in a muddled order. Basically the *order* isn't important; it is the central arguments that you need to grasp. He said he remembered the central theme, which is good, but he was worried about the statistics and names. I certainly didn't bother to remember *any* of the names. And I only tried to get the 'general idea' of the figures — that we are talking about the 1980s and about growth of between 50 and 75 per cent. Would it be worth writing down Chelsea, Liverpool, etc? Why should you? You are *not* reading to find out about these particular places but about the new trends in shopping centres.

Facts, figures and names

Should you try to remember facts, figures and names as you read?

It depends what you are reading for. Often the answer is no — you only need to get the general gist of the information. But if you think the details might be useful to hang on to, then *write them down*. Don't try to memorize them.

Bob also said that he remembered two very specific points. One of these was about shopping as a 'disease' (which was actually the opposite of Gardner's point of view), and the other was about the voyeuristic element in shopping centre culture (which is a rather marginal point). This shows how we engage with ideas which have a specific relevance to our interests of the moment; and how they stay with us, bobbing about in our thoughts, whether we choose to remember them or not. In a sense this is 'real' learning: when we read things which feed directly into our current thinking. We may not be aware of having 'remembered' them, but they strike a chord and set us thinking along new lines. However, it also shows that we cannot rely entirely on what we remember spontaneously. We need to make a special effort to attend to the main thrust of the author's argument and take down notes which capture the essential points.

Actually, how would you know how much you remember? Would it count as remembering if you found yourself quoting Gardner's views in a casual conversation — or should you be able to sit down with a piece of paper and write out all the main points? The fundamental question is whether the article has made any changes to the way you think about shopping centres and about the 'retail boom'. If it has, then these changes will remain as substantial traces in your mind of the process of reading the article. You will be able to detect this development of your ideas if you try re-reading the article at a later date, because it will be much easier to read.

Remembering what you read

The purpose of reading something is *not* to be able to store the whole text in your mind. Even an author re-reading something written some time before will find ideas he or she has forgotten ever having. If even the author is not in a position to recall in detail all that is written in the chapter you are reading, why should you want to be? What you want is to be able to 'think' with the ideas the author has presented, should you choose to.

You know you have retained some of what you have read when you can read the same piece more easily a second time, and when you can read other texts on the same subject more easily. It shows that your mind has retained some elements of the reorganization it achieved during the original reading.

The point of reading is to be able to *understand* what you read and to be able to *get back to* the ideas at some future point when you need them again. Holding them in your mind is by no means the only way. You can often construct a much more reliable route back to ideas you have been reading about by making *notes*.

KEY POINTS

Don't worry about your memory. Just write things down. It's what you understand that counts.

---

5 Taking notes

Did you have a pen in your hand as you read the Gardner article? Reading is an *active* process of *'making' sense* as you read. One way of keeping your mind active as you read is to use your pen.

ACTIVITY BREAK If you didn't take notes on the Gardner article go back over it quickly and jot down a few points.

When you have some notes answer these questions.

1 What do you think is achieved by taking notes?

2 What *uses* do you think you might have for the notes?

3 Where will you *keep* them?

4 Did taking notes *change your understanding* of the article?

5.1 Highlighting and underlining

When I was reading the article I was continually marking it with a ball-point pen. You could equally well use a highlighting pen. Some people use several colours of pen to mark for different purposes — yellow for general interest, pink for essay-related material, and so on.

I underlined only a couple of phrases in paragraph 1, but then I began to be a bit more active with my pen in paragraph 2. Figure 2.2 shows the underlining I did. How does it compare with yours? Why do you think I used double underlining in three places? 'Basic features' is what the paragraph is about. The other two phrases seemed to me to sum up what is distinctive about the new centres. (Sometimes, where the text has an argument, I find it useful to pick out the words I underline in such a way that I can read them more or less like a sentence. However, with this descriptive passage it didn't seem necessary.)

I underlined a lot of the first sentence in paragraph 3, but only 'refurbishments and rebuilds' in paragraph 4 (the paragraph seemed to be just filling in on changes to existing centres). I double underlined 'new images', 'interior styles' and 'time shopping', as these phrases summed up paragraphs 5 and 6 for me. Otherwise it was just the odd word. Paragraph 7 had such a strong 'visual' content, I thought it would be very easy to remember, so I only underlined 'themed' — to remind me what it was about. I carried on this way to the end of the article, varying my underlining depending on the nature of the material.

2 Though varied in size and style, nearly all centres offer the same <u>basic</u> <u>features</u>. Most importantly, there are <u>spectacularly engineered</u> <u>glass atria</u> or <u>glazed</u> barrel-vaults to flood the shops and walkways with <u>natural light</u>. <u>Plants and trees</u> by the forestfull are being used too, and many of the shopping centres are finished in polished steel with mirrored walls and marble or terrazzo flooring. For winter and night-time use, they bristle with the latest in <u>high-tech</u> lighting — massive <u>heating</u> and <u>air-conditioning</u> systems provide <u>perfect environmental control</u>. Those on several floors generally have opened-sided escalators, or glass-sided, wall-rising lifts to give customers a short <u>scenic ride</u>. And many have incorporated centrally located 'food courts', offering a range of 'eating experiences' where customers can sit and eat. More importantly, it's a vantage-point from which they can see and be seen, an essential element of the <u>unashamedly</u> voyeuristic shopping centre culture.

Figure 2.2 Sample of text underlined after reading

There is no *correct* way of underlining. *You* may have had excellent reasons for marking quite *different* words. It depends on what your mind focuses on as you read. I just offer my markings as a stimulus to your thoughts about:

▶ *how much* underlining you do, and

▶ *what* you choose to underline.

The value of highlighting and underlining

Does writing on a book seem rather vandalistic?

I suppose it depends whether it's yours. If it is, marking the text as you read, using a highlighting pen, or underlining key words with a ball-point is an extremely valuable way of:

▶ focusing your *attention* on the text

▶ making you *think* about what the key concepts and issues are, and

▶ leaving a *trace* on the page of the sense you have been making of the text.

When you come back to a marked text you can quickly tune into the thoughts it evoked on first reading. This is all the more true if you also write occasional comments in the margin — *questions* that come to your mind as you read, *examples* which illustrate the meaning of the text, etc.

> Marking the text is a way of moderately increasing your *time investment* as you read, while considerably increasing the pay-off — both in terms of your immediate comprehension and in terms of your long-term recall.

You don't *have* to underline as you read, and certainly not *all the time*. It can make reading too boring and slow you down too much. In any case, not all texts require such detailed attention. On the other hand, if you scan back over material you know you have read, but haven't marked, and you find that very little seems to have stuck, it can be rather disheartening. It boosts your morale tremendously to be able to see your familiar markings, offering direct evidence of the attention you have already given the text, and leading you to the heart of the argument.

5.2   Note taking proper

When you want to get seriously to grips with a text, however (say, because you want to write an essay on it, or you want to be able to answer an exam question on it), there is really no alternative to written notes. Taking notes forces you to *think*; to 'grapple' with the ideas in the text as you read them, because you have to *decide* what to write down and how to say it. Even if the notes themselves are not particularly good, the activity of writing them pushes you much further into the meaning of the text. What is more, if you read without taking notes, no matter how good your 'memory', you will find that the ideas gradually drift away from you: not simply because you 'forget', but because later reading that you do will give rise to *new* ideas which push out your present ones. You will then find that, although having read a particular book has produced some *general* shifts in your thinking, you will not be able to get back to the *details* of what went through your mind while you were reading. So although note taking is hard work and quite time-consuming, it is an extra investment which adds a lot to the value of the effort and time you are already investing in the reading.

But what kind of notes should you take? There are many different ways of taking notes, depending on:

▶ the way your mind works
▶ the kind of text it is
▶ what you want to use the notes for
▶ the amount of time you think it is reasonable to 'invest'.

KEY POINTS

Notes should *not* be simply a shorthand *copy* of the original text. They should be an attempt to pick out the 'bones' of the text — or more specifically those points in the text which are *relevant* to *your studies*.

One way to do this is to carry out the exercise already suggested in Section 3.2 — writing down key words from the first sentence (or two) of each paragraph. However that on its own would not be enough. You would not be able to make sense of the words at a later date. You need to put more of *your own thinking* into it. It would be useful, for example, to have a sentence *summarizing the main theme* of the article. Bob wrote, 'The article was about the changing face of shopping centres — how they affect us and the way we see them.' This would serve as a useful general reminder, though it would be even more helpful if it indicated *how* shopping centres are changing and *what kind* of effects they have had on us. One way of keeping a sketch of the content of the article would be to jot down notes on a card from a card index box, as in Figure 2.3.* This might provide all the notes you need.

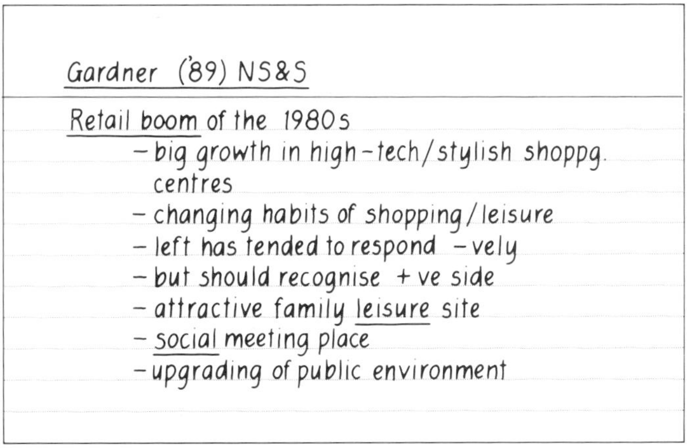

Gardner ('89) NS&S

Retail boom of the 1980s
- big growth in high-tech/stylish shoppg. centres
- changing habits of shopping/leisure
- left has tended to respond -vely
- but should recognise +ve side
- attractive family leisure site
- social meeting place
- upgrading of public environment

Figure 2.3 Card summarizing key points

On the other hand, if you really wanted to take the article apart, you could take more detailed notes by working from the markings you did as you were reading. To do this, you copy down some of the phrases highlighted or underlined and set them out on the page in a

---

* What do you think '–vely' and '+ve' mean? The minus sign is my shorthand for 'negative' and the plus sign stands for 'positive'. So '–vely' reads 'negatively' and '+ve' reads 'positive'.

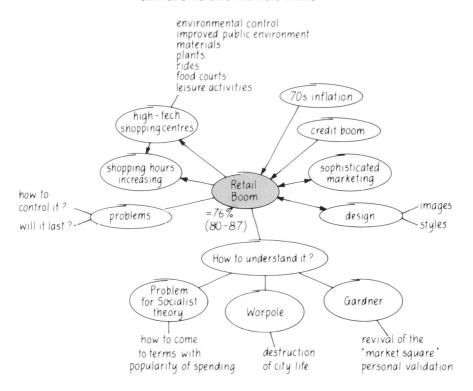

Figure 2.4 *Diagrammatic notes*

way that brings out the main themes and their relationship to each other. If you think visually and have enough time, you might want to do this in the form of a diagram, as in Figure 2.4.

Creating a diagram requires a considerable extra time investment, but it helps to clarify your thoughts. You will have to play around with methods like this for yourself, to find out whether the gain you make in being able to understand and remember an article or chapter is worth the extra cost in time and effort.

ACTIVITY BREAK   Look at Figure 2.4 carefully. Work out why I have used arrows in some places.

Notice the way the 'How to understand it' bubble acts as a second 'node', below the main one, but with its own offshoots.

Does the diagram work for you? Does it, in effect, reveal the 'bones' of the whole article?

Getting to the 'bones' of an argument

Any text has just a *few* central ideas running through it.
However, if the writer simply stated these ideas baldly in the
fewest possible words, you wouldn't be able to understand them
properly, or to see their importance and their wider
implications. So the writer puts flesh on the bare bones of the
ideas, giving examples and evidence and 'talking you through',
to show how the ideas 'work'.

Once *you* have *understood*, you don't need the 'flesh' — you
just need to hold the bones in your mind. Taking notes is a way
of making yourself *seek out* the bones so that you can finish up
with a stripped-down version of your own.

You might find it useful at times to go into more detail than in the
diagram in Figure 2.4, sketching out a whole argument for yourself
in note form, so that you can get clear in your mind what is being
said. In fact, we can present the 'bare bones' of the entire Gardner
article in note form, though you would seldom, if ever, need to go to
such lengths. I have actually done this in Figure 2.5; *not* as an
example of what *you* would want to do in normal practice, but to
demonstrate the principle of extracting the skeleton of the argument
from continuous prose and then laying it out on the page in a way
that enables you to see the structure and to follow the logical links.

ACTIVITY BREAK   Read carefully through the notes in Figure 2.5

Notice how I have placed the points in *clusters* and used arrows to
bring out the *links* in the argument. (Sometimes the arrow means
'leads to', or 'causes'. At other times it just indicates the general
flow of the argument. The upward-pointing arrow before 'long hours'
(point 14) is shorthand for 'increasingly'.) You can be creative in all
sorts of ways in making notes meaningful to yourself.

When you can see the 'bare bones' of what is being said, it is much
easier to use the material in writing an essay or revising for an exam.

There are plenty of other ways in which you could make notes on
this article. If you took your own, I'm sure they were quite different
from any of my examples. Since you don't need a detailed grasp of
theories of 'the retail boom' right now, you didn't *need* to invest a
lot of time in close reading and elaborate note taking here. In future
though, you will need to do so at certain times, so it will be useful to
'experiment' with *different* styles. You need to develop several kinds

Spend, spend, spend – Carl Gardner (NS&S, Dec.89)

1. Many new-style shopping centres – springing up – around the country

2. Basic features – spectacular engineering ⟨ classy materials / light enough for plants / rides

    – environmental control ⟨ lighting / heating

    – central food courts – (voyeuristic culture)

3. This investment → evidence of – emergence of Retail Sector – as most dynamic component of Brit econ.

4. (more evidence – i.e. refurbishment of older shopping centres)

5. Increasing sophistication of – marketing techniques

    – retail design – (huge design business now) – rapidly shifting ⟨ images / styles

6. Shopping hours – increasing – becoming major leisure industry

    – shopping centres → major pleasure sites

7. This is reflected in their designs ⟨ themes / links to leisure facilities

8. Trad. socialist theory – can only disapprove → consumption of commodities = bad

    retail boom = ⟨ cultural deviation / economic time-bomb

9. This isn't good enough – must attempt to understand ⟨ cultural / social / psychic ⟩ shifts – which make shopping an attractive activity

10. Socialist theory of – manipulation → marketing is a giant con trick – by capital – to sell commodities

    desire to consume → delusory pleasure → shopping a 'disease' (implies contempt for ordinary ways of life)

11. Worpole – destruction of ⟨ urban fabric / quality of city life

12. Problems with Worpole ⟨ High st. is not dying – but thriving / relies on a 'romantic' evocation of past city life

13. Contrary to Worpole – Shopping centres → recreate ⟨ earlier forms of city life / link-up 'market' ↔ social life

14. – in British climate – indoor 'market place' – much more effective → ⟨ long hours of shopping + Sunday trading

15. Political response of left – i.e. ⟨ Labour / TUs ⟩ restrictive/oppositional

    – admittedly there are – some real problems – in terms of – employment conditions

    – but – workg. people are also consumers – & they want shopping centres

16. These 'retail developments' → have had overall effect – of improving public environment

17. Offer ⟨ sense of validation / a better environment experience

18. What encouraged – growth of Retail? ⟨ 70's inflation → undermined saving ethic / credit boom → uncoupled – spending ↔ earning

19. Even for unemployed – spending → defiant demonstration that you are not 'marginal'

20. Problems with the 'Retail Revolution' ⟨ needs more control & planning / need to improve employment

21. Will it last? – (i.e. - survive a recession)

Figure 2.5 Detailed notes on the Gardner article (numbers on the left correspond to paragraph numbers in the article)

of note taking for use on different occasions. The notes you require for a difficult and important text will be quite different from the sentence you write to summarize an article you happened to read in passing.

What is note-taking skill?

Note taking is not a single 'skill' which you can acquire once for all times and occasions. It is a range of rather different activities, the common characteristic of which is that you are *writing for yourself* rather than for an 'audience', so you don't have to worry about 'explaining' yourself.

Note taking is more 'strategy' than 'skill'. Being good at note taking involves reading texts in an active way: thinking 'What is this about?', 'What do I want to remember?', and writing down the answers.

It also requires you to be flexible — to take detailed notes sometimes and very sketchy notes at other times. You need to keep looking back at your notes, asking yourself, 'Are they doing the job I want?', 'Could I be using my time more effectively?', and changing your approach accordingly.

Note taking is not however a panacea. You can do too much, so that studying becomes tedious. It may take away the pleasure of exploring new and interesting areas of reading. Since this pleasure is one of the main things that keeps you going, it would be fatal to allow taking notes to turn all your reading into a dreary chore. Note taking *can* make studying *more* satisfying, when it helps you to sort out the meaning of what you are reading and when it creates a tangible 'product' from your labours. But it can *also* hold up your progress and dull the attractions of studying. You have to weigh up carefully *when* to make notes, what *kind* of notes to make, and what the level of *detail* should be.

Health warning: READING IN DEPTH AND TAKING DETAILED NOTES CAN DAMAGE YOUR MORALE.

The notes in Figure 2.5 are *not* an example of what you would expect to produce from reading an article like this one. It would be crazy to spend so much time.

The *point* of looking at such full notes is to see the *principles* of setting out ideas in a structured way—and to show that you *can* represent a text in ways other than the sentences it is written in.

5.3 What is the point of note taking?

What did you write down as the purposes of note taking in response to the question at the beginning of Section 5? I have already indicated some. I will now summarize what I see as the reasons you might have for taking notes.

Focusing your attention

Making notes is one of the most effective ways of stopping your mind from wandering as you read. Michael (our fictitious student in Chapter 1) should have pitched into note taking and stopped worrying so much about what to write down. (Notes can come out in any old shape if necessary. Special techniques take time to develop.)

'Making' sense

As you write down notes, you are pressed into *finding* some sense in the words in the text. What is more, you have to formulate the ideas in the text in a way that makes sense to *you*, in terms of the way *you* understand things.

A form of 'external' memory

The notes you make act, in effect, as a kind of *extension to the memory capacity of your mind* — enabling you to have ready access to a far wider range of knowledge.

A symbol of progress

Notes provide you with evidence of the work you have done and so make an important contribution to your morale.

Preparing an essay

Making notes which draw together ideas from what you have read is an essential part of constructing an essay (see Chapter 6).

Pulling the course together

As you study a course and range over different topics and different texts, your mind becomes cluttered with disconnected bits and pieces. Making notes which summarize a section of the course (even in the form of a set of headings), helps you to create order, making the ideas less confused and more useable.

Making notes on notes

Sometimes it is very useful to bring together the notes you have already made (e.g. while you were reading) and make a new, very short, condensed version; that is, notes which summarize your earlier notes. This is a tremendous help to your learning, because it makes your mind create orderliness at a higher level in your thinking — not 'perfect' orderliness, not something you would like to show to other people, but a lot better than no order at all.

You would be particularly likely to make notes of this kind as part of your revision for an exam (see Chapter 7). But it is also very useful to try to pull things together at other stages of the course; for example, when you have finished one topic and are about to move on to another.

KEY POINTS

Taking notes helps you in many different ways. Learning when and how to take notes as you study is critical to your development as a student.

5.4 What will you do with your notes?

If taking notes is a way of 'extending your memory', then clearly you need to work out some kind of *system* for storing them where you can find them. To make a start, get hold of some folders and find shelf space, or some boxes, for storing them. You will then have to develop a filing system. It is very easy to end up with large piles of notes which are so disorganized that you never can face trying to find what you want (for instance, you may know you took notes on an excellent discussion of political legitimation in Poland, but may not have a clue where to start looking for them). When you are starting on your studies, it is hard to believe that you could ever have a problem of having too many notes. But you will waste a lot of the time you invest in *making* your notes, if you don't also invest some time in working out a simple and effective system for *filing* them.

Having stored your notes, what *uses* are you likely to put them to? As you take your notes you might think, for instance, that one day you will sit down and read carefully through them all. Perhaps you will. On the other hand, there tends to be a shortage of suitable times for doing that. Your studies keep driving you forward into new areas. There is always a new book to read, or another essay to write. Going back over old notes is seldom as pressing, or as attractive, as going onwards to something new — unless, that is, you have a specific purpose, such as looking for material for an essay, or pulling together ideas for an exam. So the fate of notes is often to accumulate dust on a shelf.

This means that there is little point in creating acres of wordage which faithfully cover all the main content of the course. Your notes are much more likely to be useful for *reference* purposes rather than as a source of extensive reading. You need to make them with this in mind. You need pithy questions, comments and summaries, though not so cryptic that they do not make sense when you come back to them. It doesn't necessarily matter if you *never* go back to a particular set of notes. The process of writing them is valuable enough in itself. However, if *all* your notes are very lengthy and unstructured you will find it difficult to make *any* future use of them. Life, as they say, is too short.

6 Conclusion

Reading is one of the central activities in most courses of study. The purpose of it is to make you *learn*. But learning is not a *passive* process. You don't just let ideas wash over you. You have to *make* sense of ideas as you read and then *use* them to *think* with.

KEY POINTS

Reading for study purposes is not simply a matter of passing your eyes across hundreds of words. It is a *set of practices* which *you develop* to enable you to *engage* with the ideas in the text. These include actively:

▶ *defining your task* as you set out to read (setting a target)

▶ *underlining or highlighting* as you read, as appropriate

▶ *taking notes*, as and when appropriate

▶ *stopping* to look ahead or back in the text when you lose the thread of the argument

▶ *checking* across to other sources as necessary

▶ *monitoring* your progress from time to time, and

▶ *changing* your approach as necessary.

As a beginner, it is worth *experimenting* with a range of different ways of doing things, so that you have a wider base of experience to work from in developing a robust, flexible, all-round style. To read effectively you have to be able to work out *what you are trying to achieve* and *how well you are progressing.* It isn't easy to make those judgements. *That* is what becoming a 'skilled' student is all about.

CHAPTER 3

Other ways of studying

1 Introduction

In Chapter 2 we focused our attention on *reading* and *taking notes*. But of course there are other ways of studying. In fact, learning is a complex and subtle process which is helped along a great deal by coming at it from several directions.

1.1 The nature of studying and learning

As I said in Chapter 1, studying is essentially to do with getting hold of new *ideas*, which involves *taking in* ideas by making sense of them, *thinking through* the ideas and fitting them alongside ones you already have in your mind, and learning to *use* the ideas by expressing thoughts and presenting arguments in speech and in writing.*

KEY POINTS

In most courses of *study* you are concerned with learning:

▶ *ideas*

▶ ways of *thinking*, and

▶ ways of *arguing*.

Reading is an excellent way of doing the first of these three things. You can approach new ideas on *your own terms* and work at *your own pace*. Provided that the text you are working on is clearly enough written, you can get a long way simply studying on your own. This is particularly true if you are fairly expert in a subject.

---

* When we talk of 'studying' we are *not* usually referring to the learning of *physical skills*. We would not tend to talk of 'studying' how to walk a tightrope, or how to juggle. For that kind of learning we would be more likely to use words like 'practising' and 'training'. You might, perhaps, think of studying as learning a lot of *information* or '*facts*', but even that is not quite on the mark. If you are learning a lot of words in order to be able to speak a foreign language, or if you have to learn your lines for a part in a play, then a word such as 'memorizing' seems more appropriate. Just *storing* up information in your memory is not at the heart of what we usually mean by studying.

You can pick up the latest book in a bookshop, or library, take it home and absorb any new ideas by yourself. On the other hand, when you are starting to study a subject as a beginner, reading on its own is often not enough. If it were, there would be no need for courses. People would learn all they needed to know simply by getting hold of the relevant books and reading them. But as we know, reading is not all plain sailing. It is only too easy to get stuck, to be baffled, to grind to a halt with your eyes no longer able to take in the words in front of you.

1.2 The value of the spoken word

Making sense of new ideas

When you read you have to be able to 'project' meaning into the words on the page. That is to say, you already have to have some notion of what the words *might* mean. But what can you do if the only clues available to you are actually in the text you are trying to read?

Learning new ideas

Making sense of new ideas has a kind of chicken and egg quality to it. You cannot make much sense of a *discussion* in your subject area until you understand the *questions* that the discussion is trying to address. But you cannot really get hold of what the *questions* mean until you have engaged with some of the *discussion*. Learning new ideas is not simply a matter of furrowing your brow, concentrating your mind, and reading systematically through a series of ideas from A to B to C and on to Z. It is more a matter of circling around picking up the gist of what is going on.

Did you ever look at 'grown-up', serious newspapers as a child and wonder how you would ever be able to understand so many difficult words? I used to think I would have to sit down one day and 'learn' them. I never did, of course. As you become a participant in the normal discourses of adult life, those words, apparently effortlessly, become part of your vocabulary. Usually, there is no specific day on which you 'learn' any particular word. The words just seem to accumulate around you.

Learning ideas is very similar to this. There is seldom a specific day when you 'learn' a particular idea. It just starts to 'turn up' inconspicuously in your thoughts. You spend time moving around within a certain sphere of ideas and gradually you become aware of what the central questions are and how the

---

> ideas and arguments work. At first everything is a mystery but, when you have moved on to grapple with other new ideas and turn to look back, what you once struggled with somehow seems much more obvious.

This need to pick up the 'general gist' of what is going on in a subject area is why the spoken word is helpful when you are learning new ideas. Lectures, group discussions, TV and radio programmes, and audio and video cassettes are all very valuable in giving you a chance to 'sit-in', as it were, and 'overhear' ideas in action. They present you with samples of the kinds of debates going on in a subject. They let you hear how the arguments work. *Even* when you get lost or confused you can still make valuable progress in:

▶ hearing *how* the *language* of the subject is used

▶ hearing the *kinds* of *questions* that are asked, and

▶ getting a sense of the *kinds* of *argument* that are used.

All these things help when you return to your reading, because they give you clues to the kind of sense you ought to be able to make from the printed word.

Driving meaning forward

With reading, the great advantage is that you can move at your own pace. The meaning of the words doesn't run ahead of your thoughts. But the corresponding drawback is that *you* have to shoulder the whole burden of pushing the meaning along. If you get tired or confused, the process of understanding comes to a halt. With the spoken word it is the other way round. The advantage is that speech has its *own* forward momentum. Indeed, when other people are doing the speaking, meaning sweeps along independently of you. The drawback is that you may not always be able to keep pace with the meaning, so that you are left floundering at times. With the spoken word, meaning is made to 'happen' as a social event, which you share in. It isn't just a private process inside your head. In this way the burden of making meaning and of driving it forward is shared with other people. You have the opportunity to be carried along a line of thinking by the momentum of a discussion.

Putting ideas to work

The spoken word also delivers ideas in a more *active* form, because they have to meet the demands of 'live' debate. If you read ideas laid out neatly in a text, you may think that you have taken in what they are about. But when you then hear an expert *speaking* with those ideas, you find they can take on a new force. You begin to realize there is much more there than you understood at first, and you begin to see new possibilities for *using* the ideas. But can you use them? If you subsequently join in a discussion and try to use the ideas yourself, you may find, as you reach for them, that they slip from your grasp and dissolve, or that they emerge in a garbled form. Only after you have engaged in batting them back and forth in debate for some time do you gradually get on to reasonable working terms with them. Later, when you come to write an essay, you struggle again to achieve a further degree of mastery over the ideas, as you use them to answer a question. By the time you have done all that, ideas which seemed quite slight and straightforward as you read them on the page will have acquired layers of extra meaning and become integrated into a whole range of other related ideas which you already held in your mind. What is more, they become 'active' ideas — ideas which *you* use to help you make sense of the world and ponder about it. They are not just something 'out there' on a page, which you chose to 'memorize'. They have become part of the way you think and understand.

KEY POINTS

Modes of study which use the *spoken word*:

▶ help you to get the *general gist* of new ideas

▶ *drive you on* through difficult arguments, and

▶ help you to build newly acquired ideas into the way you *think* about a subject.

The learning of ideas is a complex process, which does not happen in a single moment or through a single activity. It develops unevenly over time and over a range of activities, surging forward at some times and hanging back at others. Looking at learning this way, it is easy to see the value of studying in several different modes concurrently, particularly if some of the modes involve the spoken word.

2   Learning in groups

Group discussions are a widely used mode of studying, particularly amongst adults.

2.1   What does learning in groups offer?

Thinking collectively

We learn throughout our lives by engaging in discussions with other people. As well as giving us access to the ideas of *others*, conversation helps us to clarify our *own* thoughts. In the effort to explain a point, you may quite frequently hear yourself expressing ideas in a form you had not been quite aware of before. In short, discussion helps you to *think*.

Sharing the thinking load

When you are thinking by yourself you have to do two things at the same time. You have to hold in mind *what* you are thinking *about* (the frame of reference) and you have to *work through the thought itself* (the content). This puts limits on how far you can go, since it is easy to lose track of one while you attend to the other. However, when you are discussing with other people, you *share* the responsibility for holding on to what the discussion is about — the frame of reference. This means you can pursue thoughts of your own and then tune back into the discussion to remind yourself of the point of it all.

One advantage, then, of group discussions is that the 'frame of reference' is 'looked after' by the group as a whole. Another is that the frame keeps moving onwards, with the result that the thoughts in your mind are constantly being presented against a slightly different background. This shows you fresh ways of working on them. As a result, ideas which defeated you when you were reading on your own can suddenly take on new meanings; knots you have tied yourself into become loosened. That is to say, you can think in a wide-ranging and free-flowing way 'in company', so that you achieve thoughts you would never be able to arrive at on your own.

What is more, when you meet the same people regularly, the group's handling of the subject matter 'evolves'. The frames of reference become more subtle.

Collective progress

A study group which meets over a period of time gradually develops a *shared understanding* of the subject matter. The discussion doesn't go back to first principles each time. It builds on the achievements of previous meetings. This means that as your own thoughts on the subject matter are becoming gradually

---

> more developed, through working on the course, so the 'shared understanding' within the group also becomes more sophisticated and the collective frames of reference that the group constructs during discussions become more powerful. This means that you are able to take part in discussions which approach increasingly closely to the level of the ideas you are reading in the texts.

In other words, a group of students can collectively advance their level of thinking. And as a participant, your own thoughts can be worked out against an increasingly sophisticated frame of reference.

The combination of *private reading* and *regular discussions* is an immensely powerful one. The level of debate within the group benefits enormously from the individual efforts of each student in grappling with ideas in print and, at the same time, the advances in collective understanding within the group give a huge boost to private reading, by supplying a far richer spread of meanings to 'project' on to the words in the texts.

Learning to speak the academic language

The whole point of studying is to be able to take hold of ideas and put them to work for you. In the end, the most exacting way of doing this is in writing. But writing is a formal and rather disembodied way of 'talking'. It is generally easier to make your first efforts at using unfamiliar terms in an active discussion. Then you can see directly whether other people understand you. And you can find out if they use the words in the same way. As you engage in debate, you begin to get a working knowledge of how to put arguments together. You get a clearer sense of how the 'logic' of the debates is supposed to work. In fact, discussions are not only helpful in showing you how to present arguments orally; they also give you clues about how to develop your thoughts in writing.

Social support

An equally important benefit of group-based learning is that it helps to keep up your morale. Many students say that the best thing about attending a class is discovering that other students are experiencing exactly the same difficulties as themselves. It is easy to feel stupid, inefficient and inarticulate when you study on your own. It is a great relief to find that standards are quite ordinary amongst your fellow students. Just talking with others about the disarray of your study programme and your confusions over the reading, and so on, helps to put these worries into perspective. Studying is a tough challenge, and *everyone* finds it difficult. You need to keep reminding yourself of this, and talking to other students who are facing exactly the same tasks is by far the most convincing evidence.

Of course, you can do more than just commiserate. You can actually *help* each other. You can share tips about how you cope. You can exchange plans and strategies for approaching the work ahead. You can even share out some of the work. Learning does not have to be a competitive activity. You can often collaborate very effectively with other students, checking different sources of information for a project, comparing plans for an essay, or cross-checking notes from a book or a lecture. You can collaborate in purely practical ways, such as arranging for another student to look after your children on Saturday, while you write your essay, with you returning the favour on Sunday. Networks of mutual support can make the everyday challenges of study much more manageable. And when you run into a *crisis*, as most students do from time to time (pressure at work, moving house, domestic complications, etc.), such networks can make the difference between struggling through and dropping out altogether.

I have stressed the practical help you can get from studying in a group. What I have missed out is that meeting other people is an end in itself. The pleasure of social contact and of taking part in challenging discussions may turn out to be the most rewarding part of taking up study. Study classes often bring together people from a wide range of backgrounds, whose only common characteristic is an interest in the subject matter of the course. As a result, studying can be a very significant *social experience* as well as an intellectual one.

Summary

It is often hard to put your finger on what you learn from group discussions. You are unlikely to come away with lots of detailed notes. You may not come across many brand new ideas. You may find it difficult even to recall what topics have been discussed, let alone be able to summarize the main points that have emerged. But discussion is *not* a primary means of access to a formal body of knowledge. It is too fluid and unpredictable for delivering detailed points. The strength of group study is in preparing the ground for reading you are about to start, or in reworking and deepening your understanding of material you have already studied.

KEY POINTS

The value of group-based studying is:

▶ sharing the work of *advancing your thinking*

▶ practising *using the language* of the subject

▶ providing *social support* for your studies.

2.2 The nature of classroom discussion

Discussion is a highly flexible process which can accommodate a wide range of needs and interests, but it is also unstable. It can veer from the stimulating and illuminating to the dreary and stultifying and back again. In this sense it is a 'high risk' mode of study. At best it offers a great deal. At worst it seems a dreadful waste of time. It is sometimes very hard going, as you grope your way through tangled thickets of confusion, but then it is suddenly exhilarating when you glimpse a new perspective. You need to understand its inherent unpredictability if you are to make proper use of group learning, so that you don't expect too much or too little.

Discussions define themselves as they proceed. When you start on a chosen topic, the options are boundless. But as you explore one pathway you close off the possibilities of others. Every minute you spend on one issue is time denied to others. So there is always uncertainty as to how long the group should spend pursuing any given train of discussion and what would be the best direction to follow next. Indeed, members of the group will have different views on these matters. There will also be uncertainty as to what right each group member has to influence the direction of the discussion and how such influence should be exerted. Thus, the flexibility which is a core strength of discussion is also a problem. It is never absolutely clear what is and what is not a useful contribution to the discussion, or where the debate as a whole is supposed to be heading. The 'intellectual agenda' is always uncertain.

Even more tricky is the 'social agenda'. When several people are engaged in a single conversation, immediately there is the problem that *somebody* has to speak (or the conversation will cease), but only *one* person can speak at a time. How is the group to determine *who* should speak and *when*? Taking turns would be very 'mechanical'. It would work against the whole idea of pursuing a train of thought, or arguing out the differences between two views. But anything else requires group members to make judgements about the value and the timeliness of their own potential contributions. Some people are much more optimistic about this than others. Some are inclined to doubt the value of *anything* they might contribute and prefer to take the 'safe' option of staying silent. Others happily throw in thoughts without very much concern as to their relevance. So a group can establish a very uneven pattern of contributions. This is unsatisfactory for the group as a whole, in that members do not benefit from the full range of insights available. But it is particularly unsatisfactory for those members who are not getting a chance to try out their own ideas.

To establish and maintain a *social* and an *intellectual* agenda for a discussion requires some form of 'management' of the process. Overall responsibility for 'managing' group discussions often falls to the tutor. But it is not a task the tutor can accomplish unaided. It is in no one's interest, for example, to have one or two students who dominate a whole discussion, but it is very difficult for the tutor to prevent this without taking over and dominating the discussion himself, or herself. The tutor can't *make* the other students talk. A direct question to a quieter student, for instance, tends to shine the spotlight too suddenly and too brightly and creates embarrassment rather than encouragement. In the end, tutors have to rely on students coming forward more or less spontaneously to make contributions (whatever the reservations they may feel). They also value assistance in drawing out the less confident students and in keeping a check on the more enthusiastic ones. In other words, a good group discussion relies on active participation and a sense of shared responsibility.

2.3 How to enjoy taking part in group discussions

A study group discussion is a challenging social process. As students, most of us are eager to speak effectively and to show the force of our ideas, but at the same time we are concerned not to appear foolish. So we often feel quite ambivalent, particularly at the first meeting or two — keen in principle to contribute, but also quite reticent. In the early meetings it is easy to form the impression that most of the other students are cleverer, more articulate, more hardworking, and more confident than yourself. Remember, however, that most of them are thinking exactly the same about you. Just throw caution to the winds and join in. Stop worrying what the others think of you and remind yourself that they are not very concerned about what *you* say. *They* are worrying about what *they* say and what you think of *them*.

Another thing to remind yourself of is that you have as much right to take part in discussions as anyone else. A discussion is not set up as an ordeal to 'test' you. It is part of the study package you have paid your course fee for. Don't let yourself be intimidated. It is *your* discussion, arranged in order to help *you* learn. Don't seat yourself just outside the fringes of the group. Push your chair right in, so that you can see everyone's face and hear what they are saying. Give yourself a decent chance.

Saying the simple thing

You may feel that you ought to wait until you have something really important to say before taking up the group's time by speaking out — a penetrating new insight, a telling illustration of the theme, or a lucid summary of the debate. If you raise the stakes to this high level you will only create problems for yourself. For a start, it will be a very long time before you attempt to speak. As you wait, poised for the right moment, the discussion will drift on to other topics, so that when you finally speak it is no longer clear what, exactly, you are referring to. And by then you will also be too wound up by the significance of the occasion, so that you tend to say too much too quickly, and other people will find it hard to follow your train of thoughts. They will then have difficulty responding to what you have said and incorporating it into the flow of the discussion.

Rather than entering into this cycle of inhibition, it is much better to set your sights low. Just ask the simple question, make the obvious point, and offer the mundane illustration. What seems ordinary to you will often be more interesting to other people. In any case, the group does not *need* 'brilliant' contributions to have a good discussion. It just needs everyone's mind focused on the main theme and a steady flow of contributions. You all work *together* to move the discussion on to new levels of understanding and analysis. Individual brilliance isn't necessary.

In any discussion, you are likely to be confused occasionally — to be unsure of what, in general, the discussion is about or of what, in particular, has just been said. This may make you feel rather inadequate, but don't let it! You may be quite right! The whole group *may* have lost its bearings and the person who has just spoken *may* have made little sense. These things happen frequently. Simply saying that you don't understand is a useful contribution, because other people will be worrying about the same thing. Just ask, 'What are we talking about?', or 'What would be an example of what you just said?' In going back over a few points the whole group may reach a new level of clarity about the issues being discussed.

Of course, you *will* tend to be confused if you have not done any reading in preparation for the discussion. It is very important that you *try* to do the set reading in advance, or at least skim over *some* of it, so that you can tune your thoughts into the subject matter and make a useful contribution to the debate. However, if for some reason you have hit a bad patch in your studies and *haven't* managed to do the reading, don't miss the class on that account. Even if you cannot follow everything that is said, you will pick up very valuable clues which will help you to work quickly on the reading when you do make time for it.

Being a 'quiet' group member

You may sometimes find it difficult to contribute simply because so many other people are eager to speak. There isn't time for everyone to say a lot and some people are just more talkative and more thrusting in groups than others. So don't feel self-critical if you say very little in some discussions. You can get a lot from a debate by listening very closely and 'participating' silently — agreeing or disagreeing with what other people say. It certainly isn't the case that the people who speak most in a discussion necessarily know the most. You *ought to try* to join in *some* of the time. But don't worry if you find yourself cast in a relatively minor role. Groups need their support players just as much as the big shots.

Finally, if for any reason you find that you are unable to arrive in time for the beginning of a class, or have to leave before the end (which is quite common for part-time students), don't feel you have to miss the whole class. Just let the tutor know your difficulty and arrive or leave discreetly when you have to.

KEY POINTS

In group discussions:

▶ Don't be anxious about the quality of your contributions. Other people are more concerned about what *they* say than what you say.

▶ Don't wait for 'the big moment' before you speak. Just jump in; ask the *simple* question; give the *obvious* example.

▶ Share in the responsibility for keeping the group going.

Try as best you can to do the relevant reading before the class, but don't skip the class if you *haven't* been able to manage it.

2.4 Giving a 'presentation'

One device sometimes used in group discussions is to ask one of the students to prepare a short talk on a particular article, or book. This is usually intended to take ten to fifteen minutes at the start of the session, to get things rolling. In principle, it is a very straightforward task. But students sometimes get a bit overawed by the responsibility. In fact, finding a 'public speaking voice', even for such a small public, takes practice, so it is not surprising if you are a little unsettled by the occasion. Here are a few guidelines which will help to ensure that your presentation goes well.

The most important principle is to avoid being too ambitious. In ten to fifteen minutes you are not going to be able to make more than a few main points. If you allow anxiousness to push you into preparing a lot more, you will end up gabbling everything in 'shorthand', and no one will understand a word. Don't read widely round the topic. Just cover the minimum. If you are introducing a chapter of a book, try to summarize in a sentence or two what is distinctive about the book. What is the central question it deals with? How does it approach that question? Keep it very simple. Remember that although *you* may have been thinking a lot about the subject the other students have not. They will need everything spelled out slowly and carefully. Try to use examples to illustrate your points, so that others will be able to see what you are getting at. Prepare a diagram if it will make things clearer. When you have made a few notes on your topic and have decided roughly what you want to say, write down three headings (or thereabouts) on a card, and a single main point and an example or illustration under each. Then give your presentation from the card. If you try to read points from detailed notes you will lose your thread and so will your audience. (It is very difficult to switch between a talking and a reading mode.) The fewer details cluttering your thoughts the more clearly you will be able to make your points to the group.

Remember a 'presentation' is not a major event. You are just serving the routine function for the group of 'kicking-off' the discussion. For everyone else it is just another session. They will not be worried about how hard you worked or how clever you are. All they will be concerned with is whether *they* can understand what you say.

KEY POINTS

If you have to make a presentation to a seminar group don't be too ambitious:

▶ keep it short and simple
▶ use examples to illustrate your points
▶ speak from a card with two or three main points on it.

2.5 Self-help groups

All that I have said has assumed a discussion group led by a tutor. However, there is no reason why you shouldn't arrange your own discussion groups with your fellow students. You can arrange to meet at a place and time to suit your own circumstances and set the agenda to meet you own needs. You may find a self-help group even more useful than formal sessions run by a tutor.

You will need to set firm agendas for your meetings and probably to appoint a chairperson for each. No one likes to appear too thrusting and self-important, particularly when the group members don't know each other well. So it is sometimes difficult to find anyone who is prepared to take responsibility for making decisions about when and where to meet and what to discuss. If you are going to have a successful group, *someone* has to stick their neck out and accept at least a share in the role of 'leading' the group (perhaps on a 'rotating' basis). Otherwise, good intentions will tend to dissolve into indecision and disorder.

KEY POINTS

▶ Self-help group meetings are an excellent idea.

▶ But they need organizing, so work out early on how you will share out the role of 'leader'.

3 Talks and lectures

Lectures have traditionally been the main mode of teaching in higher education. Certainly, at degree level, the bulk of direct teaching has been delivered in the form of the fifty-five minute talk. However, over the last thirty years doubts have frequently been raised as to whether this reliance on lecturing is a good thing.

3.1 What do lectures offer you?

Critics have said that lectures simply 'present' knowledge instead of encouraging students to *think*; that listening is a passive and generally rather tedious mode of learning. They also suggest that students are unable to pay close attention for more than about twenty minutes, and that at the end of a lecture they are unable to recall more than a small proportion of what has been said. In spite of this, the lecture continues to be the dominant teaching method. And, in fact, students themselves do not appear to be that critical of it.* They find 'good' lectures to be good value. However, it has also been suggested that students' enthusiasm for lectures is a kind of immaturity — a yearning to be *told* things by an authoritative, parent-like figure, coupled with a willingness to believe that they are learning, when in fact information is simply washing over them. So what are we to conclude? Can so many students be mistaken about whether or not they are learning? Can it be the case that they retain very little and yet continue to come back for more?

In fact, it is misleading to think of lectures simply in terms of 'information' transmitted and remembered. The lecture is *not* a very good method of delivering a lot of *detailed information*. It is too unreliable. *Essential* information is better presented in *print*, where it can be set down correctly, where you can study it when you are ready to take it in, and where you can return to it as needed.

Lectures and learning

Where the lecture comes into its own is in helping you to understand how the *ideas* in the subject *work*. The lecturer can 'project' meaning into the words for you. The sense of the words is signalled through tone of voice and embellished with gestures and facial expression. Devices such as diagrams, slides and notes on the blackboard can also be brought into play. By orchestrating all these different means of communicating, the ideas you are grappling with in the course can be presented to you much more explicitly and forcefully. This is *not* an entirely *passive* experience. *You too have to make the effort to 'follow the argument'*. However, the lecturer can 'talk you through' from the beginning to the end of the argument, *even* if you cannot understand it all and *even* if you miss some of what is said (because your attention wanders from time to time). You can still pick up a *sense* of how the whole debate is supposed to work.

---

* Research studies surveyed by Beard, R. and Hartley, J. in *Teaching and Learning in Higher Education*, 4th edn, 1984, Harper and Row, led them to conclude that, '. . . [the] pessimistic assessment of lecturing as a teaching method proves not to be general among students . . .'.

This makes lectures an excellent counterpart to reading (where you *can* stop and think over points which puzzle you, and go back to re-read them if necessary, and where you have time to make notes thoughtfully). When you are learning unfamiliar material, *both* approaches are useful. One drives you on into new territory; the other lets you get your bearings and take time to map out the ground around you.

Far from depositing a mound of information in your head, the main effect of an excellent lecture might be to shake up all your thinking on a subject, so that you are not sure *what* to think. You might simply end up with a whole lot of new questions in your head. But these questions could be exactly what you need to help you make more sense the next time and you pick up a textbook. Lectures, when given well, help you to 'get inside' the discourses of the field you are studying. Their purpose is *not* to make sure that every point in the lecturer's notes ends up in your notes. (In the age of the photocopier there are much easier ways of doing that.) What they offer is 'live' discourse; words spoken in a social setting, which engage directly with the thoughts in your mind.

The role of 'tutor talk'

I have been talking exclusively in terms of lectures. But all the points made apply just as well to shorter, or more informal, talks by teachers. The contribution the teacher has to offer in summarizing at the end of a classroom discussion, for example, is to take some of the *ideas* that have been floating around in the discussion and show how they can be made to work in terms of the central *questions* and *arguments* of the subject matter. In other words, the teacher can take the *ideas produced within the discourse of the classroom* and show how they work *within the more formal discourses* of writers and researchers on the subject.

KEY POINTS

The strength of the lecture lies, not in presenting information to you, but in:

▶ engaging your mind with the debates going on in the subject

▶ showing you how the explanations work

▶ letting you hear how the language of the subject is used.

3.2 Problems of learning from lectures

The most pressing practical problem when you are listening to a lecture is that it sets you three challenging tasks to do *simultaneously*:

▶ You have to *attend* to and *make sense* of a line of argument.

▶ You have to *think* about what is said.

▶ And you have to *take notes* of some kind.

Of course, you can't actually do more than *one* of these at once. So the best you can aim for is to switch quickly from one task to another. In an odd way the urgency of the struggle to cope with this mental juggling act is helpful. By putting you under pressure, lectures force you into taking leaps and short cuts. These force you to seize the initiative in 'making sense' of the subject. When you are reading you may tend to hold yourself at a respectful distance from the ideas in the text, painstakingly summarizing them in note form. In a lecture you haven't time for that. You just have to pitch in and make what sense you can quickly, because the scraps you get down are all you will take away with you at the end. You have to learn to think on your feet.

But how do you develop this juggling act? Clearly you cannot afford to leave the primary task of *attending to the lecture* for very long, or you will lose the drift of the whole argument. On the other hand, you are bound to miss *some* of what is said, because listening 'intelligently' will make you stop and *think* from time to time (as you make connections with other ideas already in your mind). You have to find out how to make a trade-off between listening and thinking which enables you to keep in touch. In fact, the most significant thing you can do to keep your mind on the lecture is to develop a good note-taking strategy.

Since the notes are made in time 'stolen' from listening and thinking, it matters a lot how time-consuming and how effective your note-taking strategy is. You have to weigh up quality against speed. To strike a suitable balance you have to think about your broad objectives:

▶ what is your *purpose* in being at the lecture at all, and

▶ what do you hope to gain by making *notes*?

You will then need to try out a number of different approaches and afterwards look back over your notes to see whether they serve your objectives.

3.3 Practical advice

There is no single 'best' way of taking notes. Some people scribble busily throughout the lecture and write several pages, while others take down no more than a few key points set out diagrammatically. Both of these approaches can be very effective. It depends on the *context* in which you are attending the lecture, on the *kind of lecture* it is, and most of all on the way *you* work and learn.

How many notes do you need?

If your course uses lectures as the main source of information, then you may have to write down a lot to be sure of getting hold of what you need. On the other hand, if the lectures are backed up by handouts and by good textbooks (or better still by 'teaching texts', structured to help you to learn), then you may need very little in the way of a written record.

Equally, if the lecture itself is delivered in a formal and monotonous way and is packed with detailed information, you may find that you have to write down a lot just to keep track. If, on the other hand, the lecturer has a lively style and gives striking examples and illustrations of the main points, you may find that you learn a lot by concentrating on listening and just writing the occasional notes of the key points and the topics covered.

The most important factor, though, is you.

What sort of lecture listener are you?

Do you tend to daydream in lectures? Do you tend to feel anxious as to whether you are understanding enough? Are you the sort of student who prefers to rely on the printed texts for any ideas you need to work on in detail, so that you can concentrate on listening in lectures? Do you feel confident that a few phrases here and there will be enough to remind you of the points you need to hold on to (for your next essay, say)? Or do you find it too difficult to decide *which* points are important as the lecture is in full flow? Do you feel that unless you are writing most of the time you will miss something crucial?

You need to analyse your own reactions to listening to lectures, so that you develop a note-taking strategy which suits *you*.

If writing a lot helps you to allay anxiety and if it keeps you actively 'working' with what is being said, rather than just letting it wash over you, then it may be the right approach for you. On the other hand, if you try to write *everything* down, you will probably learn very little during the lecture itself. Most of your work will still lie ahead of you at the end, in that you will then need to read the notes to find out what is in them. This will be quite difficult and time-consuming, if you didn't have time to spare to take in the central theme of the lecture. It is worth stopping to ask yourself whether, in practice, you will find time to read your voluminous notes. Perhaps it doesn't matter, if the writing helps to keep your mind on the job. However, if you do decide that you are *not* likely to make much sense of mountains of notes, this releases you from the burden of writing endlessly and allows you to listen and take notes more selectively. Your only problem then is what to select.

How do you know which points to write down?

In fact, the beginning and the end of a lecture are particularly important times for note taking. At the start you are likely to be able to get down 'the point' of the lecture. Indeed, the lecturer will often give clues in the form of notes on the blackboard or handouts, which reveal to you the broad structure of the lecture. At the end, you should try to draw out some conclusions. Again, the lecturer may give you direct help with this by summarizing. For the first and last ten minutes, then, you might set yourself the task of taking quite full notes, while allowing yourself to be more relaxed and your note taking more sporadic in between. All you may need are a few headings and the occasional word or phrase to remind you of the general area covered and the main themes. Note down any *examples* and *illustrations* that the lecturer gives. They will help to remind you of the workings of the arguments and explanations. Often you won't need more than a word or two to bring these back to you. On the other hand, when you want to note a key point which is more abstract, you may need to get the whole thing down in detail, if you are going to be able to make sense of it afterwards. Note the names of major writers who are mentioned and the dates of their work. This will help to give you a sense of who the main figures are in your field of study and enable you to make connections with what you read in the texts. Make a point of writing down any questions or comments that occur to you as you listen. After the lecture, you may find that your comments are more use to you than the words of the lecturer in reconstructing what was going through your mind at the time.

If you take listening and thinking seriously, you cannot expect to make very full notes in a lecture. And in fact the process of *deciding what is important* enough to write down and what is not may actually be more valuable to you than the notes you end up with. It keeps your mind alert and makes you think about the subject.

Styles of note taking

What you select to write down and *how you position it* on the page will impose a structure on the material presented in the lecture. This in turn will help you to understand it and to remember it. Don't be stingy with your paper. Spread your notes across the page generously and use dividing lines, arrows, brackets, boxes, and so on, to emphasize divisions and links in the material. You might, for example, put your own remarks and queries over to the right-hand side of the paper [or enclose them in square brackets, like this].

Some people find it helpful to use diagrams, putting the topic of the lecture in a circle in the middle of the page and then drawing lines branching out for various sub-topics as they arise. (See Chapter 2, Section 5.2 for examples of different note-taking styles.)

Of course, you cannot expect lecture notes to have as much structure and clarity as notes you make when you read. The emphasis is on speed. A very simple but important technique is to develop your own shorthand. For example:

Asch (52): expt. – gp. pressure

line lengths – approx. 1/3 of subjs. accept gp. judgmt.

This is short for:

In 1952 Asch reported carrying out an experiment to explore the pressures group opinions exert on people. He used a series of groups of eight people. The members of a group would be asked to say which of three lines on a card was the same length as a line on another card. This was repeated for a series of cards. However, seven of the group had been briefed in advance and at a secret signal these seven began to pick a wrong line, to see what the other person (the *subject* of the experiment) would do. This was repeated with many groups. In about a third of cases the subjects went against the evidence of their own eyes and agreed with the group.

In my shorthand, 'expt.' stands for experiment, 'gp.' for group, 'subjs.' for experimental subjects, and so on. The lecturer might spend ten minutes or more describing the details of this experiment, but these few abbreviated words would be enough to bring the crucial features back to me. And, if I happened to experience any difficulty in recalling what the experiment was about, I have the name Asch and the year he published the report, so I would be able to look up the details in a textbook if I needed to.

Using a cassette recorder

In recent years some students have developed the practice of making sound recordings of lectures. Not all lecturers are comfortable with this, as it tends to make the lecture feel less spontaneous. It also raises doubts about the purposes these recordings serve. At worst, someone might intend to have a series of recordings typed out and then sell the transcripts to prospective students as a substitute for attending the 'real' lectures. However, if we ignore such potentially underhand uses of 'bootleg' recordings, we are left with the question — is the cassette recorder a useful and legitimate learning aid?

One thing that recording *can* achieve is to remove anxiety about missing important points. This leaves you free to listen and to make only very brief written notes. In other words, it is a way of solving the problem of having three things to do at the same time. However, by taking this pressure off you, the recorder may also lower your concentration during lectures and let you off the hook of struggling to construct sense. Then there is also the question of what to do with a recording afterwards. Do you play it back right through, pausing the tape to take detailed notes and to think through difficult points? This could be an excellent way of consolidating your learning. You might even listen with a group of fellow-students and have discussions about key points. But have you the time? Should you be moving on to read the textbooks instead of poring over the details of past lectures? Sitting through a lecture once is hard enough. Is lining yourself up for a double dose a sign of masochism?

By 'fixing' the lecture in the form of a permanent record, you destroy its ephemeral nature and make it more like a textbook. The words the lecturer happened to use will take on an importance they were never meant to have. And instead of letting the words float through your mind and out, leaving a residue of *ideas* behind, you find yourself lumbered with the words themselves and the job of extracting the ideas.

The danger with the practice of recording lectures is that you might be lulled into a false sense of security. You might find you put off the crucial job of *understanding*, thinking that 'one day' you will really take the time to work on all your recordings in a concentrated way. You might also be tempted to write essays by pasting together 'quotes' from the lectures, instead of learning how to say things for yourself. So before deciding you want to use a cassette recorder, check, first, that this is acceptable to the lecturer and, secondly, be sure that you are not using it to avoid facing up to the necessary hard work of studying. On the other hand, using recordings constructively could be a useful way of consolidating your learning.

Making notes after the lecture

An hour spent at a lecture is a significant investment of your study time, but the return may seem disappointing if, a day or two later, you cannot recall what the lecture was about, or make much sense of your notes. However, you may be able to increase the yield a great deal by making an additional time investment immediately after the lecture. If you make the time to write a short summary of the main points of the lecture (say ten lines), you may be able to convert scrappy notes into a much more intelligible record. It is sometimes said that what you get out of lectures is not determined by what you do *during* the lecture so much as by the work you put in before and after. On some courses, it is suggested that you should put in two hours work outside the lecture theatre, preparing and consolidating, for every one spent in it. Whether this is a reasonable rule-of-thumb for you depends a lot on the nature of the course, but it is important to remember that, unlike school, where what happens in the classroom is the main content of the course, lectures are generally intended as an *adjunct* to work which you are expected to be doing elsewhere.

KEY POINTS

▶ Be clear in your mind as to *why* you are attending the lecture and *what* you want to take away from it.

▶ Develop a flexible way of working which you can change depending on the kind of lecture it turns out to be.

▶ Take account of your *own habits* (e.g. you may tend to daydream), and develop a note-taking strategy which helps you to concentrate.

▶ Don't attempt to write down 'everything'. Listening is your main job. Try to make brief notes which pick out the main themes and key points.

▶ If you write a summary shortly after the lecture it will greatly increase the value of having attended.

4 Learning from TV and radio broadcasts

4.1 What do TV broadcasts offer?

Most of us learn a great deal from the TV and radio these days. However, when you watch a nature documentary, a historical reconstruction, or a report on drug smuggling, you are learning in a very different way from when you are listening to a lecture or reading a book.

***

Learning from TV

With a book or a lecture, you attend primarily to a sequence of words and *you* then have to connect these abstract words with 'real life'. On TV you see pictures and hear sounds which give you the sense of actually 'being there'. The 'real world' seems to be very powerfully present *even* when you are looking at something you could never see by 'natural' vision, such as a hugely magnified insect in a flower, or the inside of a living human organ. You don't have to *struggle* to hold your focus on the central subject matter. All your most basic processes of perceiving and experiencing the world are brought into play more or less effortlessly. What is more, any *narrative* which is then overlaid discussing and explaining what you are being shown is given a ring of 'authenticity'. (Of course it's true, you can actually see it.)

***

When words and images are carefully synchronized so that ideas are presented at exactly the moment they are relevant, the abstract explanation has an immediate impact as a reasonable and convincing account of what you are watching. You see the starving people in the refugee camp and the bags of grain being unloaded and you hear the voice say that Western countries are doing all they can to help. You have a much greater sense of the urgency of the crisis and the scale of the relief operation than you would if you just heard, or read, the story in words. Moreover, if reality is a bit complicated to take in, the programme can switch to an animated diagram in which a simplified representation demonstrates how you are supposed to understand the process in question. You see a map with shaded bits and arrows showing where the grain is being distributed. It looks and sounds such an impressive account of the events that it is easy to forget that it is *just* an account, a *version*, of what is going on. It is easy simply to absorb the message about the generosity of the West, without stopping to ask questions about how famines arise in the first place and why some countries have surpluses of food while others have famines. As a medium for putting across a line of argument, TV is potentially immensely powerful.

Its power makes TV appear a very attractive medium for teaching, especially for presenting and explaining complicated subjects, where many different aspects of the world need to be considered at the same time. Instead of *just* examining a particular case study, or *just* looking at a table of figures, or *just* following a line of explanation, you can cut back and forth quickly between all three, or even superimpose one on top of another.

'Dynamic' knowledge

TV is particularly valuable in understanding the *dynamics* of processes. With writing or speech alone, it often takes many words to represent the unfolding of a dynamic process. Verbal explanations tend to have a somewhat *static* quality. Moving pictures offer great potential for representing the world in terms of 'processes' rather than 'objects'. Thus TV can develop and convey a different kind of knowledge from 'book knowledge' — a more rounded and dynamic understanding.

4.2   Problems with learning from TV

It might sound from all this as though TV is the ideal teaching medium. So it is interesting to note that the Open University, which was originally conceived of as the 'University of the Air', actually allocates a much larger portion of study time to reading than to watching TV. To some extent this is attributable to the much higher cost of delivering TV teaching. On the other hand, surveys of student opinion have found that printed teaching texts are consistently the most popular components of Open University courses. For some reason the TV programmes, with all their latent powers, do not impress the students as much as the more traditional printed word.

The lack of impact is due in part to rather mundane factors, such as the difficulty of remembering to tune in at the right times, or conflicts with other family members over channel choice. It may be hard to watch in the right kind of atmosphere for serious study. With a lecture, the formal setting and the ritual of turning up and sitting in respectful silence help to create the frame of mind you need for studying. Watching TV in the sitting room with other people around you, the phone ringing, the next-door neighbour calling to borrow some milk, and so on, may make it very hard to concentrate sufficiently.

Such distractions aside though, the very power of the medium can be a problem. Because of the high cost of making TV programmes, a great deal is often condensed into a short space of time. With your eyes and your ears at work and with images, information and arguments all being presented at once, you are often hard-pressed

74

simply following. This makes it very difficult, for instance, to take any notes — there is just too much to record. Consequently, at the end of the programme you may find, when you try to recall the content, so much has happened that you don't seem to be able to put your finger on any of it. This can create a sense of loss of control. Reading texts may be difficult, but at least *you* are in control of the process. You can stop to think and make connections. TV can by contrast be an unsettling medium to learn from, because it sweeps you along and you can't quite be sure what you are learning or what you think of it. You come to the programmes with high hopes, but may end up feeling vaguely dissatisfied.

In a funny way it often seems easier to enjoy Open University programmes which are for other courses than the one you are studying. Perhaps this is because you are not going to have to write an essay on what you see. After all, the end-product of your work as a student is to write essays and sit exams. That is to say, you are required to work with the written word, and the more dynamic and rounded knowledge you have gained through TV may be very difficult to 'cash in' for credit.

Written knowledge and aural/visual knowledge

The discourses of the academic world are built upon the strengths of the written word; the opportunities for detailed and unhurried analysis and for 'freezing' propositions into a timeless form. TV, on the other hand, is a more 'plastic' medium for representing the world and communicating ideas about it and, as such, provides opportunities for complex and dynamic ways of understanding. However, these do not necessarily engage easily with the more formal and rigorous discourses developed through writing. Whether the newer medium will eventually give rise to academic discourses of equivalent weight to the existing print-based ones (or even supersede them) is impossible to say. But for the time being you as a student are left with the problem of translating the insights and understandings gained from TV into written arguments. This isn't to say that the TV-derived insights and knowledge are not helpful. They remain — at a deep level — part of the intellectual apparatus you use for making the world make sense to you, just as your own direct experience of the world provides such insights and knowledge. It is simply that knowledge at that level is hard to connect with academic knowledge, and it often takes a long time to percolate through to the point of engaging effectively.

The Open University often takes account of these difficulties in learning from TV programmes by providing extensive printed notes, sometimes including exercises. These notes help you to find the links between 'screen knowledge' and 'print knowledge', so that they can work together.

4.3 What do radio broadcasts offer?

Radio programmes offer some of the same possibilities as TV for bringing 'live' segments of the world to you; for example, presenting you directly with the spoken words of a manager and a union leader giving an account of a strike. However, without the visual component radio has to work much harder to achieve the full sense of 'being there'. So radio generally leaves 'expeditions into the world' to the TV and conforms to the model of 'conversation', or chat. Consequently it is often closer to the more formal debating format of mainstream academic discourse.

Learning from radio

Radio is often used to bring the equivalent of a short *lecture*, or a *discussion* between two or more 'experts', into your home. Here it has the advantage that it is a less intense medium than TV. It is much more feasible to sit with a note-pad in hand and take notes. And it tends to be easier to concentrate on *abstract arguments* because you are not attending to visual images at the same time. A philosophical debate, for instance, can be very arresting, when you have nothing but the words to focus on. There are other ways of making a virtue of the absence of 'interfering' visual images. Poetry readings, for example, can play directly on your imagination, as indeed can readings from novels and plays. And musical performances can be distilled to the pure sounds. In fact, radio encourages you to give your whole attention to exactly what the teacher intends.

In some ways, radio is 'friendlier' than TV — more like someone chatting to you as you go about your business — whereas TV demands your whole attention and works on you in so many ways at once. Certainly radio is a much cheaper and less complicated medium. This has encouraged its use for fairly low-key, conversational style programming, such as the arbitrary chitchat of the radio DJ, or 'phone-in' programmes. Such programmes can give radio an immediacy and raw authenticity which glossy TV programmes tend to lack. Educational radio sometimes builds on this by broadcasting 'magazine-type' programmes, which keep you up-to-date with new developments and which let you 'tune in' to the thoughts and feelings of teachers and other students. If you are a home-based learner, you tend to miss out on a lot of very useful background know-how about the course and the subject matter, which full-time students pick up in passing, between lectures, in the coffee bar, and so on. Radio programmes of a less formal kind can help to fill that gap and lessen the feeling of isolation in your studies.

4.4   Problems with learning from radio

With radio programmes, some of the most persistent problems are again very mundane ones. It is very easy to forget to tune in at just the right moment. Indeed, it may even be a problem tuning into the right waveband, since radio programme information tends to be tucked away in very small print. What is more, educational broadcasts tend to get squeezed into unpopular times after midnight and before breakfast, which are times when many people would feel much more comfortable sleeping in their beds, rather than poised with pen and pad trying to focus on a high-powered discussion. And when you *have* made such sacrifices to listen to a programme, the chances of it meeting your heightened expectations are considerably reduced. In fact, the kind of chatty, informal programme which radio is potentially *good* at may be the last thing you feel is worth losing sleep for. To put this point more generally, one of the problems with learning through broadcasts is that you are not studying at the time you would choose. At least with a book you can pick it up when you feel ready and stop reading when you choose.

When it comes to actually listening to the programmes, the problems are fairly similar to those of listening to lectures (see Section 3.2). Though, if anything, radio speakers experience even greater pressures than lecturers to pack a lot into a short time. And without the social context and the visual presence of the speaker it may be harder to grasp the arguments presented.

4.5   Suggestions for learning from TV and radio

When you study from TV you are hard-pressed to do more than watch, since the medium is so intensive. Most of your scope for improving your use of programmes lies in what you choose to do before and afterwards. As with a lecture, you need to be well-prepared if you are to gain full benefit, so you should make a point of reading any programme notes beforehand. Also, a skim through relevant course texts will help to remind you of the central issues and bring them to the front of your mind ready for action. After the programme, spend fifteen minutes trying to note down major points.

This will help to *translate* what you have learned into the 'written' form of knowledge that the rest of the course requires.

Of course, if you have a video-recording machine, you can transform the process of using TV material, by *taping* the broadcasts and playing them back to yourself at leisure. This allows you to control the pace at which you study and helps to offset the 'intensity' of the medium. You can switch the programme off to think and write notes, and you can replay a difficult section until you have understood the point. You can also return to the programme for material for an essay. Repeated viewing allows you to squeeze out the full value of the multiple channels of information in a TV programme. The only catch is that it is very time-consuming, though it may be well worth it if you are struggling with the printed texts and need some help in making the subject make sense.

With radio broadcasts, as with lectures, your main strategy for effective listening lies in taking notes. (Again, you should make a point of reading any programme notes beforehand, and you should try to write an overall summary of the programme afterwards.) However, as with TV, the most radical approach is to *record* radio broadcasts on to cassette, so you can listen at your own chosen time and pace and as many times as you want. You can play the cassettes as you peel the potatoes, or on your way to work, so creating new areas of study time. But most important, you take the pressure off yourself as you listen to the programmes. You don't have to worry about whether you might miss the essential point. You can decide to listen once for the general message and then again to take notes, and you can replay the difficult bits any number of times. You may not *want* to go over every programme in such a detailed way, but the fact that you *can* allows you the freedom to listen with full attention knowing that you can choose what else to do afterwards.

KEY POINTS

▶ To learn effectively from TV and radio broadcasts you should prepare in advance by reading any notes supplied and by skimming the relevant sections of the course.

▶ You can greatly increase the benefit you obtain from programmes by spending time afterwards writing down the main points you picked up.

▶ With radio you can take notes as you listen, but with TV it is often hard to do more than watch.

▶ Learning from TV and radio is transformed if you can record the broadcasts and replay them in your own time and as often as you want.

5 Other study media

We shall look briefly at a few other ways of studying. I shall simply pick out a few of their features without going into detail about problems they present or suggestions for using them.

5.1 Audio and video cassettes

Teaching cassettes are often designed for an 'interactive' mode of study. They may, for instance, set exercises to do, where you switch off the cassette to write some notes, or look something up in a book, or carry out an experiment, before returning to the cassette for further discussion. The audio cassette, in particular, is a relatively cheap and uncomplicated technology and, as such, is useful for informal interactive exercises. You might, for example, be asked to look at a complicated table of figures, or a map, or a picture, while the voice on the cassette 'talks you through' the important features. An audio cassette can also be used to introduce you to the central ideas in a text. Then, after you have done the reading, you return to the cassette to hear the main themes discussed again, so that you can check that you have been picking up the right meanings from the text. Using cassettes 'interactively' with texts helps to vary the texture of your studies, offering a change of activity and a change of pace.

Video cassettes are considerably more expensive to produce and supply and so are used to present 'rich' material worthy of repeated viewing. In fact, they offer exciting prospects of bringing 'the world' to you in a form that you can study in detail in your own home. For example, on a course on child development you can be supplied with recordings of young children at work or at play, to study closely and use as a basis for carrying out project work. Or a course on teaching can use a video showing samples of teachers in action for extensive discussion and analysis. A drama course can give you excerpts from performances of plays to explore in depth, and so on. These opportunities for close, careful and repeated observation enable you to make links between the 'real' world and the formal ideas you read in the texts; links which would otherwise take a lot of time and experience to establish.

The main problem with using cassettes is the amount of time they tend to consume and the attendant worry that you are not spending enough time doing 'core' study activities, such as reading and essay writing. Finding your way around them can also be a little irritating, since they do not have page numbers like books. Otherwise, they tend to be more or less self-explanatory in use. As time and resources are set aside for developing their uses, they will no doubt become more widespread and increasingly helpful.

5.2 Residential schools

Some courses offer short residential schools of a week or a weekend in length. These often require a substantial commitment of time and money on your part, so it is worth pointing out their purposes. The greatest benefit of attending a residential school is that it allows you to become completely immersed in your subject for a few days. When you have been grappling with the texts on your own at the same time as struggling with a crowded life, it can give an enormous boost to your general grasp of the ideas, arguments, language and theories of your subject matter to work at them 'full-time' for a few days. It is also possible to carry out certain kinds of exercises (such as simulating a political crisis) with large groups of people and the time to spare. And sites such as a university campus can allow access to facilities such as laboratories and an academic library, which you might never normally be able to experience. It is very valuable too to mix with a number of different tutors who can offer a wide range of knowledge and opinions, instead of always dealing with the same one.

These are the formal benefits of residential schools. But there are other equally important informal ones. When you study mainly on your own at home, it can be hard to establish a sense of being a 'real' student. Your studies can seem like a slightly unusual hobby perched on the edge of your 'normal' life. Being with a large group of other students helps to put your studies in their proper place as a very important part of your life. You gain the support of being part of a large body of people who share your concern to understand the world better and are prepared to give serious attention to it. You also pick up a great many ideas on how to cope with your studies, as well as moral support from sharing experiences with others. Many students find that a residential school is the best part of the course and that it transforms both their approach to their studies and their understanding of the subject.

5.3 Project work

Some courses have a substantial 'project work' component. This allows you to choose an area of special interest to you, setting your own targets, posing your own central questions, and seeking out your own sources of information. Undertaking a project changes your status *vis-à-vis* the subject, in that *you* take an active role in conducting an enquiry and 'creating' knowledge, instead of being presented with it. This gives you insight into the nature of knowledge. You begin to understand the process through which it is produced. When all goes well, project work creates a high level of motivation, gives a great sense of achievement, and produces a very deep kind of learning.

However, project work is not a bed of roses. There are many points at which beginners tend to run into trouble. Most students start out being too ambitious. Some have great difficulty in defining in detail what the project is actually about. Then there is the time-consuming process of getting hold of information, followed by a lengthy stage of analysing it. Finally, there is the challenge of writing the whole thing up. In other words, project courses should not be undertaken lightly. There is much opportunity for losing direction, losing heart, and using up huge amounts of time. Project courses place you and your life under considerable strain. Basically they offer all the rewards and the problems of studying in general, but writ large. So before plunging into a project course seek advice from a tutor, or read a guide on project work. Make sure that you have plenty of time ahead of you as you start. Be modest in your aims and take *very seriously* all *deadlines* for project outlines, draft reports, and the like. Project work could be the pinnacle of your educational experience, but you will need all the foresight and all the support you can get.

5.4 Computers and study

Whole books have been written on the role of computers in education. This is just a sketch of some of their present uses and future potential.

Word processing

One way in which the spread of desktop computers has had a profound impact on education is through their use as *word processors*. The sheer speed with which you can get words down and then move them around transforms the writing process. If you can't type, the computer can teach you relatively quickly and easily. When you produce your essay in this way, the quality of presentation of your finished document gives an uncanny authenticity to the words you have tentatively formulated. Having said this, not everyone finds that they can accomplish mentally demanding writing on a word processor. Others find they write too much because it is so easy to produce words, or they keep moving bits around until their writing loses its coherence. So word processing is not necessarily the perfect answer for every writer and every circumstance. But if you are expecting to do a lot of writing in the near future, and you don't already use a word processor, it is certainly worth investigating the possibilities. You may be able to get access to a computer at work or at your local college, or you might want to look into buying your own for use at home. On the other hand, like many students before, you can get along perfectly well without.

Information

A place where you are very likely to come across a computer is in any large *library*. Nowadays library *catalogues* are increasingly held on a computer system. This has transformed the activity of hunting for relevant books, journals and articles, which is one of the basic processes of studying and of academic research. It is now possible to carry out searches for source texts much faster and more flexibly than before. However, beyond that, the computer will increasingly be capable of use as a source of information itself. Some encyclopaedias and dictionaries are already available on compact discs, allowing instant access to the very topic or phrase you want. There are enormous potential benefits in being able to access information in this way (rather than waiting endlessly for books to be returned to the library), though developments of this sort are at a very early stage as yet.

Data banks

For social science students there is the exciting prospect of being able to have access to large collections of *social data*. You can then ask statistical questions directly, instead of having to work with tables in the form in which they happen to be presented in a particular research publication. This promises to turn the statistical side of the subject from a somewhat tedious and technical topic into a much more active and creative one. A further revolution on the statistical and data-handling side of the subject is the potential for setting up statistical 'models' of the world, with which you can 'interact'. With these you can make decisions, feed information in, and find out the result. For example, you can have a computer model of a national economy set up such that teams of students can compete at 'running the economy', thus testing out their understanding of economic principles.

Learning from computers

Two other areas where the potential of computers in education is being explored are the possibilities of *computer-aided learning* and the uses of *computer conferencing*. For certain fairly well-defined fields of knowledge it is possible to write computer programs which 'teach', in the sense that they explain things and then set you tasks. The computer checks your answer and if you have made a mistake you are given extra explanation and practice. Producing programs of this kind is very labour intensive and therefore expensive. Moreover, the potential for teaching broader and more abstract conceptual material this way (such as the main content of a humanities or a social science course) appears to be fairly limited, so it seems unlikely that you would study this way to any great extent in the immediate future. Turning to *computer conferencing*, this involves students with home-based computers being connected through the telephone system to a central computer. This allows all the participants in the scheme to send messages to each other. A few Open University courses are already experimenting with the potential of computer conferencing for holding something like a tutorial discussion by means of the computer link. In effect, the computer acts like a classroom noticeboard on which people pin messages. Somebody puts up a message with a question and then other students, or the tutor, put up other messages in response. The idea is that members of the group check the 'noticeboard' every few days, to read the new messages that have been put up in the various currently active 'conversations', and to add any comments of their own. It remains to be seen how well teachers and groups of students can develop the conventions, habits and discipline to make the system really useful. It is already clear that, as well as the potential for sending blinding flashes of insight, the conferencing system offers the same opportunities as conventional noticeboards do for trivial communications. Indeed, the quantity of such communications tends to be much greater, and they are more difficult to wade through. Clearly the idea of having 'conversations' with people of similar interests scattered across the country (or even in other countries) is an intriguing one, but students will have to develop a new range of study skills to exploit this potential.

Whether or not you decide to fling yourself enthusiastically into the world of computers, it is worth taking the time to acquaint yourself with some of the things they can do and to explore their relevance to your studies.

6 Conclusion

This brief review shows that there is already a lot more to studying than simply reading a book or listening to a lecture. Moreover, there is every reason to assume that the range of alternative ways of getting hold of knowledge and ideas will continue to grow. As a student, you can expect to spend your time on a range of different activities, some of which will not feel very much like 'studying' as we have traditionally understood it. Accordingly, you will need to develop a wider range of skills and a flexible attitude to your studies. With luck, the pay-off will be that studying will be more effective and more fun.

CHAPTER 4

Working with numbers

1 Getting to know numbers

In Chapter 2, I talked as though reading necessarily involved words and sentences. However, we live in a society where a great deal of information is communicated in the form of numbers. Sometimes these numbers come singly, as when the newsreader tells us the number of casualties after a hurricane. Sometimes they come as sets of numbers which are presented together, such as the cooking instructions for a chicken, giving temperatures and times and weights. And sometimes a lot of numbers are put together in the form of a chart or graph, such as the diagrams on the TV news which summarize the results of the latest political opinion poll, or which show how the pound has been rising or falling against the dollar.

Many of these sorts of numbers are so familiar that you have learned to take in their meaning without stopping to think about it. When the weather forecast in the newspaper says it is going to be 30°C or 86°F today you *immediately* know it is going to be hot; and you have a much better idea of *how* hot than if the forecaster simply said, 'It will be hot'. Yet in making instant sense of these small clusters of numbers, letters and symbols you bring into play a lot of knowledge and experience. To interpret the information you have to know:

▶ that '°' stands for 'degrees'

▶ that degrees are units of temperature

▶ that 'C' stand for 'Celsius' and 'F' for 'Fahrenheit'

▶ that Celsius and Fahrenheit are temperature scales

▶ that figures for temperatures on the Fahrenheit scale are much larger than figures for the same temperatures on the Celsius scale (e.g. 30°F is very cold whereas 30°C is hot)

▶ what it feels like when the temperature is in the 30s C, or in the 80s F.

After years of exposure to weather forecasts, all this knowledge is something you take for granted. You are not aware of being an expert at reading this particular form of numerical representation.

To take another example, if you are a tennis enthusiast, a newspaper report reading 'Becker beat Chang 7–6, 3–6, 4–6, 7–6, 6–1' would present you with no difficulty. The numbers would convey a lot of information to you. They would tell you that it had been a long match; that the first and fourth sets had been so close that they had to be decided by the 'tie-break' system, being narrowly won each time by Becker; and that Chang had been ahead after winning the second and third sets but had collapsed rather rapidly in the fifth set. You would know that each pair of figures represents a tennis 'set' and that in each pair the first figure is always (by convention) the number of games won by the eventual winner of the match, while the second is the number of games won by the loser. Similarly, if you were watching tennis on TV and you glimpsed a scoreboard showing the information set out in Figure 4.1, you would, as a tennis follower, quickly register that the game was in its third set, Sabatini having won the first 6–3 and Sanchez the second 4–6. You would also see that Sanchez was winning the third set by 3 games to 2, but that Sabatini was leading the current game by 30 points to 15.

6	4	SABATINI	30	2
3	6	SANCHEZ	15	3

Figure 4.1 *Information conveyed by numbers*

The point I am making here is that it is quite normal in everyday life, nowadays, to be expected to take in numerical information. In most walks of life it is assumed that you know that 10% stands for ten per cent and that you know what it means if you are offered a 10% pay rise.* You are expected to become familiar with quite complicated tables such as bus and railway timetables, which lay out information so that the *position* in which each figure is placed is very important in interpreting its meaning (for example, you see that the figure 7 at the right on a timetable is under the heading 'Platform', and so you understand that it must be telling you where to find the train). *So long as you understand the conventions* and have plenty of *experience* of reading such information, it is something you can do very easily and quickly. Indeed, it is a blessing

---

* Do you need refreshing on percentages? If you started with 30 pupils in your class and there was a 10 per cent increase in the numbers, you would then have 33. Ten per cent means 10 for every hundred (*centum* is Latin for a hundred). To work out what 10 per cent of something is, you multiply it by 10, then divide by 100. (Similarly, to calculate 6 per cent you multiply by 6 then divide by 100.) If you multiply 30 by 10 you get 300 — then dividing by 100 you get 3. So, if your increase is 10 per cent, you have 3 more to add to your original 30, making 33.

to both the givers and the receivers to be able to transmit detailed information so efficiently. Living in a complicated society like ours involves a great deal of co-ordination of our activities. It presumes the ability in each of us to inform ourselves of the details of what is going on around us, so that we can adapt our actions to suit the requirements and the opportunities life presents. At the very least, being able to read the time (both from a digital display and from a clock face) is a basic skill for social survival.

So far so good. We can all cope with very basic numerical information. We know how to cope with turning on the TV in time to catch the 9 o'clock news (though perhaps if your digital watch is reading 21:00 it might cause a moment of doubt). But when you come across a *new* kind of numerical information, particularly if the layout is rather complicated, it tends to mean very little to you. Your eyes simply glaze over and you look at something else? Why?

Why numbers can be difficult

Numerical information is information in a very condensed and highly *abstract* form. A number on its own means very little. You have to *learn* how to read it. You have to find out both *how* the number is used (i.e. what the conventions are) and *what* the number stands for. Thirty years ago, 5/- was a very meaningful sign in Britain. Now the convention for representing that quantity is 25p or £0.25. It is hard to imagine 5/- being the 'natural' way of writing it, we have learned the new conventions so thoroughly.

Numbers of any kind are only meaningful to people who have learned how to read them.

Each time you come across a *new* kind of numerical information, the question arises as to whether it is worth making a fresh investment in learning how to make the numbers meaningful to you. Since there is so much numerical information around these days, the answer will often be no. You are unlikely to have the time to discover the significance of *all* the numbers you come across on the backs of bottles, on the packaging for technical equipment, in the financial pages in newspapers, and so on. On the other hand, within any given area of knowledge there is quite often a *general* level of *numerical 'literacy'* which is taken for granted. So if you intend to become a regular participant in discussions within that field, then you have to take the time and trouble to develop the relevant 'numeracy'. If you want to play stocks and shares, for example, you have to be prepared to *learn* how to read the Financial Times Share Index.

KEY POINTS

In order to be able to use numerical information you have to *invest some time* in learning:

▶ *how* the numbers are being used, and

▶ *what* they are being used to represent.

Numeracy

'Numeracy' is not a single ability which you either have or don't have. It is the *skill, experience,* and *knowledge* you need to *'read'* the *specific kinds of numbers and tables, used within a particular field of discussion.* You can be 'numerate' in one field, such as betting on horses, but 'innumerate' in another, such as accountancy. As we have already seen, we *all* display a wide-ranging 'numeracy' in our daily lives, without even noticing it. We tend to be much more aware of the numbers we *don't* understand.

When you become a student you are, by definition, moving into unfamiliar territory and, in so far as the subject you are studying makes use of numerical representation of information, *you will have to make a time investment in order to acquire the relevant numerical 'vocabulary' and the conventions of presentation.* At first, new uses of numbers may be difficult to make sense of, but as you get practice, reading numerical information eventually becomes 'second nature', like reading the time or taking in the forecast temperatures for the day.

1.1 Numbers and studying

In many subjects of study you will come across numerical information in various forms. However, you may find you are tempted to skip straight past the numbers, tables, and diagrams because they don't immediately convey a lot to you, and because of the initial effort required to learn how to read them. Don't skip! You need to have access to that information.

> ## *The temptation to skip tables*
>
> Remember that in academic study, as in other walks of life, numbers can give you a lot of detailed information very quickly and efficiently. The time you invest in learning how to read tables and diagrams will *save* you a lot of time in your future reading. You will become informed much more precisely and much more rapidly once you can take advantage of these numbers. What is more, you will be able to make you *own* interpretations of the information, rather than relying on the judgement of others.

This doesn't mean that you have to become a statistical wizard. Some people *do* choose to specialize in working with numerical information. But many students require little more than a very basic idea of how to set about reading a table of figures, or a graph. *You* will acquire this basic level of skill provided that, as you come across tables and diagrams, you are prepared to take a careful look at them. It takes a little time before you feel comfortable and confident with all kinds of tables, but it *will* come with practice. To begin this process, we shall look at an example.

2   Describing the world

One of the aims of academic enquiry is to be able to *describe* aspects of the world — to sketch out key features and to outline what is going on.

Imagine you were asked to *describe* ways in which British society in the 1990s is different from that of fifty to sixty years earlier. One very obvious feature you might pick on is the impact of modern technology. You might, for instance, point to the changes brought about by the enormous growth in electronic communications.

As soon as you take time to think about it, it is clear that developments in communications have made huge and fundamental differences to the way societies work. Take the growth of *television*. This has had an enormous impact on the patterns of domestic life. It has dramatically changed the way we spend our time within the home. Indeed, it has encouraged us to *stay* at home for our entertainment and made us less dependent on the communities around us for supplying our links to the world at large. It has also imported ideas from 'the world out there' — the high pressure, glossy world of public broadcasting — directly into our living rooms. This in turn has brought about huge changes in politics. The way politicians and policies come across on TV has become more important than political activity at a local level (this is, after all, the age of the film star president). And the medium of TV has itself constantly undergone changes. For instance, the development of *video recorders* has given us more control over our use of the TV; and now the coming of *cable* and *satellite* TV presents us with another great upheaval in our relationship with 'the box'.

You might also want to consider the impact of the spread of the *telephone*. It is inconceivable that we would have such enormously complex business and government organizations without rapid communications provided by the telephone. Neither would our international trade nor political links have anything like the same character. Distances which separated whole civilizations for centuries have been made irrelevant for many purposes. And this erosion of the significance of distances is also experienced at a personal level. You can keep in regular touch with distant relatives. You can phone for help in an emergency. You can even do your shopping by telephone. If we add to these telephone links the potential of the modern domestic computer, then the possibilities for planning and organizing our lives from within our own homes become quite staggering. It is possible for some people to do quite sophisticated technical jobs from a home base and at the same time to be in direct touch with an employer miles away. When it is as easy to deliver a piece of work to the other end of the country as to the other end of a corridor, then the nature of work organizations is put under enormous pressure to change.

Let us stop at this point and simply draw the conclusion that electronic communications have made an enormous contribution to shaping the kind of society we live in. We have enough material here to be able to write at great length about important and fascinating aspects of our society and about the lives we live within it. And thus far I have described these changes in our society without making use of *numbers* at all.

However, it would not be unreasonable for someone reading all this to say: 'Hold on! How do you *know* that all this electronic equipment is as widely used as you imply? You *say* that "everybody" has a TV these days, but perhaps lots of people choose *not* to have one, or can't *afford* one. What evidence can you offer? Just how many homes actually contain these various items of electronic equipment? I want to know the scale of all these changes before accepting that they are so significant.' To answer questions like these we are going to need some numbers.

Why use figures?

It adds a great deal to the force of your description of any aspect of the world if you can present some figures which will give an indication of the *dimensions* of what you are talking about.

---

3   Describing with tables

In fact, we need to look up some social statistics.* I found a relevant table of figures in a copy of the weekly magazine *New Statesman and Society*. You can see it in Figure 4.2.

Ownership of communications and information facilities among households in selected income groups

Weekly income: £	Percentage owning: TV	Telephone	Video recorder	Home computer
60–80	96.9	67.4	12.6	3.3
100–125	98.1	76.7	21.2	7.6
150–175	97.7	76.3	31.6	9.6
225–250	97.5	87.3	43.5	21.2
325–375	98.0	94.1	56.5	26.5
550+	98.4	98.2	64.8	28.8

Source: *Family Expenditure Survey 1986*, Table 3, Department of Employment, 1988

Figure 4.2 *A table taken from* New Statesman and Society, *30 June 1989*

ACTIVITY BREAK   To help you to tackle the table constructively I have set some questions. Work out the answers by studying the table shown in Figure 4.2. Write them down, so that you can check them against mine when you have finished.

1   (a) What is the lowest figure for TV ownership?
(b) What is the highest figure for TV ownership?
(c) Would it be reasonable to say that almost everyone has a TV?
(d) Does owning a TV depend on income level?

2   (a) What percentage of households in the lowest income group have a phone?

* Originally, 'statistics' referred to the collecting and analysing of facts about the *state* (or the society). Nowadays the word 'statistics' is more specifically associated with *numbers*; particularly with techniques for working on large sets of numerical data and presenting summaries of their main features.

Finding your way round a table of figures

It is easiest if we take a specific case. Take Question 1(a): What is the lowest figure for TV ownership?

The second column from the left of the table is the one you should look at. It is headed 'TV' and above that is says 'percentage owning'. This means the figures in this column tell us 'percentages owning TV'.

If you look down this column, you will see that all the figures are in the high 90s. If you ignore the numbers after the decimal point, you will see that they are all 96, 97, or 98. 96 is the lowest (though of course there is not much in it since 96.9 is very nearly 97).

If you then read across to the left of this figure of 96.9 you will see that in the 'Weekly income' column we have 60–80. There is a '£' sign at the top of this column which tells us that this means people with an income of £60–80 per week. Referring to the title at the top of the table we see that the figures are for *ownership among households.* So we are being told here that, *of households which have an income of between £60 and £80 per week, 96.9 per cent own a TV.*

If you read across the top row of figures, the other three columns tell you the level of ownership of telephones, video recorders and home computers for this £60–80 income group.

The rest of the table gives you the same information for the other income groups.

(b) Can you express this as a *fraction* (roughly)?
(c) What fraction (roughly) of households in the next-to-lowest of the income groups shown here *don't* have phones?
(d) Do *most* people have phones?

3   (a) What income level do you have to go to to find more than half the households owning a video recorder?
(b) What proportion of the wealthiest households have a video?
(c) Do families with low incomes manage to buy a video anyway?
(d) Do most people have a video recorder?

4   (a) Do low income households have home computers?
(b) Roughly what fraction of the next-to-highest income group have home computers?
(c) At what income level does the biggest leap in computer ownership happen?
(d) Is owning a home computer related to level of income?

5 Leaving out TV, for the other three types of item there tends to be a fairly steady increase in ownership as you move to higher levels of income. Where is the exception to this?

6 Are *all* income groups represented here?

7 (a) When was this information gathered?
(b) When was it reported?
(c) Why do you think the dates are different?

3.1 Answers to the quiz

1 (a) 96.9 per cent — for the £60–80 weekly income group. If you didn't get this answer read the box above.

1 (b) 98.4 per cent — for the wealthiest income group (i.e. those with £550 per week income, or more). If you have not chosen the same answer as I have, hunt back through the table to see where my figure comes from. Then try to work out how I arrived at that figure.

1 (c) Yes, it would. Only 2–3 per cent of households are without a TV. This is the case for all income levels.

1 (d) No — TV ownership is not related to income level. Owning a TV is almost universal; and where there are slight variations between income groups the differences are unevenly spread across the income levels (e.g. the second *lowest* income group — £100 to £125 — has the second *highest* level of ownership, 98.1 per cent). These small variations look like *random* variations. They do not suggest a trend. If another survey were done, we would expect the numbers to be slightly different because of chance variations, and thus the order of the groups would tend to switch around.

2 (a) 67.4 per cent.

2 (b) ⅔ or two-thirds. 66.7 per cent is two-thirds.* Since 67.4 is very close to 66.7, for all practical purposes you can say that two-thirds of this group have phones.

2 (c) A quarter of the £100–125 income households don't have phones.

2 (d) This is a difficult question. Certainly the majority of people have phones, because even in the lowest income group two-thirds

---

* You can check this. One third is 33.3 and if you double that it comes to 66.6. This is almost the same as 66.7 (the small difference is due to rounding-up from 66.66 to 66.7). If you add three thirds together, i.e. 33.3 per cent + 33.3 per cent + 33.3 per cent you get 99.9 per cent, which is virtually the same as 100 per cent.

have a phone — and in the highest income group virtually everyone does. However, below the average income level, a *quarter* or more of households are *without* a phone (according to the article in which the table appeared, the average income in 1988 was £218). So it could be rather misleading to say that *most* people have phones, since that might lead you to ignore the substantial minority of households (at least an eighth), which do not.

3 (a) £325–375. For all the income groups below this level, fewer than half the households have a video recorder.

3 (b) Nearly two-thirds (64.8 per cent).

3 (c) Some low income families *do* own a video — 12.6 per cent or about an eighth.* But it would certainly be misleading to assume that a video recorder is something that virtually all families manage to afford regardless of how low their income is.

3 (d) No. In fact, making a rough summary of the figures in the video recorder column, it is clear that fewer than half of all households had a video at the time of the survey.

Percentages and fractions

It is useful to be able to switch back and forth between fractions and percentages because, although percentages are more accurate, you can begin to lose touch with what the figures mean. If you remind yourself from time to time that 50 per cent is the same as a half, that 75 per cent is three-quarters, that 20 per cent is a fifth, and so on, it helps to fix in your mind the kinds of quantities you are dealing with.

---

4 (a) Generally no. However, a very small proportion of households in even the lowest income group do have computers.

4 (b) A little over a quarter of the households in the £325–375 income group had a computer at the time of the survey.

4 (c) The biggest rise in computer ownership appears between the £150–175 and the £225–250 levels of income (from 9.6 per cent to 21.2 per cent).

4 (d) Yes. There is a clear relationship between levels of income and ownership of a computer.

---

* A quarter is 25 per cent, so an eighth is half of 25 per cent — in other words 12.5 per cent.

5 The 'blip' in the otherwise fairly steady rise in ownership at successive income levels comes in the *telephone* ownership column. The ownership level for the £150–175 income group is slightly lower than for the £100–125 income group.

'Blips'

Picking out 'blips' is one of the 'tricks of the trade' of table reading. You scan down columns and across rows, looking for patterns of steady rising or falling. Wherever you find a 'blip' it is worth stopping to take a closer look and to think what might have caused it.

In fact, what we have here is a levelling off, rather than a drop (since 76.3 is scarcely different from 76.7). We would need to make further enquiries to find out whether there is a reason for this. On the other hand, it might well be due to chance. Perhaps with another survey we would find the blip disappears.

Sampling errors

If you follow the political opinion polls, you will know that every now and again a freak result comes up. Most surveys rely on studying a *sample* from a given *population**, or group of people. This means that the researchers could be unlucky and by chance pick a lot of people of one kind and fail to pick many of another kind. This will bias the results.

There are several ways of trying to avoid being misled in this way. One is to make the sample very big, since the effects of chance *ought* to even out when you select lots of people to be in the sample. On the other hand, big samples are very expensive, so another safeguard is to do small surveys on several occasions to check whether you get the same results. The variations in results that you get from different samples are called *sampling errors*.

*(*Note:* The total number of people in any particular group is known in statistics as a 'population'. All the students in the Open University are the 'population' of OU students. Some populations are very small, such as the population of internationally ranked British tennis players. To find out things about that group you wouldn't need to 'sample' them. You could study every member of the population individually. Others, such as the population of people who use supermarkets, are very big, so it would be impossible to study more than a small sample of the total population.)

KEY POINTS

▶ You need to be cautious when you are reading tables.

▶ Remember that the figures are only *approximations* to 'the truth'.

6 No we *don't* have all income groups represented here. Presumably for purposes of cutting down the size of the survey, or of making the table easier to read, we have been given figures for 'selected' income groups. However, looking at the information in front of us, it seems unlikely that we are missing anything important. The trends in each column look very smooth and solid. It is most improbable that data for the missing income groups would do more than fill out the picture we already have. It is worth noticing, though, that the 'bands' of income are not all the same size, nor evenly spread apart. You can see this clearly in the diagram in Figure 4.3. The higher income bands are broader and spread further apart.

Figure 4.3 *Income groups shown in the table in Figure 4.2*

7 (a) The survey was carried out in 1986. It is obviously *very important* to know this. Most of my remarks have been in the present tense. But really I *ought* to have been using the *past* tense. (It will be even further in the past when you read this. Did you look inside the front cover of *this* book to see when it was published?) The market for home computers has grown enormously since 1986, so *that* column of figures is certain to have changed considerably. Also, video recorders, as a relatively new technology, are likely to have spread to many more households since this survey.

7 (b) The Department of Employment reported on the survey in 1988, two years after the data were collected. And the *New Statesman and Society* article used the data halfway through the following year. So there was a fairly long time-lag between the gathering of the information and its discussion in public.

7 (c) Large surveys take a long time to carry out. The initial design of the survey, the choosing of people for the sample, the filling in of questionnaires (and perhaps some interviewing) are all big jobs. Then the data have to be coded, entered into a computer and analysed,

and finally a report has to be written, approved and published. Certain kinds of standardized surveys, such as political opinion polls, are carried out relatively quickly. But in general it is quite usual for there to be a long delay between the gathering of information and its general availability.

Out-of-date data

Social statistics are almost always 'out-of-date', simply because of the time it takes to collect, process and publish the information. This is something you have to look out for when you examine tables.

On the other hand, just because information is not right up-to-date doesn't mean it isn't worth looking at. You can never get *exactly* the figures you want. And *some* information is a lot better than none. The table we have been looking at has enabled us to answer a lot of useful questions, even if we have had to put a note against our findings, to the effect that there are likely to have been important changes since the data were collected.

It is usually the case that you have to work with data gathered by someone else, for some other purpose, some time ago. You haven't the time, or the resources, to gather for yourself all the figures you might like to have. Research is very expensive. The trick is to learn how to make intelligent use of the data that other people collect.

3.2 Summary of tips for table readers

Take your time and be cautious

As I have said, numbers are a very *abstract* and *condensed* form of information. They can tell you a great deal in a very compact and efficient way. But, with any table you want to read intelligently, you have to allow time to 'get on the inside' — to 'feel your way' round the figures and the words, so as to be sure that you know exactly what kind of information you are looking at. It is easy to be misled by numbers. You need to approach them in a careful and questioning frame of mind. There is a lot to learn from most tables if you take the trouble to become familiar with them.

Finding your way in

It is often a bit difficult to get your first grip on a new table. When you look at the headings and labels they may be a bit too cryptic to take in on their own. Often the best way in is to pick on one or two of the *numbers* and see if you can work out what they stand for by checking across to the left-hand edge and the top edge of the table. Try to cross-check against what you know of the 'real world' to see if the figures as you understand them seem likely. (For example, in the table we have been looking at, does it seem likely that 96–98 per cent of all groups would have TVs? – yes it does!) If you seem to be making a plausible reading of the figures then try some other checks. If the proportion of people owning a video recorder in the highest income bracket is 65 per cent (note I have rounded 64.8 upwards to 65), and in the lowest bracket is 13 per cent, what would you expect the figure for the middle groups to be? Halfway between would be 39 per cent. Well the two middle groups fall either side of that figure, so that looks fine.

If the figures seem to make sense, then scan across some of the rows and up and down some of the columns to see whether you can see any patterns in the way the figures rise and fall – in other words, look for any 'trends' in the figures. If you *can* spot *patterns*, think whether *they* seem to make any sense.

Reading the words

When you have had a good look at the *numbers*, go back to the *words* to check *them* more thoroughly. Once you have something of a feel for the figures, the significance of the main title of the table will be clearer to you. You also need to check the headings of the columns carefully. Make sure that you are clear what the units of measurement are. Are you dealing with numbers of people, or numbers of millions of people, or percentages of people – with pounds, or millions of pounds? Then look at any other notes that go with the table. Who collected and published the data and when? You may find that you need to change your understanding of the numbers in the table once you have read the small print that goes with the table (as, for instance, was the case with the information on when the survey data was collected).

Extracting information

When you have satisfied yourself that you really *have* grasped what the figures in the table mean, then you are ready to start pulling out what you want to know:

▶ Look for the highest figure and lowest figure in each row to see what the range of variation is. Then do the same for each column. Are any of the highs and lows surprising?

▶ See if you can find an interesting trend. If so, how could you summarize it in a few words?

▶ Are there any 'blips' in the trends? If so, can you think of any reasons for them?

▶ Try quickly to summarize for yourself in words the main patterns which emerge from each of the rows and columns of the table.

What I have been outlining here is the 'super de luxe' treatment. You won't have time to look at *every* table you come across in loving detail. However, you should make a point of building up your experience in reading tables, by picking on one from time to time and really giving it the full treatment. Once you are used to reading tables, you will find you become quite comfortable with them.

KEY POINTS

▶ Take your time and be cautious.

▶ Look fairly quickly at the main headings of the table. Then pick on one or two numbers and check what they seem to be telling you. Does the table 'make sense'?

▶ Go back to the words round the edges of the table and at the heads of columns and read them carefully, to be sure you know what you are looking at.

▶ Read any footnotes.

▶ Scan for interesting data — horizontally along the rows and vertically up and down the columns. Check for:

high and low points

trends

blips.

▶ Summarize for yourself the main conclusions you think can be drawn.

4 Describing with diagrams and graphs

The table we have been studying indicated to us that there are some clear links between levels of income and ownership of certain items of electronic communications equipment. We can *show* the nature of these relationships much more clearly if we turn the table into a *picture*. Figure 4.4 shows exactly the same data as Figure 4.2, but presented in the form of a bar chart. To help you to check this I have repeated Figure 4.2 on the same page.

Ownership of communications and information facilities among households
in selected income groups

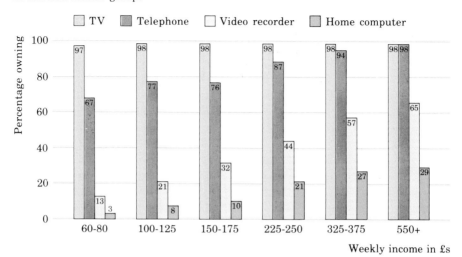

Figure 4.4 The same data as in Figure 4.2, shown in the form of a bar
chart

Ownership of communications and information facilities among households
in selected income groups

| Weekly income: | Percentage owning: | | | |
£	TV	Telephone	Video recorder	Home computer
60–80	96.9	67.4	12.6	3.3
100–125	98.1	76.7	21.2	7.6
150–175	97.7	76.3	31.6	9.6
225–250	97.5	87.3	43.5	21.2
325–375	98.0	94.1	56.5	26.5
550+	98.4	98.2	64.8	28.8

Source: *Family Expenditure Survey 1986*, Table 3, Department of Employment, 1988

Figure 4.5 A repeat of Figure 4.2, so that you can cross-check the numbers
with Figure 4.4

ACTIVITY BREAK To check that the bar chart is nothing more than
the data from the table presented in a different way, try comparing
the numbers in the two. Look at the top row of numbers in Figure
4.5. Find the figure 96.9 per cent, which as you know is the
proportion of people in the lowest income group who have TVs. If

you 'round' this to the nearest whole number, it comes to 97 per cent. Now look at the top of the left-hand bar in Figure 4.4. Again the figure is 97 per cent — so this vertical bar stands for all the people in the lowest income group who have TVs. The key at the top of the chart tells you this. Now check the first figure in the next column of the table. It shows a 67.4 per cent level of ownership of phones. This rounds to 67. On top of the second bar you will see 67. Quickly check all the numbers in the table to convince yourself that they are the same as in the chart. Make sure you agree that the key at the top of the chart agrees with the headings in the table.

The way the bar chart works is to take the first income group and draw four bars representing ownership of TV, phone, video and computer next to each other. After a gap you get the four bars for the next income group; then again for the third income group; and so on through all the six income groups.

To make use of the chart you scan from left to right and back again, looking for patterns. I hope you agree that the trends show up extremely clearly. You can see that the TV bar is almost the same for all groups, but that the others get steadily bigger as you move from left to right. This shows us what we had already learned from the table — that ownership levels for phones, videos and computers are related to income, whereas TVs are almost universal. However, the diagram brings the message out much more clearly and forcefully. That is the basic purpose of presenting data in diagrams rather than in tables. If you choose the right kind of diagram, it makes the *patterns* in the data very much clearer and more obvious.

In fact, the bar chart is not the only type of diagram we can use to display this data. We can just as easily use a graph, as you will see in Figure 4.6.

ACTIVITY BREAK   Again try cross-checking some of the numbers from Figure 4.5 to Figure 4.6, to convince yourself that we are indeed looking at the same figures presented in a different way.

For instance, does the figure 28.8 per cent for ownership of computers in the top income group show up in Figures 4.4, 4.5 and 4.6?

If anything, the trends show up even more clearly in the graph than in the bar chart. You can see, for example, the steady rise in ownership of video recorders as you move from low incomes on the left to high incomes on the right. And the 'blip' we noted in the

Ownership of communications and information facilities among households
in selected income groups

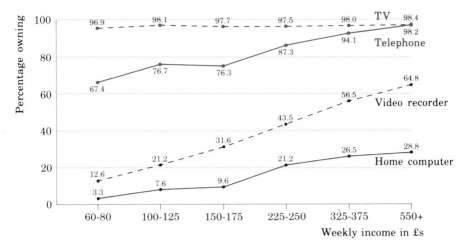

Figure 4.6 The same data as in Figure 4.5, shown in the form of a graph

phone ownership figures is much more obvious. In fact, the graph is
so clear and direct in its display of the trends that you might ask
why anyone would bother with the bar chart.

The main reason for preferring a bar chart is that it is not quite so
abstract as the graph. When you can see solid bars representing all
the owners of phones in each group, it reminds you that the chart
represents lots of real cases of people with phones. In fact, the bar
chart gives you a better picture of the *overall quantity* of electronic
communications equipment owned in each income group. You can
see immediately that the high income group at the right owns a lot
of everything, while the low income group on the left owns TVs and
phones rather than videos and computers. That information is there
in the graph too, but it doesn't show up so clearly. With the graph,
the figures are condensed to just a set of points, so you have to work
a little harder to remind yourself what the picture is telling you. So
long as you are clear what the points stand for, the graph is, in a
way, a purer representation of the trends.

Another thing the graph does is to make it easy to predict what the
levels of ownership might be for other groups who were left out of
the original table. For example, if you look along the line for video
ownership to the point halfway between the £100–125 group and the
£150–175 group, it suggests that, for the group in between (i.e. the
£125–150 group), we would expect about 26 to 27 per cent to own
videos. In other words, we can 'read off' predictions from a line
plotted on a graph.

One more thing we might want to do, while we are looking at the trends on the graph, is to ask: 'What about the unevenness in the bands of income groups? Perhaps the shape of the graph would be different if we showed the income groups the "proper" distance apart?' To do this, I took the middle point of each income group — e.g. £70 per week for the lowest group — and re-plotted the graph. (I had to make up a number for the top group since it didn't have an upper limit, so I made it £600). This gives the graph in Figure 4.7, which is just the same as Figure 4.6, except that the points are more stretched out to the right-hand end, to reflect the real widening of the income bands. Instead of nearly straight lines pointing upwards to the right, we get curves which appear to be gradually *flattening* off. Whereas the first graph implies that video ownership goes steadily up as incomes go up, the second suggests that video ownership might peak at about 70 per cent. And computer ownership might not reach much higher than 30 per cent however high the income group you study.

Ownership of communications and information facilities among households in selected income groups

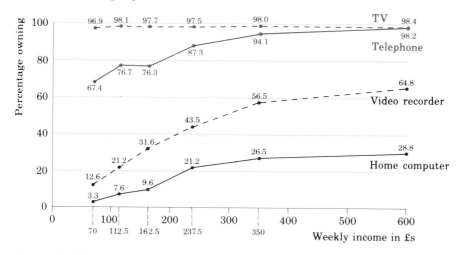

Figure 4.7 *The same graph as Figure 4.6, but with income groups spaced out to show the 'real' differences*

ACTIVITY BREAK   Now that you have three different diagrammatic versions of the original table, look back carefully over all three.

If you could choose only one of them, for the purposes of explaining this data to someone else, which one would you choose?

What do you think are the particular advantages of that form of presentation?

What would you be missing out by not having the others?

Do you think it would be easier to use one of these *diagrams* to explain the data, rather than the *table* of numbers?

Do you know anyone who would be prepared to listen? Perhaps you could try explaining the data to them, to demonstrate to yourself that you understand them.

KEY POINTS

▶ Sets of numerical data can be presented in many different ways.

▶ Although they may *look* very different,
- tables of numbers,
- bar charts, and
- graphs

can all be used to present exactly the *same* information. They are just different ways of trying to sketch a picture using numbers. Which you choose is largely a matter of deciding what kind of presentation will best show up the features you are most interested in.

4.1 Summary of tips for reading graphs and charts

My advice for graphs and charts is very similar to that for tables of numbers.

Take your time and be cautious

Graphs and charts *ought* to be easy to read, since the whole point of turning figures into diagrammatic form is to bring out their meaning more clearly. However, like numbers, graphs and charts are highly abstract representations, which attempt to summarize certain aspects of the world in a very condensed form. Consequently they require a degree of mental effort on your part to bridge the gap between the formal pictures on the page and the aspects of 'reality' that they stand for. As with tables, it is important to approach graphs and charts *carefully*, allowing yourself time to 'get the feel' of what you are looking at. Don't *assume* you know what a graph is about. Take a thorough look.

Finding your way in

The sheer visual impact of a diagram can make it difficult to look *past* the pretty lines and shading to the underlying message. As with tables, it is a good idea to look quickly at the main headings and then focus on a point here and there to check what you are being told. Pick on one of the bars and tell yourself what it stands for; for example, 'this bar tells me that 65 per cent of the highest income families own video machines', or 'this line shows that phones reach the same level of consumption as TVs in the highest income groups'. Scan your way around the diagram — up and down and from side to side. Check that it makes sense in terms of what you already know of the world.

Reading the words

When you feel reasonably comfortable with what the diagram is about, examine in more detail the words written around it; the main headings, the 'key' to shading, and the axes. The 'axes'* are the bottom edge (the horizontal axis, or X-axis) and the left-hand edge (the vertical axis, or Y-axis) of the diagram. The *axes should always be labelled* to tell you what units you are counting in. In Figures 4.4, 4.6 and 4.7, for example, the horizontal axis is 'Weekly income in £s' and the vertical axis is 'percentage owning'. Read any small print by the diagram to be sure you don't draw wrong conclusions from it.

Extracting information

When you are sure you know what the chart or graph is all about, then start to check the main trends it seems to suggest. Jot down for yourself a few conclusions that you think can be drawn. It often takes a little time before you begin to grasp the full extent of what the diagram has to tell you. However, it is worth the effort, because information held in the form of a graph is highly patterned; and since our memories work by finding patterns in information and storing them, graphs are all set up ready to be stored. As a result, it can be a lot easier to remember information you have taken in from a diagram than information from a table, or from a text.

KEY POINTS

When you are reading diagrams or graphs you should:
- ▶ take the time to get a 'feel' for what the diagram is telling you
- ▶ pick on one or two points and make sure they make sense
- ▶ read the words around the edges very carefully
- ▶ look for patterns, peaks and troughs, and blips.

---

* 'Axes' is the plural of 'axis', not 'axe', and is pronounced *axees*.

4.2 Where have numbers taken us?

We started with some questions about the extent to which modern communications technology has contributed to the dramatic reshaping of our society and the lives we live. The table we have been looking at, in various different disguises, cannot take us to the end of the line in establishing answers to those questions. We would need to look at a whole lot of other numbers to get a satisfactory picture. In any case, numbers are never the whole answer. Nevertheless, the numbers in the table have taken us quite a long way. They have shown us that it *is* reasonable to assume that TV is more or less universally available throughout British society as a means of communication (whether it is a *powerful* means, or even an *effective* means, could only be established through further research). On the other hand, the numbers suggest that when people talk enthusiastically about the 'electronic village' of the future — in which we are all busy organizing our lives on computers, which link us to each other and to work organizations — they are for the time-being talking of a minority, and in the main a well-off minority. These are important things to know.

4.3 Not all data are numbers

We have focused on numbers in this chapter because making use of them requires specific skills, which you may not have had a chance to pick up before. However, you should not conclude, from all the attention we have been giving to them, that numbers are more important than other kinds of information. Even in a subject like 'social science', you should not assume that the word 'science' automatically implies numerical measurements. Don't fall into the trap of thinking in terms of the equation:

Social *science* = research = data = numbers

A science is not *all* about research. Research is certainly important in any field of science, but so is *constructing theories*, so is *thinking* about ideas and explanations and *applying* them to 'real life'. Research becomes a sterile 'end-in-itself' if it loses touch with these other equally important activities.

Secondly, research is not simply about 'producing *data*', or facts. Research is always linked to testing out *theories*. There is an infinite number of possible facts to record. The only thing which makes fact-gathering useful and manageable is the *theory* shaping the research.

Thirdly, 'data' are not exclusively 'quantitative data' (i.e. in the form of numbers). Much of importance in social research, for instance, is in the form of qualitative information. You would know next to nothing about the significance of TV in our society if all you collected were quantitative data. You would also need to collect qualitative data by talking to people, watching TV yourself, reading what the newspapers say about TV programmes, and so on. The figures for owning TVs and viewing programmes are only a small part of the picture.

So while it is important that you gradually become fairly competent at examining tables, you should not let this numbers business get out of proportion. To be able to summarize some aspects of the world in numerical form is a valuable part of the process of enquiring into it and explaining it. However, a subject like social science is far from being suited only to 'number junkies'. The words far outweigh the numbers.

5   Try out your skills

You have been introduced to two common types of diagram, the bar chart and the line graph. There is one more which we should look at because it is also widely used. It is called the 'pie chart' or 'pie diagram' and it is probably the easiest of all to read. So here is a chance to try out your diagram-reading skills. Look at Figure 4.8 and see if you can work out what it tells us (before looking at the Activity Break).

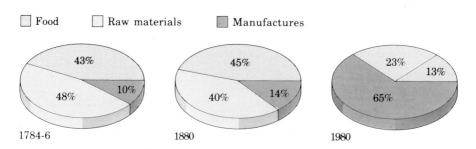

Source: based on Mitchell, B.R. (1988) *British Historical Statistics*, Table 5, Cambridge University Press

Figure 4.8 *Pie chart showing the relative money value of imports into Britain of different categories of goods in 1784–6, 1880 and 1980*

ACTIVITY BREAK   Look at the pie chart in Figure 4.8 and then answer the following questions:

1 What major changes have there been in the pattern of importing into Britain over the last 200 years?

2 Have they been slow and steady changes?

3 In 1980, did Britain import less food than in 1880?

1 It should be fairly obvious how to read this diagram. In the first period, 1784–6, the largest slice of the import pie was for raw materials (nearly half), closely followed by food, with manufactures a very small slice. By 1880, manufactures had grown a little and raw materials had fallen somewhat. But by 1980 manufactures had expanded enormously to take up two-thirds of the pie. With the pie diagram in front of you, you can see very clearly the enormous growth in the *importance* of manufactured imports over the 200 years, and the decline in the *relative* importance of food imports.

2 We have not got a lot to go on here because of the very large time gaps between the three dates. However, it is clear that there was not very much change in the pattern in the first hundred years. The main shift was during the second hundred years.

3 What this chart *doesn't* tell us is that we import less food than we did (it was a trick question). Since there is a great deal more trading and transporting of goods in general than 200 hundred years ago, the whole import 'cake' is certain to be *much* bigger now than it was then. We cannot tell from this diagram *how* large the quantity of

There is no perfect table or diagram

Keeping the pies the same size has made it easy to compare the proportions of the slices from one date to another. However, we have no information comparing the overall sizes of the three pies. We could have made the pies different sizes to represent the overall volume of trade in £s, but then the 1784–6 one would have been minuscule compared with the 1980 one.

You never get something for nothing with tables and diagrams. Every way of presenting figures has its advantages and disadvantages. You have to decide what you want to bring out most clearly.

food imported is compared with 200 years ago.* All we can see is the *relative* importance of food imports compared with the other two categories.

I hope you found you could make some sense of this chart without too much difficulty and that you remembered to look carefully at the information accompanying the diagram.

6   Conclusion

If you are new to tables and diagrams you will have done some hard work in this chapter. Perhaps some of what you have attempted has baffled you. If so, don't worry about it. Any course you attempt that requires you to work with numbers is likely to give you further assistance. Indeed, there are many other interesting and valuable things to learn about statistics, tables and diagrams, but you will have these explained to you as you need them. All I have been aiming for here is to begin the process of building up your skill and experience. I hope you will also feel encouraged to develop the habit of stopping to look carefully at tables and diagrams and to work out what they mean, rather than skipping over them. As you have seen, tables and diagrams offer you a lot of information in a very compact form. If you follow the basic steps outlined here you will soon be able to make yourself familiar with the common ways of presenting numerical data. Then you will be in a position to start finding things out for yourself instead of waiting to be told.†

---

* In fact, that would be fairly tricky to assess, because the units we would have to measure in would be money, and money has changed dramatically in value in the last 200 years.

† When you feel ready there are plenty of data available in publications such as *Social Trends* (Central Statistical Office, London, HMSO), which is published annually and is held in university and college libraries, or in the shorter *Key Data* (Central Statistical Office, London, HMSO).

KEY POINTS

▶ Making sense of numbers is a normal part of modern life.

▶ The ability to work with numbers is more a matter of building up experience with specific ways of using them rather than some special 'gift'.

▶ You have to be prepared to 'invest time' in learning how to read unfamiliar kinds of numbers, tables and diagrams.

▶ If you invest this learning time, numbers can give you a lot of information very quickly and effectively.

▶ Numbers help you to give weight and form to descriptions of society by showing the dimensions and the scale of social phenomena.

▶ You need to be careful when you read tables — approaching them in a spirit of exploration and questioning.

▶ When you approach a new table you need to:
  – focus on a few specific numbers and work out what they stand for
  – check all that is written above and below the table and along the edges
  – scan for patterns, trends and blips
  – be aware that the figures are no more than 'approximations to the truth', so draw conclusions cautiously.

▶ When you approach graphs, charts and diagrams you do much the same as for tables.

▶ Graphs, charts and diagrams help you to 'see' the patterns in sets of numbers.

▶ Because of this they also help you to *remember* information.

▶ The following are common types of charts and diagrams:
  – bar charts
  – line graphs
  – pie charts.

CHAPTER 5

What is good writing?

1 The importance of writing

Of all aspects of studying and learning, perhaps the most challenging is writing. This is no accident. The reason why writing is especially demanding is that it forces you into a very deep and powerful kind of learning. In the previous chapters we have been talking in the main about how you 'take in' ideas from books and so on. However, as I said in Chapter 3 (Section 1.2), until you have made the effort to *use* the ideas of the subject to *say* something for yourself, you cannot really be said to have 'learned' them. The ideas only become a properly functioning part of your thought-processes when you can call on them in *expressing* yourself to other people. Just as you don't know your maths until you can solve mathematical problems, so you don't know your social science or your humanities until you can use the ideas to *argue* a case. One valuable way of doing this is by discussing them with others, using the spoken word. But an even more exacting way is to use the ideas in writing.

1.1 What is an essay?

There are various kinds of writing that a course of study might involve, such as diaries, reports of projects, and so on. In this chapter, however, we are going to concentrate on the essay, since that is the most common form of writing in the social sciences and humanities. The word 'essay' originally meant a *first attempt* or a *practice*, but it now has the more general meaning of *a short piece of writing on a specific subject*.

KEY POINTS

An essay should:

▶ begin with a *title* which sets out the issues that it will deal with

▶ take the form of an *argument* which leads the reader from the title at the beginning to a conclusion at the end.

1.2 Why write essays?

Essay writing is not simply a chore you endure for the purposes of *assessment*. As I have said, it is an essential part of the learning process. When you look back over a course, you will find that the subjects on which you have written essays are the ones that you remember best and understand most clearly.

However, there is another kind of learning through essay writing which is equally important, and that is the *development of your writing style*. In our kind of society, being able to write clearly and persuasively is a very valuable 'skill'. It puts you on a much better footing with other people if you can represent your point of view forcefully in writing. Indeed, though you may have started your studies with the idea of finding out about certain things, you may eventually discover that the most valuable thing you have gained is the ability to write much more effectively. This is equally likely to be true whether you start with a rather weak writing style or with a well-developed writing style. Whatever point you start from, there is always valuable progress to be made.

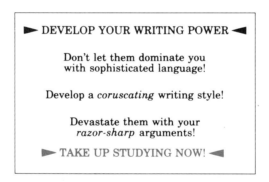

► DEVELOP YOUR WRITING POWER ◄

Don't let them dominate you
with sophisticated language!

Develop a *coruscating* writing style!

Devastate them with your
razor-sharp arguments!

► TAKE UP STUDYING NOW! ◄

KEY POINTS

Writing essays is a very important part of studying for three reasons:

▶ it enables *assessment* of your progress
▶ it deepens your *learning* of the subject you are studying
▶ it strengthens your general powers of *self-expression*.

Writing tends then to be both the most demanding and at the same time the most rewarding part of any course of studies. Because of this it is not just an extra you can fit on to the end of your other study activities, in your spare time. Essay writing requires you to make a substantial investment of your time and effort. It also requires you to think hard in working out *strategies* for approaching the task.

1.3 How to develop your essay-writing ability

To be able to develop your skill in writing essays you need to address two basic questions:

▶ What does a good essay look like?

▶ How do you set about producing one?

We shall consider the first of these questions in this chapter and the second in the next.

Reading guide There is a lot to think about in this chapter, particularly if you work carefully through the examples and activities. You will probably get most out of it by reading it in stages. I suggest you take it in five chunks:

1 Up to the end of Section 2.2

2 Section 2.3

3 Section 2.4

4 Section 2.5

5 Sections 3 and 4.

Alternatively, just stop reading in close detail when you feel you have gone as far as is useful for you at present and skim the rest of the chapter, looking at the boxes. You can then come back to it at later points in your studies, when you are ready to work on new aspects of your writing.

2 What does an essay look like?

One of the most perplexing things about writing essays is that you are seldom offered much insight into *what* you are setting out to produce. Writing tends to be a very private process. You know very well what *your* essays look like and what your tutor says about them, but you have very little idea what *other people's* essays are like and what comments *they* receive back. You are told, perhaps, that your essays ought to be more structured, or that you need to be less subjective, but you don't really know what a more structured or a more objective essay would look like. Your tutor is able to pass judgement on your essay by *comparing* it with lots of other essays, but *your* conception of the task is usually restricted by having seen only your own approach to it.

2.1 Looking at other people's essays

One of the most valuable aids to developing your essay-writing ability is to have the opportunity to see how other students have responded to the same task; not because you want to *copy* someone else's style, but to broaden your vision of what is *possible* when you are answering an essay question.

Getting help from other students

If you are studying with other students, you could arrange to meet from time to time to read each other's essays — or, if you can't meet, you could exchange essays by post. This is *not* cheating. It is a way of gaining insight into the strengths and weaknesses of your own writing, by comparing your approach with that of your colleagues. It is unlikely that you could copy other people's styles even if you tried. Nor would you want to, since it is *your* style you are aiming to develop.

Admittedly, the idea of letting others see your work is rather daunting at first but, once you have broken the barriers of privacy, other students can often be at least as useful as a tutor in giving you new ideas of ways forward.

Let us take up this notion by looking at some short essays written about the Carl Gardner article you read in Chapter 2. The writers were adult students on a 'return to study' course, who were given the following task:

Write a short essay of about 300 to 500 words on the following:
Is the rapid development of new 'high-tech' shopping centres a bad thing? Discuss in the light of Carl Gardner's article.

ACTIVITY BREAK   Read the essays by Sam and Ann on pages 115–17.

1 As you read, mark any places where you have difficulty getting the point. Write any questions, or other points that come to you, in the margins. Pencil in any alterations you think could usefully be made. *You will feel freer about doing this if you can work on photocopies of the essays.*

2 When you get to the end of the essays, take a sheet of paper and write two headings: *Strengths* and *Weaknesses*. Note down the good things about Sam's essay and the weak points.

3 Do the same for Ann's essay.

4 Imagine you are their tutor. Try writing a few sentences to each of them to help with their future writing.

5 Try to weigh up the quality of these essays:

▶ Do you think one of the essays is better than the other?

▶ Can they be good in different ways?

▶ Overall, do you think that they are good essays or bad?

▶ How much of that is to do with the quality of the *ideas* in the essays and how much to do with how they are *presented*?

6 Finally look back over:

▶ your lists of strengths and weaknesses

▶ your advice to the two students, and

▶ your conclusions as to the overall quality of the essays.

Can you draw any general conclusions about the qualities a good essay should have?

7 Write the heading *Qualities of a good essay* and see what you can jot down under it.

Learning to 'judge' writing

This is a demanding activity. You may find you can't (or don't want to) do all of it at this stage in your own writing development. However, *it is worth trying to do as much as you can*. It will be time well invested, because you need to develop your own ability to see what works in writing and what doesn't. It is not helpful to try to learn *formal 'rules'* of writing. Instead, you have to become a *reasonably good judge* of real pieces of writing, including your own. 'Marking' other people's writing is a very good way of broadening and deepening your grasp of what you are trying to aim for in your own writing.

Here are two of the essays I received. They were handwritten, but otherwise they were exactly as you see them. The first, which arrived about five weeks late, came with this letter:

Dear Andy,

Sorry about the delay in sending you this essay. I have found it hard to write, as I have not written an essay since leaving school some 15 years ago.

Yours sincerely

Sam

Sam's essay

Is the rapid development of new 'high-tech' shopping centres a bad thing? Discuss in the light of Carl Gardner's article.

Carl Gardner article on 'high-tech' shopping centres raises some interesting points. First is the way which the British public now regards shopping as their favourite leisure activity after holidays and TV. Spending up to a whole Saturday shopping while 10 or 15 years ago it was half a day.

Second there has been an huge raise in sophistication in both marketing techniques and retail design which has helped to boost retail sales by 76 per cent between 1980–89. Also an increase in retail space of 50 per cent, easy availability of credit has helped the raise in retail sales.

Third Carl Gardner describes the new 'high-tech' shopping centres how they varied in size and style, spectacularly produced glass atria or glazed barrel-vaults which helps to use natural light for the shops and walkways. How the centres offer the perfect shopping environment day or night, all types of weather. The centres are air conditioned, well lihted and are well heated and traffic free.

Fourth is that the main work force tends to be part-time, low pay women workers, on the back of these workers the retail boom of the 80's has been built.

Is the rapid development of new 'high-tech' shopping centres a bad thing? Well there is lots of good things going for the new centres such as traffic free, a good shopping environment for all types of weather.

Some of the bad points are that the main part of the work force tends to be women who are low-pay, part-time without the benefits of sick pay, penisons or any employment protection.

The new centres use sophisticate retail and marketing techniques to relieve shoppers of their money, to almost con people in buying things they don't need. Trying to turn shopping in to a leisure activity.

Also offering easy available credit facilitys with their 'in house' credit cards with high interest rates and high spending levels. Also taking all major credit cards.

Ann's essay

Carl Garner, has written a very interesting article in which he puts forward his own views and those of others, concerning the development of new types of shopping centres. In order to assess whether these developments are, on balance a bad thing, it is necessary to look at the various advantages and disadvantages that such hi-tech shopping centres have.

There are several ways in which the new style shopping centre seems favourable. They are plesant surroundings in which enables people to shop in all seasonal weather. Emphasis, on style and design, with the inclusion of many leisure facilities in these centres, reflects the majority of people's views of shopping in the eighties. The demand in stylish shops with equally stylish environments brings about a complete change to what many shoppers are used to. The article suggests that people are spending more time shopping and these hi-tech centres definately create the right atmosphere for pleasurable shopping. One social aspect of these centres enables people to meet friends whilst enjoying themselves, shopping has taken on a new meaning and has never been regarded in this way before. Mr Gardner believes that it is the new style centres that have brought these changes in peoples view of shopping.

Mr Gardner, also argues that these new retail developments have helped to bring about improvements in facilities for the centres and surrounding areas, such as old style high streets, in order to compliment the new shopping areas. Therefore these centres offer the customer a great deal in terms of environment and design and they fully reflect the current retail boom in a favourable way.

However, there are also some disadvantages expressed in the article, some of which are the view of other authors, but with whom Carl Gardner does not agree. One is the idea of manipulation of the customer in the development of new style shopping centres, that is people are being used in order to maintain desired consumption.

Labour views these developments unfavourably but Gardner seems to argue against left wing views.

Ken Warpole, puts some strong views against these shopping centres that are present in the article. In which he maintains that the retail boom, as reflected by hi-tech centres is causing a division among people who can and cannot afford to buy and this in turn is leading to an increase in crime. Town centre life is also being ruined by schemes and developments by these hugh, fully automated shopping centres. Gardner, however presents strong arguments against these ideas by saying the remarks are old fashioned and giving examples of successful city centres which also have out of town developments.

On an individual level these centres rely on low paid female labour working long and arduous hours, for people who may not necessary be purchasing goods but just browsing, which incedently can be much more pleasant in such surroundings. There may reach a crisis point when retail development gets out of hand and reaches a saturation point, or when spending is reduced by political manoeuvers.

Although there are some arguments against the hi-tech centres Gardner, himself largely regards them in favourable terms and argues against the views of others who find them disadvantageous. Therefore these centres really are not such a bad thing, in the light of the article.

I shall now pick out what struck me as I read these two essays. I expect you have picked out many of the same points, since there is no great mystery about what is good writing and what is bad. Good writing is easy to read and makes sense. Bad writing is unclear and confusing. It keeps making you stop to try to work out where you are going.

2.2 Critique of Sam's essay

What is the most striking difference between Sam's essay and Ann's? To me it stands out a mile. Ann's has an *argument*, whereas Sam's is simply a list. Ann has worked out a sequence of points, which have logical links between one and the next. Her essay has a clear structure:

▶ an *opening* paragraph

▶ a section arguing in *favour* of high-tech shopping centres

▶ a section arguing *against*, and

▶ a final paragraph which *returns to the question*.

Sam, on the other hand, has picked out some useful points, but hasn't been able to devise a sequence for presenting them to us. It isn't obvious *why* he *starts* with the point he does, and when he *finishes* there is no sense of having reached an *ending*. When, in the fifth paragraph, he poses the question as to whether the shopping centres are a bad thing, he can't work out what to do other than to repeat the points he has already made.

It is actually quite hard to read an essay of this kind, even though the sentences are fairly simple, because there is no thread of meaning to guide your thoughts from one point to the next. Each point hits you abruptly on its own terms and adds nothing to the preceding points. A longer essay written this way would be unreadable.

This reminds us of an essential feature of any essay.

KEY POINTS

Essays have to have an *argument*. (They have to lead from an initial question to a conclusion.)

It isn't particularly easy to define exactly what an argument is, but it's what Sam's essay hasn't got. To illustrate the point more forcibly, I shall take the very same points as Sam and wrap them in an argument, so that you can see the difference. In doing so, I have moved some of the points around to make a more natural flow in the sequence of points. Take, for instance, his third paragraph:

Third Carl Gardner describes the new 'high-tech' shopping centres how they varied in size and style, spectacularly produced glass atria or glazed barrel-vaults which helps to use natural light for the shops and walkways. How the centres offer the perfect shopping environment day or night, all types of weather. The centres are air conditioned, well lighted and are well heated and traffic free.

This reads much more easily if it is reworked like this:

These new high-tech shopping centres vary in size and style, but they tend to involve spectacular glass atria which allow the use of natural light for the shops and walkways. They are also air-conditioned, well lighted, well heated and traffic free. In effect the centres offer the perfect shopping environment, day or night and in all types of weather.

This gives us a paragraph which is *about* something. It is about the attractions of the new shopping centres. The paragraph now says, in effect, 'The new shopping centres offer X and Y, which means they are attractive because they provide Z.' Moving the middle sentence to the end and giving it a new beginning makes it act as a summary of the other two, and the points now flow from one to the next.

Now that I am clear what the paragraph is about I can use it as part of a larger argument. For instance, I can use it as a link between paragraphs one and two. I then have a paragraph *introducing* the new centres, followed by one about *why* they are attractive, which leads to one about *how* this change has come about. Extending this process, I worked out a rough sketch of an argument which uses all Sam's main points. It looks like this:

Outline for a revised version of Sam's essay

Para. 1: *The emergence of shopping as a leisure activity —why?*

Para. 2: *Because shopping centres have taken the drudgery out of shopping and put in glamour and entertainment.*

Para. 3: *But why has **that** change happened? — Because the 80s credit boom led to a retail boom and the big operators are cashing in.*

Para. 4: *So retailers and shoppers are happy — where's the catch?*

Para. 5: *Poor jobs — people being 'conned' into buying what they don't need — indebtedness — slump.*

Para. 6: *So although shopping centres seem attractive — they are sowing the seeds of hard times to come.*

ACTIVITY BREAK   Read this outline carefully and check that you can see how the argument flows.

Having sketched this outline, I wrote the whole essay out again, mainly using Sam's original words but adding in some new bits to link the points together. Here is how it came out (the bits I have added are highlighted):

Revised version of Sam's essay

Carl Gardner's article on 'high-tech' shopping centres raises some interesting points. Perhaps the most striking is the way in which the British public now regards shopping as its favourite leisure activity after holidays and TV. Whereas shopping used to be a 'chore' reserved for women, we now find all the family spending up to a whole Saturday shopping (10 or 15 years ago it was half a day). Why should this great change in habits have come about?

119

Gardner suggests it has a lot to do with the environments in which we now shop. He describes a new breed of 'high-tech' shopping centres. They vary in size and style, but most of them feature spectacularly produced glass atria or glazed barrel-vaults which allow the use of natural light for the shops and walkways. These centres are air-conditioned, well lighted and traffic free. In effect the centres offer the 'perfect shopping environment' day or night and in all types of weather. In a cold, wet and windy climate this represents a major change to the experience of shopping. Instead of being drudgery left for the hard-pressed housewife, it has become a 'fun' activity the whole family wants to join in.

But why have these changes in shopping environments come upon us so rapidly? Gardner argues that we are witnessing a retail boom, riding on the back of an upsurge in the availability of credit. The retailers have been quick to respond to this increase in spending power and we have seen a huge rise in sophistication in both marketing techniques and retail design which has helped to boost retail sales by 76 per cent between 1980 and 1989.

Clearly the big retailers are happy with the boom in sales, and (judging by their popularity), the new shopping centres, with their attractive environments and their leisure orientation, are what many people want. So is everything in the garden rosy?

In fact serious objections have been made to these new developments. Firstly, the work they have created has been for women, who are poorly paid part-time employees, without the benefits of sick pay, pensions or any employment protection. Secondly, the use of sophisticated retail and marketing techniques to relieve shoppers of their money, amounts almost to 'conning' people into buying things they don't need. And thirdly the easily available credit facilities create potential problems of indebtedness for the shopper and of slump for the retailers when the limits of credit are finally reached.

It seems that, while shoppers are able to enjoy the immediate illusion of prosperity in comfort and style, the new high-tech shopping centres are creating poor jobs and at the same time sowing the seeds of hard times to come.

I hope you can see a difference with this revised version. I am not suggesting it is by any means perfect, but it is certainly more of an 'essay' now because it has an argument.

ACTIVITY BREAK Go back over the revised version of Sam's essay and look carefully at the changes.

In each case, check whether you can see:

▶ *why* I thought a change was needed

▶ *what* I was trying to achieve in making the change, and

▶ *how* I set about doing it.

Refer to Sam's original as you go along, so that you can compare the impact of each version. Scribble down your thoughts as you work. (Again, it will be useful to work from a photocopy.)

> ## *Creating a flow in your arguments*
>
> Giving this detailed attention to the mechanics of constructing a flowing argument out of a set of separate points is extremely valuable in building up your own skill in constructing an argument.

I will now give you my own version of why I made the changes I did.

I liked Sam's opening sentence. It was nice and direct, so I kept it. But to avoid simply launching into a *list* as Sam did, I decided to emphasize the first point *because* it was first, so I suggested it was a particularly *striking* point (i.e. you should have a reason for putting that point first). But I then felt I had to indicate *why* it is a striking point, so I added the bit about shopping having been a *housewife's chore*, to bring out the contrast with the new *family-at-leisure* image. Then, having started with the topic of changes in shopping habits, I needed to find a way of using it as a launching pad for the next paragraph, so I posed the question as to why the changes had come about.

This set me up for using Sam's third paragraph (which we have already discussed) as an explanation of why shopping might have become more popular. But I needed to start with a sentence which would pick up the thread from the end of the previous paragraph, so I cast the opening sentence of the new paragraph in the form of an answer to the question I had just asked. The reorganized paragraph works well as a quick sketch of the attractions of the new centres. However, I again felt it would be necessary to emphasize to my reader just *why* these 'controlled' shopping conditions were seen as so attractive, so I added Gardner's points about the British climate. I then made explicit the link between the pleasanter conditions of shopping and its new-found popularity, in order to remind the reader where we had started from and where we had now reached.

Spell it out

Be aware that your reader cannot see into your mind. He or she may not be able to see connections between points which seem perfectly obvious to you.

When you are writing it is always safer to spell out quite clearly how your points are meant to link up to each other.

By the end of paragraph two we already have quite a nice little piece in its own right:

▶ a description of a new social trend

▶ a question as to its origins, and

▶ a partial answer to that question which incorporates a description of another social trend.

There is a sense of completion at this point.

That is why the next paragraph starts with a question. I wanted to disturb the apparent completeness of the previous two paragraphs, so as to give some forward impetus again. So I pointed out that we have only moved the question about causes one stage along the line. We now need to ask *why* all these new shopping centres are springing up. This is the cue for bringing in the points about the expansion of credit facilities and the subsequent retail boom. Again, I changed the order of Sam's points, taking the availability of credit first, because I could use it as an explanation of the changes in marketing and retail design.

Of course, the essay is supposed to be about *whether the new style shopping centres are a bad thing.* By now I had covered all Sam's points in *favour* of the shopping centres, so I thought it would be a good moment for speaking directly to this central question and then switching to consider points against. In other words, this would be *the turning point of the essay.* I had not previously reminded my reader of the issue posed in the title, nor had I signalled that we had been going over the points in favour of the new centres, so I felt it was now necessary to erect a really clear 'signpost' to say just this. I put in an extra paragraph to do the job.

Signposting

Signposting is extremely important. Readers easily get lost while following you in your journey across a range of ideas. You need to be very generous in supplying pointers as to where you have come from and where you are going.

ACTIVITY BREAK Go back to the fourth paragraph of the revised essay. Check whether you think it does its job in *signposting* the shift of tack from points *for* to points *against*.

I then decided to put all of Sam's points *against* the shopping centres into a single paragraph, since they were so short. This time I decided to stick to the 'list' format (i.e. firstly, secondly, thirdly), as it would let me handle the points quickly. In any case, I couldn't see a neat and obvious way of linking them logically.

When to use lists

Listing points *can* be useful, when you want to get through a number of them quite quickly. The problem with Sam's essay was that listing was the *only* organizing principle. There wasn't any explanation of *why* the lists were there.

I started the paragraph by signalling that I was moving on to some arguments *against* the centres. Then I tried to make the argument behind each of the objections clear (particularly the one about credit facilities, where Sam had forgotten to give us any idea of why that might be a problem).

Finally, I added a paragraph to serve as a *conclusion* to the essay. Sam's essay just stops without any hint of having reached a particularly important point. I wanted to give a sense of having arrived somewhere with the argument. To do this, I needed to remind my reader about the central question of whether the shopping centres are a bad thing. I could have done this directly by saying, 'Are we then to welcome these new shopping centres or should we attempt to resist them?' — but as it was only a couple of paragraphs since I had raised the question, I decided it would be enough just to refer back to the image of the happy shoppers and set against it the image of hard times to come. In fact, I ended on a note which sounds '*anti*-shopping centre' because I thought this was a satisfactory way of resolving the argument of the essay. However, I could just as easily have concluded on a positive note. For instance, I could have stressed that, in spite of the problems, a lot of people are enjoying the new opportunities. In this kind of exercise, it doesn't matter too much *which* way you play the argument out. So long as it hangs together and makes sense, you have done your job.

Conclusion

An essay should end by taking a brief sweeping look back over the argument of the essay and also a look back to the *title* of the essay. The conclusion should show the reader how the discussion in the essay has 'answered the question'.

You do not have to come to a definite position on one side or the other. You can simply point out the case on each side. But you must try to show that the whole trip has been worthwhile — that the time spent following your argument has indeed taken the reader closer to the issues contained in the title. A conclusion doesn't need to be particularly grand, but there should be a sense of having reached an ending.

I think you will agree that my revised version reads like a completely different essay from Sam's original, although there is not really anything in it that Sam hadn't thought of. The difference is in the organization. I hope this detailed reworking of the essay has given you an idea of what is meant by having an *argument* running through an essay. I hope it has also shown you what is meant by giving an essay a *structure* — that is, a beginning, a middle and an end. These are not, however, notions you can expect to pick up all in one go. It takes plenty of practice to develop a quick eye for argument and structure.

2.3   Other points about Sam's essay

There are, of course, other aspects of Sam's essay which could be improved.

Sentences

Sam clearly has some idea of what a sentence is, because he uses some perfectly good ones. On the other hand, he seems rather shaky with other sentences. Let us look at an example:

Spending up to a whole Saturday shopping while 10 or 15 years ago it was half a day.

This is punctuated as a sentence, in that it starts with a capital letter and ends with a full stop. But a sentence should be a self-contained unit of sense. It should make sense read out on its own. This does not. On the other hand, it would be very easy to turn it into a proper sentence.

If you put 'They spend' in place of 'Spending', it becomes a sentence. It has a subject ('they'), and a verb ('spend'*). However, Sam's error here is basically one of punctuation rather than sentence structure. He should have put a comma, rather than a full stop, before 'spending' and a small 's' instead of a capital 'S' at the beginning of the word. This group of words makes a perfectly good subsection of a larger sentence; it is just that the punctuation is misleading.

Sentences

Every sentence needs a verb — a 'doing' word — and (virtually) every sentence needs a subject — the person or thing which is 'doing'.

In — 'She rang the bell.' — 'she' is the subject (because she is 'doing' the ringing) and 'rang' is the verb (because that is what she was 'doing'). A simple test you can apply if you are not sure whether you have written a sentence is to ask, 'Does it have a verb and a subject?' ('does have' is the verb in that sentence; 'it' is the subject).

We could get very technical on the subject of grammar, but fortunately it is quite possible to use grammar effectively without knowing the rules in a formal way (just as you can live within the laws of the land without actually knowing their details). Many people can 'hear' whether a string of words is a sentence or not because it 'sounds' complete if it is. They don't have to stop to think whether there is a verb or a subject.

If you find it *isn't* obvious to you, even when you read your work out loud, then you need to get some direct assistance with grammar, either by going to a local class, or by getting a book on the subject. You will find it very difficult to develop your writing style until you have a reasonable feel for what a sentence is.

---

* Spending isn't a verb. It acts more like a noun. You couldn't say 'They spending Saturday shopping' because 'spending' won't do the job of a verb. You *could* say 'Spending is wasteful'. Here 'spending' is the *subject* and 'is' is the verb.

Grammar is not a subject we shall go into in detail in this book. However, you can check your own grammar to a certain extent by reading what you write aloud. If you read each sentence by itself (i.e. from one full stop to the next), you will often be able to 'hear' where something is missing or where there are too many complications. You need a practical ability to judge what works — not a detailed knowledge of English grammar. This will develop spontaneously as you get more practice in disciplined reading and writing. But if you find that you need more direct help, ask you local library or bookshop to show you what books are available.* Better still, the library should be able to give you information about any local classes. You may, for instance, be able to get some help from an Adult Basic Education project operating in your area.

Punctuation

What I have said about grammar also applies to punctuation. Again, you should be able to pick up most of what you need to know as you progress with your studies, but if you find you need more help, get a basic English book.

Punctuation

Punctuation is the system of signals you give to your reader to show how the grammar of the sentences is supposed to work. The basics are the capital letter at the start of a sentence and the full stop at the end. You use commas to mark off any sub-segments of the sentence, to divide up lists, and so on.

ACTIVITY BREAK   What is wrong with the following 'sentence'?

'Also an increase in retail space of 50 per cent, easy availability of credit has helped the raise in retail sales.'

Can you turn it into a 'proper' sentence?

Again, Sam has the wrong punctuation. There should be a full stop after 'per cent', and 'Easy' should have a capital 'E'. The last part is a whole sentence in its own right ('availability of credit' is the subject, 'has helped' is the verb).† However, there is still a problem with the first part. Again, there is no subject or verb. It should read, *'There has* also *been* an increase in retail space of 50 per cent.'

* One such book is Redmayne, E. and Redmayne, J. (1981) *Basic English*, Macmillan Education. Another is Collinson, D.J. (1987) *Writing English: A Working Guide to the Skills of Written English*, Wildwood House.

† Also, it should be 'rise' rather than 'raise'.

There are other similar examples, such as the very strange sentence at the start of the third paragraph, which has a complete break in the flow of sense between the words 'style' and 'spectacularly', as though they are tacked together from different sentences. However, it would take too long to unpack all these problems here. It will be more useful if you simply look carefully at how I have rewritten these faulty sentences and check how they have been made to work.

Consistency

A common problem is to have different bits of a sentence which do not match up. What is wrong when Sam writes, 'Well there is lots of good things going . . .'? He should have said 'there *are* lots'. 'Is' is *singular*, whereas the 'things' are *plural*. You have to make up your mind whether you are talking about one thing or lots of them.

Another common slip is to get the tenses wrong. Sam, for example, wrote of the new shopping centres 'how they varied in size and style'. 'Varied' is the *past* tense. But these are *new* centres which are just being built. It must be more appropriate to use the *present* tense and say that they 'vary' in size and style. These may seem small points, but I am not picking on them just for the sake of it. Inconsistencies fuzz the meaning as you read. They slow you down and distract you from picking up the meaning of the sentences. Reading is hard enough, without constantly stumbling over distractions along the way.

Tenses

The tense of a verb is its setting in time. For example, 'I shout' is set in the present. 'I shouted' is set in the past. 'I will shout' is set in the future. There are other possibilities, but you don't need to worry about them. The main point is to be *consistent* in using tenses. Decide whether you are discussing the past, present, or future and then stay there, unless you have a good reason for shifting.

Colourful popular phrases and 'slang'

Some terms you use in everyday life look weak and out of place in an essay. It isn't that they are 'bad' language, so much as that they carry a lot of associations and local meanings, and consequently are not exact enough for the purposes of arguing a case in an essay.

Terms like 'street cred', or 'wimp', for example, emerge in popular speech and take on a richness of meaning as people find new ways to use them. Vibrant and useful though such 'living' language is, it tends to be too loosely defined and unstable for making crisp, precise points in a written argument.

This is something you get a 'feel' for as you practise your writing. However, just to signal the point, consider Sam's piece about:

*. . . marketing techniques to **relieve shoppers of their money**, to almost **con** people . . .*

Sam is making a serious point and I found that it distracted me to see it addressed half-jokingly, using the ironic slang of 'relieving' shoppers of their money.

If, for some reason, you *deliberately* choose to use an everyday expression, then put quotation marks ('. . .') around it, to show you are conscious of the departure from form. This would apply to the word 'con'. It is perfectly appropriate to use the term in this particular essay (it is, after all, taken from the Gardner article), but I would put quotation marks around it.

Evidence

At some points Sam slips in items of information that are not from the Gardner article. This gives rise to a problem because we, the readers, are in no position to judge their reliability. For instance, he says that shopping centres are 'traffic free'. I'm sure he's right, but it is an *assumption* and he should signal this somehow — for example, by saying '*presumably*' traffic free, or '*usually*' traffic free. At another point he talks of the employees being 'without the benefits of sick pay, pensions or any employment protection'. This sounds plausible, but it is stated here as fact, without any indication as to where this information comes from. Either Sam should have qualified what he said by saying 'in all probability without the benefits . . .', or if he *did* know this information on good authority he should have let us know the source.

Although you may not have thought about it while you were reading, Gardner's article presented us with a lot of information drawn from research — such as data about the growth of the retail sector, plans for new shopping centre developments, national shopping habits and attitudes to shopping, and so on. To avoid being too boring in a weekly magazine, he has presented it in a non-technical, chatty way. However, one would assume that, if challenged, he would be able to tell us how he came to know each item of information he gives us. If this had been an essay rather than an article, we would expect to be

2 WHAT DOES AN ESSAY LOOK LIKE?

told exactly where we could find this information for ourselves (see Chapter 6, Section 5.2).

In your own writing you are pretty safe if you base an argument on information you have picked up from an article in a reputable magazine or journal. However, you would normally be expected to give the readers the *source* of your information, so that they can judge for themselves its reliability (and if in doubt go back to the original to check). But in a case like this, where so much is being drawn from one source, you don't have to say so every time. The occasional 'as Gardner points out' will do.

Presentation

Another feature of Sam's essay is that it has some fairly obvious slips of the pen — words like 'lihted' and 'penisons', which I think he would have noticed were wrong if he had read it through. It is almost unbearable to read what you have just written. However, a tutor is bound to find it harder to make sense of what you are trying to say if there are huge slips of the pen all over the place. And while tutor's usually make allowances for slips here and there, if you want your writing to have its full impact you really cannot afford to omit to read your work carefully, correcting any blunders.

Spelling mistakes

Sam has spelled a number of words wrongly. How important is this? Do you lose marks for bad spelling?

In principle, the answer is no. You shouldn't actually lose marks. However, it is hard for a marker not to be influenced by very weak spelling (nor indeed by very poor punctuation). It detracts from the general impression created by the essay.

If you are chronically poor at spelling, don't worry that it will prevent you making progress. But don't be entirely blasé about it either. It is worth making an effort to look words up in a dictionary if you are not sure about them. And it would be a very good idea to make a list of the words you regularly get wrong and attempt to learn them.

On the other hand, it isn't worth setting out on a huge campaign to memorize string after string of words. In general, the more you read and write the more you will develop a sense of the broad (though rather unreliable) rules of English spelling. If you need more intensive help on this front try working with a 'basic English' book.

129

How good is Sam's essay?

I have given Sam quite a hard time, so I will leave the critical analysis there. But before moving on I want to emphasize that, although I have spent a lot of time pointing to faults in Sam's essay, I still thought it was a very useful first effort. He had clearly done the reading and spent a lot of time trying to work out how to approach the essay. It isn't at all easy, when you are working from a complex article like the Gardner one, to distill it down to a few sentences of your own. I thought Sam had extracted a useful set of points, but he had wilted under the strain of finding a way to put them together.

I thought he had enough of an idea of how sentences work to build up an effective style, once he had sorted out some of the technical points. As he said in his letter, he hadn't written anything for many years. This was like the first day at a keep-fit class after fifteen years of sitting with six-packs of lager in front of the TV — not particularly impressive. I have no doubt that with a little time and determination he would become a very effective student. It is not particularly obvious at this stage, but the signs are there.

What advice did you decide you would have given Sam? I thought you might like to see an extract from the letter I sent him when I returned the essay.

Warning: PLEASE NOTE THAT I SPENT A GREAT DEAL LONGER ON THE MARKING AND ON THE LETTER THAN I WOULD NORMALLY BE ABLE TO DO AS A TUTOR. DON'T EXPECT YOUR OWN TUTOR TO BE ABLE TO WRITE AS FULLY AS THIS TO YOU.

Dear Sam,

Thanks a lot for sending me your essay. I guess it must have taken some time to work up the nerve to do it, if it's so long since you have done any writing. Your essay shows a lot of promise but at the same time the rustiness of someone coming back to writing after a long lay off. Basically this is a very useful start. It is always important just to get your first essay sent off, so that you set down a mark against which to measure your progress.

Your opening sentence gets you off to a brisk, businesslike start and I thought you made a very interesting choice of first point to make (because in many ways this is the core theme of Gardner's article). In fact you picked out a lot of key points from the Gardner article and I could tell from the way that you had set them out that you had an idea of how they could be put together to answer the question. However you obviously had difficulty in finding a way to weave them into a flowing argument — and you ended up essentially listing them as a sequence of separate points, which makes them quite difficult to read. In other words you have done well with the **content** *of the essay, but you need practice in* **planning** *a structured argument and leading your 'reader' through that structure.*

Otherwise, your writing shows a reasonable sense of the basic structure of sentences and an attractive purposefulness of style. However you tend to make mistakes in places, so you would probably find it helpful to read your essays out loud to 'listen' to whether the sentences always 'work'. As I have shown on the essay itself, sometimes your sentences and your punctuation don't match up. Each sentence should start with a capital letter and end with a full stop and it should make sense read out on its own. Look carefully at the changes I have made to your punctuation — taking particular notice of where the sentences begin and end. If you are uncertain about any of this ask.

I am sure that you will be able to make big strides with your essay writing, since you take an intelligent and thoughtful approach to it. You have already taken the biggest step in sending this to me. Now try to get as much writing practice in as you can. You will soon find you have more control over your powers of self expression. If you don't make this effort, you will find you are frustrated by not being able to get the credit you deserve for your ideas . . .

2.4 Critique of Ann's essay

I have already said that Ann's essay is quite a lot better than Sam's because it has a structure and an argument. It also shows a more thorough grasp of the main points of Gardner's article and it keeps attention well focused on them. Generally, I found the use of language clear, direct and purposeful and the whole piece has a nice steady pace, giving each point time to strike home before moving on. All in all it was a good solid first essay, though as always there is plenty of scope for improvement.

In fact, I think the impact of the essay could be sharpened quite dramatically by a bit of reorganization and playing around with the choice of words.

Punchy openings

The introductory paragraph, like the concluding one, is rather bland and dull. To sharpen it up I thought Ann could have left out most of the first sentence, because it isn't really relevant to answering the main question. On the other hand, she could have emphasized the *speed* and the *immediacy* of the changes under discussion, so as to grab the reader's attention (since new shopping centres are not in themselves a rivetting topic). Also, it isn't *several types* of centre that Gardner is talking about; it is *one particular type*. Then I would add a sentence to broaden the scope of the discussion, to stress to the reader again that we are concerned with more than just describing some new shops. Ann's second sentence is in a way a 'truism'*. Of *course* you have to look at the advantages and disadvantages of a thing if you want to know whether, on balance, it is good or bad. So I added 'in some detail' to my revised version of Ann's essay, to make it seem a little more worth saying. Basically then, I would try to put a bit more bite into the opening paragraph — to get down to business a bit more quickly.

Openings

There is a lot to be said for brisk, direct, punchy openings to essays. You need some kind of scene-setting, to launch your reader's thoughts in the right direction for following your argument. But there is no virtue in a lot of formal 'throat clearing' and 'unaccustomed as I am to public speaking . . .'. The first sentence should grab your reader's attention. It should bear some relation to the title of the essay and should be doing important work for your argument. It doesn't have to be flamboyant or fancy. It should just get down to business quickly.

The second paragraph also suffers from the same general softness of focus. To sharpen the opening of Ann's essay, I would change the first two paragraphs as follows (bits I have added are highlighted; bits I have left out are crossed out):

Carl Gardner ~~has written a very interesting article in which he puts forward his own views and those of others, concerning~~ draws our attention to the rapid development in recent times of a new type of shopping centres. In his view these rather spectacular examples of large-scale investment are part of wider changes in the economy and in society in general. In order to assess whether these developments are, on balance, a good or bad thing, it is necessary to look in some detail at the various advantages and disadvantages that ~~such~~ the new high-tech shopping centres ~~have~~ offer.

* A truism is a self-defining truth — something which isn't worth saying because it says nothing which isn't contained in the very words used. Take, for example, the statement, 'The sun never shines at night'. What *is* night? It is precisely that time when the sun isn't in the sky. So this statement tells us nothing.

There are several ways in which the new style shopping centres seems ~~favourable~~ attractive. They ~~are~~ provide pleasant surroundings ~~in~~ which enables people to shop in all ~~seasonal~~ weather. They emphasise ~~on~~ style and design ~~with the inclusion of~~ and include many leisure facilities ~~in these centres~~, reflecting the ~~majority of people's views of shopping~~ tastes of many shoppers in the eighties. ~~The demand in~~ In fact it seems that the spread of the new stylish shops along with their equally stylish environments ~~brings~~ has brought about a complete change ~~to what many shoppers are used to~~ in habits and attitudes regarding shopping. We are witnessing the emergence of a new 'retail culture'. ~~The article suggests~~ Gardner reports evidence that people are spending more time shopping and ~~these hi-tech centres definately create the right atmosphere for pleasurable shopping~~ that it is now one of our favourite leisure activities. ~~One~~ What is more, the social aspect of these new centres enables people to meet friends ~~whilst enjoying themselves~~ in public places and in comfort. As a result shopping ~~has~~ is ~~taken~~ taking on a new meaning ~~and has never been regarded in this way before~~ in people's lives; a meaning which, according to Gardner, harks back to the days of the medieval market. ~~Mr Gardner believes that it is the new style centres that have brought these changes in peoples view of shopping.~~

Choosing the right word

Ann has a tendency to pick words which do not quite do the job she wants. For example, 'have' is a rather tame word at the end of paragraph one. 'Offer' or 'present' would give more of a sense of these 'advantages and disadvantages' being *thrust* upon us, rather than an impression of sitting patiently waiting for us to notice. Again, in the first sentence of the second paragraph, 'favourable' doesn't seem quite the right word — it means pleasing, or promising, which seems a bit weak in this context. 'Attractive' or 'beneficial' would give a sharper bite to the sentence. And in the next sentence, 'provide' or 'offer' would be more punchy than 'are'.

A sentence later Ann talks of people's 'views' of shopping, when it seems that she specifically means their 'tastes'. In the next sentence, however, there is a more seriously 'wrong' choice of word, when she talks about 'the *demand* in stylish shops', which doesn't make a lot of sense on first reading. After studying the drift of the paragraph, I decided that what she was really talking about was the *spread* of stylish shops. This substitution makes quite a difference to the impact of the sentence, but to me it makes more sense. To give a final example, the last sentence of paragraph three starts with 'Therefore'. 'Therefore' is a word you use towards the end of a sequence of fairly tight logical points, when you are claiming that you have *proved* your case (e.g. You are rich; but you do not work; *therefore* you must have inherited a fortune). Here Ann has not set out enough argument to claim to be *proving* a case. She is simply *summarizing* the arguments in favour of the shopping centres. All she needed to say was 'thus', or 'we see then that'.

Choice of words

Obviously, as you are writing, you have to use the words that come to you. You would suffer from verbal constipation if you stopped to worry about every word. However, when you are reading over what you have written, you should check that you have conveyed the meaning you intended. The exact meaning of the words you use tends to be more important in writing than in speech.

In the long run, your studies will increase your sensitivity to the shades of meaning which words carry. In the short term, all you can do is just get on with your writing, but make a point of looking up words in the dictionary when you are doubtful.

Sentences

Ann has a much firmer grasp than Sam of the basic requirements of a sentence. The essay is entirely composed of proper sentences. On the other hand, some of them are a bit ungainly. For example, take the one at the start of paragraph four:

However, there are also some disadvantages expressed in the article, some of which are the view of other authors, but with whom Carl Gardner does not agree.

There is *too much going on* in this sentence. It needs breaking into two, or straightening out in some way. For instance, Ann could simply say: 'However, as others have pointed out, there are also disadvantages.' I think this covers the same ground as the longer sentence and is much easier to grasp. If sentences are very long, you tend to lose hold of the meaning as you read them. The later bits drive the earlier part out of your head. For example, this sentence of Ann's is both too long and too complicated:

On an individual level these centres rely on low paid female labour working long and arduous hours, for people who may not necessary be purchasing goods but just browsing, which incidentally can be much more pleasant in such surroundings.

Writing in simple sentences

A sentence is a self-contained unit of meaning.

An essay is an *argument* constructed by putting a sequence of these units one after another. The meaning should flow from one sentence to the next, carrying the argument forward.

If you lapse from the sentence format the meaning becomes fuzzy. The flow of meaning starts to diffuse and leak away. You want reasonably short, simple, solidly constructed sentences which will give reliable service in carrying the meaning forward from one to the next.

Argument and structure

Although I liked the broad outline of the structure of Ann's essay, I thought it could be sharpened up and delivered more smoothly.

ACTIVITY BREAK   Take your photocopies of Ann's essay and of my reworking of it (on pages 138–40), so that you can follow my discussion of it carefully, cross-checking between my suggestions and the original.

I have already suggested giving more bite to the opening by drawing in Gardner's broader theme concerning the changes going on in our society. And I sharpened the second prargraph in a similar way by highlighting more explicitly the changes in people's habits, tastes and values. Note that if this is done clearly in the middle of the paragraph we don't need to come back to it at the end, so we can lose the last sentence. Also, I felt that Ann was on the wrong track in saying that shopping had 'never been regarded in this way before', since Gardner drew interesting parallels with medieval and Mediterranean markets. I would prefer to rework the sentence to draw in this point here.

Her third paragraph needs to signal more clearly that the scene of the discussion is now shifting to the high streets and the impact there of the new competition. It also needs a crisper last sentence summarizing the arguments *in favour* of the new shopping centres. The first sentence of the next paragraph then acts as the pivot, swinging us round to consider the arguments *against* the shopping centres. Then this and the next two paragraphs need sharper endings which bring out the argument and counter-argument more succinctly. That is, paragraph four needs to explain Gardner's objection to the concept of 'manipulation'; paragraph five needs to be clearer about his counter-argument to Worpole; and paragraph six needs to draw out more clearly the point Ann is making about shoppers only 'browsing'. Finally, I would recast the last paragraph to produce Ann's conclusion with more conviction.

Making cuts

I chopped out Ann's point about a 'crisis' in retail development, because I felt it needed more space if it were to be developed sufficiently to make sense. In any case, we have enough material without it. This does *not* mean that it is an unimportant point. It could easily be made the *central* point of the whole essay if that was what you decided. However, the essay already has a nice tight line of argument and doesn't need this extra theme.

When you are planning an essay, you have to make hard choices as to which points to work with as your central ones and which ones to chop. Essays are made worse, not better, if you try to cram everything in. It is not a matter of how *much* you can squeeze into your essays — it is *how well they read as arguments*.

To show how this tightened up version of Ann's argument looks, I have set it out in detail. (Numbers at the left refer to sentences in my revised version. Highlighting indicates additions.)

Outline plan for revised version of Ann's essay

PARAGRAPH 1 — INTRODUCTION

1 Gardner draws attention to new shopping centres

2 these are part of wider changes

3 we need to weigh up the pros and cons

PARAGRAPH 2 — ARGUMENTS FOR new shopping centres

1 there are several pros

2 pleasant surroundings — all weather

3 the emphasis on style, design and leisure reflects popular tastes

4 the spread of stylish shops and environments — has changed habits and attitudes re. shopping

5 we are seeing the emergence of a new retail culture

6 people spend more time shopping — it is now a favourite activity

7 social aspects — people can meet friends

8 shopping has begun to take on a new meaning (medieval market)

PARAGRAPH 3 — ELABORATION OF ARGUMENT FOR

1 *impact beyond the centres themselves*

2 *new develpmts also spur on improvements to existing high streets etc.*

3 *picture of improvements everywhere*

PARAGRAPH 4 — FIRST ARGUMENT AGAINST (capitalist manipulation)

1 *however there are disadvantages too*

2 *idea of increased manipulation*

3 *customers being 'conned' to maintain high levels of sales*

4 *Gardner disapproves of this view of people as idiots*

PARAGRAPH 5 — MORE ARGUMENTS AGAINST (urban decay)

1 *attack from Worpole — new style shopping causes division amongst haves and have-nots*

2 *which causes increased crime*

3 *town centre life is being ruined*

4 *Gardner gives examples where this has not (he says) happened — and argues that in fact public environments are improving*

PARAGRAPH 6 — MORE ARGUMENTS AGAINST (poor jobs)

1 *moving to the individual level — centres rely on low-paid female labour — long unsociable hours*

2 *is it worth it when people are often only browsing?*

3 *how to weigh leisure interests — against creation of poor jobs?*

PARAGRAPH 7 — CONCLUSION

1 *Gardner accepts some of these arguments against — but sees the arguments for too.*

2 *If his account of the benefits is correct then centres are not entirely bad.*

Health warning:*DON'T* THINK THAT YOU HAVE TO MAKE OUTLINE PLANS AS ELABORATE AS THIS BEFORE YOU WRITE *YOUR* ESSAYS.

I only did this very detailed plan for the purposes of analysis. I would *never* bother to make a sentence by sentence plan before writing. You need much more sketchy plans for writing (see Chapter 6, Section 2.4).

ACTIVITY BREAK Look back over this outline plan and notice how the sentences and paragraphs work together.

Look at the way *each sentence does a job* — it delivers a specific point — and the sentences are grouped together in clusters to form paragraphs.

Then notice how *each paragraph also does a job* — it presents a group of related points which together form a specific segment of the argument. Follow the paragraph headings to see how each takes us a stage further in the argument. I have stuck to the basic paragraph structure created by Ann, but I have tried to bring out the 'story line' of the argument more clearly. Each point now takes its cue from the previous one and is the springboard for the next.

Read through the outline again and see whether you sense that continuity. Notice particularly the places where I have decided to make changes to the original.

One main point per sentence

If a sentence delivers two points, consider splitting it in two.

For example, I have split the second sentence of Ann's fifth paragraph into two. This allows the point about *social divisions* to be established in its own right, before going on to deal with the conclusion Worpole draws about *crime rates*. It is possible to accept one of these two points without accepting the other, so it is useful to have them set down separately. The reader can then examine the logic of each before being committed to the whole package.

KEY POINTS

Arguments read more easily if you take the points one at a time. Allow one sentence for each point.

Revised version of Ann's essay

When I wrote out the whole revised version of Ann's essay, it looked like this (bits I have added are highlighted):

Carl Gardner draws our attention to the rapid development in recent times of a new type of shopping centre. In his view these rather spectacular examples of large-scale investment are part of wider changes in the economy and in society in general. In order to assess whether these developments are, on balance, a good or bad thing, it is necessary to look in some detail at the various advantages and disadvantages that the new high-tech centres offer.

There are several ways in which the new style shopping centres seem attractive. They provide pleasant surroundings which enable people to shop in all weather. They emphasise style and design, and include many leisure facilities, reflecting the tastes of many shoppers in the eighties. In fact it seems that the spread of the new stylish shops along with their equally stylish environments has brought about a complete change in habits and attitudes regarding shopping. We are witnessing the emergence of a new 'retail culture'. Gardner reports evidence that people are spending more time shopping and that it is now one of our favourite leisure activities. What is more, the social aspect of the new centres enables people to meet friends in public places and in comfort. As a result shopping is taking on a new meaning in people's lives; a meaning which, according to Gardner, harks back to the days of the medieval market.

Furthermore Gardner argues that these changes are not only affecting the centres themselves but are spreading elsewhere. The new shopping centres have helped to bring about improvements in facilities in older shopping centres and in the high streets, as they compete for custom. The picture he paints is of standards improving everywhere; of new opportunities for family life in public places.

However, as others have pointed out, there are also disadvantages. One argument concerns the increased opportunity for manipulation of the customers in the new style shopping centres. On this view people are being seduced and deluded in order to maintain high levels of consumption. Gardner on the other hand suggests that this line of thinking implies contempt for ordinary people's tastes and values.

Another line of attack comes from Ken Worpole, who maintains that the retail boom, as reflected by high-tech centres, is causing a division between those who can and those who cannot afford to buy. This in turn is leading to an increase in crime. What is more town centre life is being ruined by the competition from these huge, fully automated shopping centres. Gardner, however, gives examples of successful city centres which also have out-of-town developments and argues that the quality of public environments and urban life is in fact improving rather than declining.

But apart from these broader issues, at an individual level these centres rely on low-paid female labour working long and unsociable hours. Can this be justified when many people are not purchasing necessary goods but just browsing? How are we to weigh the leisure *interests of the mass of consumers against the creation of yet more work which is unnecessary, underpaid and intrinsically unsatisfying?*

Gardner recognises the force of these doubts and criticisms directed at these recent developments in retailing, but argues that the positive benefits should also be properly understood. If we accept his arguments about their contribution to a general improvement in quality of the public environments now available to many people, we surely cannot regard the new high-tech shopping centres as essentially a 'bad thing'.

How good is Ann's essay?

As with Sam's, I have now given Ann's essay a fair old bashing, so again I must hasten to confirm that I did think it was a very useful first essay. What advice would you have offered her? In fact, it isn't easy to take other people's views on your own writing. How do you think she would have felt as she read my letter?

Dear Ann,

I was most impressed with this essay. You had clearly made a good job of reading and thinking about the Gardner article and of thinking your way into the essay. The general organisation of the essay was very well worked out. You covered your points in a sound and unhurried way, developing the logic as you went along. Your writing was generally clear and direct, with good linking between the more theoretical analysis and the real world.

At times I though you had not quite got hold of the word or phrase you needed, so I have suggested alternatives. This is not necessarily because yours was 'wrong', but because I thought you could make a point more sharply with a different word. Try reading these sentences out with your wording and then with mine and see if you can 'hear' the difference I am suggesting.

Occasionally you tend to make your sentences somewhat longer and more complicated than a reader can easily follow. A good motto is — always go for the shortest sentence you (reasonably) can — at least at this stage when you are building up a new style.

Here and there you could tighten up the logic of your argument — sometimes just by cutting a few words out — sometimes by changing things around a little. I have tried to show how in one or two places.

*You did a very good job of keeping your sights on the Gardner article, but your tone is sometimes a bit **too** respectful towards him.*

This is just a matter of style, which you will gradually pick up with practice. For example, I have suggested a modification of your opening sentence which, I think, puts you on a more matter-of-fact footing with him, as well as getting down to the real business of the essay more quickly.

All in all this is an excellent effort.

2.5   Extracts from some other essays

The two essays we have examined have demonstrated some important points about writing, but I would like to show you extracts from three others drawn from the same group of students, so that you can glimpse a wider range of styles.

Extract from George's essay

. . . [Gardner] goes on to describe how the urban populace live in a world of mediocre housing, in dreary towns of poor design, who become so gratified and ever so excited and no doubt salivate about the mouth at the merest thought concerning a new shopping centre. Oh come on! If these people, I suggest, had such a low quality of life, then they would hardly be the type to spend a whole Saturday in a shopping centre; because if they can't afford to pay better rent or mortgage rates then how could they frequent such a hard sell centre with any regularity.

Finally we are told that the arrival on the economic scene of easy credit, was in some way the weapon which helped to free the populace from it's financial bonds. This in turn coincided with a massive rise in unemployment and according to Gardner, people bought goods merely to display that they were a part of the 'Dominant Culture' and not to be confused with the unemployed. He underlines this theme by suggesting that just the act of buying was what mattered. In answer to this all I can say is that Gardner with these beliefs is placing himself firmly in a minority of selfish, egocentric, meanminded individuals and that a statement of that kind isn't fit to be spoken by a juvenile . . .

Extract from Yasmin's essay

The article introduces us to the new high-tech shopping complexes, which are sprouting up like magic mushrooms in Britain, in euphoric terms. They are designed to transport the shoppers away from their urban mediocre dreary surroundings, into totally controlled spectacularly engineered exciting new environments. Glamour and glitz to match Holywood's best spectaculars, shoppers will be confronted amongst palatial surroundings themes ranging from Roman forums to Mediterranean villages are already on offer. The disoriented consumer will thus be encouraged to stay longer and buy more, not only spending their income, but with easy availability of credit, well beyond their income. With the current sharp rise in interest rates effecting mortgage repayments these shopping trips could end up giving people painfull withdrawal symptoms.

Extract from Ken's essay

Dear Fred,

I have just read Carl Gardner's article on the growth of 'High Tech' shopping centres springing up in our cities and towns, and as you live in a small village you can be grateful that you may never be tempted into becoming a 'Shopping Junkie'. I think the high financiers of the retail industry will look for more lucrative sites. Anyway a couple of points for your perusal as I know you don't read the New Statesman & Society, *although with this article I would have liked a Technical Glossary to aid me in reading . . .*

ACTIVITY BREAK   What is your reaction to these three extracts? Do you think they look promising?

The first two writers are more fluent than Sam or Ann. In fact George writes with considerable flair. He has a good range of vocabulary and a very purposeful and engaging style. I was particularly impressed by his ability to set a line of argument running and stay in control of it as he moved from point to point. I'm not saying the arguments themselves were 'good' but it was easy to read them and to see what he was driving at. However, in spite of these strengths, I think the essay is a poorer one than Ann's. Why? Because he has become carried away with his own argument.

George's essay is entirely lacking in *objectivity*. He makes no effort to present a fair and balanced analysis of the issues raised by the Gardner article. Indeed, I doubt whether he was able to take in much of what Gardner was saying because of his own very strong reactions to the subject matter. As a result *I* found it quite hard to read what *he* was saying. I felt he was trying to browbeat me. He set about attempting to demolish Gardner's case by attributing all sorts of beliefs and ideas to him and by assaulting his character. This is a perfectly normal way of writing in some newspapers. However, the conventions of *essay* writing are that you should treat arguments fairly and persuade by force of reason rather than emotion. George leaves us no room for manoeuvre with our own thoughts and reactions. He is telling us exactly what to think. That is not the relationship to establish with your readers, because the only people likely to read what you have to say will be those who know already that they agree with your views. You need to set up a more equal and respectful relationship with your audience. Arguing your case is *not* a matter of making a furious assault, but of carefully taking your reader through a series of ideas.

Arguing

Arguing in an essay is not at all the same thing as 'having an argument' in everyday terms. When you hear two people 'arguing' in normal life, there is often a hint of *anger* and *confrontation* in the air, of *stubbornness, irrationality, wild generalization* and *emotion.* Your argument in an essay should aim at the opposite of these. You should try to be *objective, precise, logical,* concerned to back your case with *evidence,* and to be *open to doubt and criticism.*

Objective

A key technique in everyday arguing is to try to get people to 'sympathize' with you and then imply that they should therefore accept that what you say is true. In other words, you try to win over their emotional support first and hope that they will then, out of loyalty, accept that your thought-processes are sound. In an essay, however, the assumption is that ideas must 'stand on their own feet'. They should be able to survive detailed logical inspection, unsupported by emotional commitment. You have to write about your ideas *as though you don't care about them* — as though you are just drawing them to the attention of your reader out of a sense of fair play.

Precise

Another technique in everyday arguing is to use words very loosely, stretching them to cover all sorts of ideas, so that the resulting vagueness as to what you are saying will blind people to the inconsistencies of your position. In essays, by contrast, you are expected to be careful about the way you use words. It matters which words you choose in making a particular point. (That is why I changed quite a number of words in Ann's essay. Similarly, Yasmin uses a word like 'euphoric' in a context where all it does is confuse her point. Who is euphoric? — the retail giants? — the shoppers?)

Logical

Essays are supposed to be based on reason and logic. Your points shouldn't just be scattered around. They should follow some sort of sequence, such that your reader can see the

---

connection of one point to the next. Rather than throwing a handful of gravel at your target, you mould together a few good sized stones in a lump of clay and then take careful aim. The accumulated force of several connected points focused into a concerted attack is immensely more powerful than a welter of separate ones. This is why you have to try to make sure that your ideas fit together smoothly; that the overall effect is *convincing*.

Concerned with evidence

Your other weapon besides logical reasoning is to provide evidence to support your case. You cannot expect your reader to believe what you say simply because it is *you* saying it. You have to show your *grounds* for saying it. Gardner, for example, draws on *survey evidence* showing that our national shopping habits are changing. George, by contrast, in attempting to ridicule Gardner's claims, takes no notice of the evidence offered. He doesn't try to suggest ways in which the evidence might be suspect, or how Gardner's interpretation of its meaning might be wrong. Nor does he offer any alternative evidence. Consequently, in spite of his energetic mud-slinging, in the end he makes no impact on Gardner's basic point.

Open to doubt and criticism

Finally, your arguments should be presented in the spirit that they are unlikely to be the whole story. You don't have to be cringing and apologetic about what you say. But you need to be capable of seeing some strength in alternative views. Gardner, for example, attacks some of Worpole's case quite sharply, but also concedes that there is something in what he says. It is part of the spirit of operating in a world of logic and evidence that you acknowledge that *new* evidence and *new* arguments will emerge and that you may, quite legitimately, change your mind when they do.

Here is part of what I wrote to George:

Dear George,

I thoroughly enjoyed reading this essay. You have a remarkably powerful way with the written word and you obviously have very strong and well developed views on social issues. There is a muscular dynamism in your attack on the subject matter and a purposefulness which is most impressive. On this evidence you will be capable of great things in your studies. On the other hand, I didn't agree with a word. I thought you were far more unfair on Gardner than he was on those he criticised. In fact I felt you had fundamentally misread the intended thrust of his argument . . . You may not agree with his views, but I think they deserve more serious attention than you give . . . In general your style was a very good one for a newspaper article, but rather too flamboyant and aggressive for an essay. You call on your reader's sympathy as you evoke hate for the enemy. But you should be calling more on reason, on argument and evidence. You imply that you disbelieve the evidence offered by Gardner, but you give no evidence yourself to counter his claims . . . I am simply pointing to dangers of running a very strong and emotionally based line of argument in an essay.

Anyway the important thing is that you are able to bring formidable powers of thought and of self expression to bear on your studies. With strengths like that to deploy as you study, you will do very well . . .

Turning now to the extract from Yasmin's essay (which was in fact the first paragraph of it), what struck me was that she was *trying* just a bit too hard to impress. She obviously had a good grasp of what the Gardner article was about and plenty of confidence about weighing into a discussion. She was well aware of the need to capture her reader's attention and then follow a line of argument, but she hadn't quite managed to establish a comfortable relationship with her reader. Somehow I felt a bit overwhelmed by the dash and the swagger. Why 'magic' mushrooms? What does she mean by 'in euphoric terms'? Can a shopping centre really be as glamorous and glitzy as a Hollywood spectacular? I found I was distracted by these thoughts, instead of following the argument carefully. And in any case I felt that, in all the excitement, some of the sentences had been concocted too hastily, so that they didn't quite say what they were meant to say. I felt more comfortable with the solid steady pace of Ann's essay, even though it was less elegant in its use of language. What is more, I think that Yasmin got caught up in the flow of her own rhetoric and lost track of her intended plan of attack. Her basic essay structure is a tried and trusty one:

para. 1: introduction
para. 2: points for
para. 3: points against
para. 4: conclusion

However, by the end of her introductory paragraph she is already spilling over from her general description of the new shopping centres into the points against, which rather confuses the flow of the argument.

So although Yasmin had a lively attitude to the subject and wrote about it thoughtfully, it would have been easier to follow her arguments if she had been striving less for effect and had concentrated more on getting her points across. When you are impatient to show your flair for the subject, it can be hard to accept the role of a beginner and recognize that an essay is an *exercise* in learning to argue precisely and logically, not a major contribution to a national debate. Basically Yasmin has not yet found quite the right 'voice' for her writing.

'Speaking' to your 'reader'

Writing is a very special form of 'conversation'. You are talking to someone you cannot see and who never answers. But you know he or she is 'listening' and reacting mentally to what you say. *You* have to take all the responsibility for deciding *what* is to be discussed and *how*, and for sustaining the other person's *interest*. You are also responsible for establishing the *relationship* between you and the 'listener'.

This is one of the trickiest things about writing. You have to convey a sense of *who* you are assuming your *reader* is, and of the *frame of mind* in which he or she will be approaching your words. You also have to convey a sense of *who you are claiming to be*; from what position you are 'speaking'. Are you speaking as an expert on the subject under discussion, as a witty entertainer, as a patient explainer, or what?

There are two basic issues here. You have to develop a sense of your 'audience' and of the right 'tone of voice' in which to write.

A sense of 'audience'

Who are you to assume your audience to be when you write an essay? Is it someone who is very learned and critical or someone who knows nothing and couldn't care less about the subject? The standard formula is to say, '*Write for the intelligent person in the street*'. In other words, assume that your reader has *not* read the books you have been studying, but that he or she is *interested* in the question posed by the title of the essay and is *capable* of picking up your arguments quickly, provided you spell them out clearly.

Your writing 'voice'

Who are you to present yourself as? Basically you are expected to be a calm, detached observer, pointing out to an equal (who happens not to be informed on the subject) some arguments which are relevant to a question you are both interested in (i.e. the question in the essay title). It is not easy to find a comfortable writing 'voice'. It may take several essays before you can settle on a satisfactory one. One of the main reasons

---

146

for getting stuck at the start of an essay is the difficulty of trying to work out where you are 'coming from'. Sometimes you have to take several shots at your opening before you can find a voice with which you can proceed.

Ken appears to have had even more difficulty establishing his relationship with his audience, for he has resorted to the format of a letter-writing relationship. Instead of writing to a 'general' reader, he is writing to one specific person. This makes the relationship easier to 'imagine' and allows him to draw on the familiar language and conventions of letter writing. It may be a good way of overcoming the difficulty of getting started if you are very new to essay writing, although it is rather unconventional and might take some tutors by surprise. Ken will very soon need to find some other way to 'imagine' his audience, so that he can construct his arguments in a more general and less personalized form.

3   What is a good essay?

This detailed analysis of the essays has enabled us to pull out some very important points about the nature of essay writing. Moreover, it has allowed us to do it in a *practical* context where we could look at the strengths and weaknesses of various ways of writing in *real* terms, not just as formal rules and abstract ideas. Now, however, we need to summarize. To begin the summary, we shall return to the question I posed at the end of the first Activity Break. What are the qualities of a good essay?

If you attempted that part of the activity you will find it useful to have your notes by you now, so that you can check how far your own insights correspond to my analysis. The reason I suggest this is that I suspect that you already have a fairly well-developed idea of what good writing is. I don't think the point of a chapter like this is to tell you much that is devastatingly new to you. It is to bring into a sharper focus what you already know and to provide a set of working concepts so that you can apply your 'native' intuitions more effectively as you work on your own writing. It is one thing to be able to spot when *someone else's* writing is boring or confusing, but quite another to be able to pinpoint *why* and to avoid making exactly the same mistake *yourself*. See how closely your own list corresponds to the one overleaf.

KEY POINTS

The criteria of good essay writing

When a tutor reads your essay he or she will be asking the following things:

▶ Have you *answered the question* in the title?

▶ Have you drawn on the *relevant parts of the course* for the main content of your essay?

▶ Do you show a *good grasp of the ideas* you have been studying *in the course*?

▶ Have you presented a coherent *argument*?

▶ Is the essay written in an *objective analytical* style, with appropriate use of *evidence* etc.?

▶ Is the essay *well written*? (i.e. is it easy to read?)

We have already touched on many of these, but let us take a brief look at each.

3.1 Answering the question

An essay can be good in almost every other way and yet be judged to be very poor because it ignores the question posed in the title.* In an essay at adult level you are never just 'writing all you know' about a subject, or simply 'describing' something (as you might do say in a school essay about 'What I did on my holidays'). You are being set a specific problem to think about in the light of what you have been studying. Your task is to argue a case in relation to the question posed in the title. Everything you say in the essay should be relevant to that task. It isn't enough that a point you make is interesting to *you*. You have to convince your reader that the point has some bearing on the title and is therefore worth his or her attention. Life is too short to read every interesting sentence. Each sentence has to be relevant to the key issues the reader is grappling with.

That is why it is a good rule always to write the title of the essay across the top of your opening page. It reminds you where your

---

* Actually it would be more correct to say 'fails to address the *issues* presented in the title', since not every essay title actually contains a *question* as such. However, it sounds more abstract and formal put that way. In fact, there is usually a central question underlying an essay title, even if it happens to be set in a form other than a direct question, so it is generally easiest to think in the terms 'Have I remembered to answer the question?'

reader is starting from as he or she launches into reading your essay. And you must always stick exactly to the title you are given — not devise a modified version of your own. (You may be interested to know that George had invented an entirely new title for his essay — 'Gently letting down the tyres of a right wing vehicle' — which may be more catchy than the original, but it also gives some clues as to why his essay ended up giving so little serious attention to the central issues raised in the Gardner article.)

A tutor faces a demanding job assessing and commenting upon your essay. The job is made possible by setting it up in a tightly defined way, so that it is clear what has to be done in order to show a certain level of mastery. This is the purpose of the title and the reason you have to work to it at all times. Tutors can be quite impatient if you insist on showing them a whole lot of knowledge and skills other than have been asked for.

3.2 Drawing on the course material

Unless you are taking a course in creative writing, essays are generally intended to help you consolidate what you have been studying. You are not being asked to answer the question in the title 'off the top of your head', or on the basis of prior knowledge. You are expected to take the essay as an opportunity to scan back over what you have been reading and extract relevant material. The tutor marking your essay will already have in mind a range of course material that could be brought into an answer to the question. If you miss out *some* of the important ideas and information it may not matter, provided you have made good use of *other* material from the relevant part of the course. If, on the other hand, you attempt to answer entirely on the basis of knowledge drawn from outside the course, you will run into trouble. It is often very difficult for a tutor to evaluate your account of material he or she is not familiar with, and there is unlikely to be time to read the sources. If you answer in this way, you focus attention on what you *haven't* done with the relevant material in the course. It is a very common tale of woe to hear a student say that the one essay topic in a course on which he or she already knew a lot was the one which received the lowest mark, while the essay rushed through the night before going on holiday was marked the highest. It seems that, in the context of a course at least, a *lot* of knowledge can be a dangerous thing, in that it tempts you into overlooking the new knowledge available to you in the course.

3.3   Showing a good grasp of the ideas in the course

To show the tutor your grasp of the ideas you have been studying you have to express them for yourself *in your own words*. Certainly your tutor will be looking out for signs that you have a grasp of the central points. In Ann's essay, for example, she showed that she understood Gardner's key point about shopping taking on a new meaning in people's lives. On the other hand, she was rather vague about Gardner's relationship to left-wing views of shopping, which suggests that she hadn't really got that part of his argument sorted out.

The point of the essay is to show that you understand how the arguments in the course work and that you can apply the ideas to examples of your own. The tutor has to be able to see your own thought-processes at work. What you must avoid doing is to *copy* directly from the texts, because that suggests you are incapable of using the ideas for yourself.

The temptation to 'plagiarize'

In writing an essay you are often working with ideas and terms you are not familiar with. This makes producing a clear, coherent argument very difficult and you may become nervous as to whether you will 'get it right'. Some students are tempted to 'lift' sections of words from the textbooks to be on the safe side. This 'lifting' is known as *plagiarism*.

To some extent Sam's essay shows signs of this. There are several strings of words which appear almost exactly as they do in Gardner's text. For example, he says:

'Third Carl Gardner describes the new "high-tech" shopping centres how they varied in size and style, spectacularly produced glass atria or glazed barrel-vaults which helps to use natural light for the shops and walkways.'

The original text reads:

'Though varied in size and style, nearly all centres offer the same basic features. Most importantly, there are spectacularly engineered glass atria or glazed barrel-vaults to flood the shops and walkways with natural light.'

Instead of setting out to describe the main features of the centres in his *own* words, Sam has selected from and re-jigged Gardner's. It doesn't 'sound' natural and it doesn't read well. Words like 'spectacular' give the game away, because he doesn't use words like that elsewhere.

Tutors are usually very familiar with the difference between the way students write and the way experienced authors write, and soon notice when there are lurches between an 'expert' style and a 'beginner' style. A particular giveaway is when most of the words are as in the original except for one or two (changed for camouflage purposes), which stick out like sore thumbs because they are in a different style. Another is when smoothly flowing sections are interspersed with short stuttering link phrases. It seems that most people write particularly badly when they are attempting to cobble together somebody else's words. Because you are not in control of 'making' the sense as you write — but clinging desperately on to the coat tails of someone else's thoughts — plagiarizing actually makes your writing worse.

Basically there is only one way to learn to 'use' ideas in writing and that is to practise expressing ideas in your own words. They may come out badly to begin with, but like a learner in any field (whether driving, playing an instrument or tap-dancing), you have to be prepared to make simple mistakes and look like an idiot. It is through exposing your weaknesses that you learn how to do something about them.

Writing in your own words

Do not rely heavily on copying out segments from the printed texts:

1 *It does not 'read' well* as a form of writing. Because you are not developing a thread of meaning as you write, but stitching together segments of meaning collected from elsewhere, the sentences read very jerkily. In fact, frequently they don't make much overall sense at all. Consequently you are unlikely to get good marks with this approach.

2 Your *tutor cannot* judge how well you understand the course and *give you appropriate advice and support*. Indeed, when the tutor spots what you are up to (and it is not hard to tell), he or she will be inclined to assume that you understand very little and so mark you down.

3 *You do not learn about the ideas and terms in the course* unless you try to use them for yourself.

4 Most important for our present purposes, *you do not develop your own writing style*. So long as you are parroting other people's words rather than expressing thoughts for yourself, you

are locked into a sterile and tedious process which gives no exercise to your capacity to link your own thoughts with words. You are in danger of remaining a beginner, a non-writer, for ever. As in swimming, you don't begin to learn until you have the courage to take your feet off the bottom.

3.4 Presenting a coherent argument

This is closely linked with answering the question. The *essence* of the essay is that it sets out to be an argument on the issues raised in the title. Even if you have a lot of the right material in your essay, it will not be judged a good one unless that material is organized so that it hangs together.

This is precisely the trouble with Sam's essay. His list of points was of little use to us his readers because we couldn't see what they were there for. However, when I reorganized these points within an *argument* they were fine. To develop an argument in your essay implies two things:

1 You need to *sort out* your points into groups, so that they can be presented in a *structured* way, giving the essay a *beginning*, a *middle* and an *end*.

2 You need to keep a *thread of meaning* running through your essay. What this means is that each sentence should flow on from the previous one, with adequate *signposting* to help your reader follow the moves you are making.

In fact, presenting a coherent argument is also closely linked with showing your grasp of ideas. One of the reasons *why* your writing tasks are set in the form of an argument is because that makes you *use* the ideas you have been studying to *say* something. Anyone can *copy* material from books. The point of an essay is to make you *think*. When you present a coherent argument you are showing that you can *take hold of the ideas* and *organize* them to do some work for you.

3.5 Adopting an objective, analytical style

An essay should argue by force of reason. In everyday life we often prefer to rely on emotional force. Consequently you may have to make deliberate efforts to develop a writing style which is cool, dispassionate and fair to all sides. If you want to dispute a claim made by someone else, you are expected to use argument and evidence, rather than setting out to cast doubts on your opponent's character. You should be *respectful* to other writers. You should assume you are writing as a member of a community of equals, all of whom are intelligent, open-minded and fair. You should write on the assumption that your reader is also one of this community and that he or she will be interested in your *reasons* for holding the ideas you do. Don't assume that your reader is interested in the ideas *because* they are *your* ideas.

3.6 Writing clearly

A final point which emerged from our analysis of sample essays was that a good essay is *easy to read*. Grand sounding phrases and elaborate sentences do not make an essay impressive. *Clarity* and *succinctness* are what win a reader over. Ease of reading is achieved at several levels.

Technical considerations

Handwriting: At the most obvious level, ease of reading depends on the quality of your handwriting (unless you type your essays). You cannot do much about the basic character of your handwriting in the *short term*. None the less, you can undoubtedly make it more or less legible depending quite simply on the time and care you take over it. Since you spend a lot of time putting an essay together, it is a waste if the essay is then misunderstood merely because the writing is misread — and it would be an angelic tutor who was not at least a little impatient at having to spend ages poring over every other word trying to make it out. It is worth investing the extra time and trouble to make the best job you can of your writing.

For the *longer term*, try to get someone to read a sample of your writing and tell you which letters are the most difficult to make out. Then you can practise forming those letters slightly differently — say, rounding them a little more, or closing the tops of a's so that they don't look like u's. Changing your handwriting is a long process, but it is by no means impossible. However, you should not despair if your handwriting is poor. Most tutors have, in the course of duty, had to become experts in deciphering all kinds of scrawl and will usually do their best not to be too influenced by barely legible writing.

Layout: Again, in a very obvious way, your essay is made easier to read by setting it out neatly on the page. You need to use lined A4 paper and leave generous margins, so that the tutor can write comments if necessary. Write on one side of the paper only (this makes it easier to cross-refer from one section of the essay to another); leave spaces between paragraphs, and so on. It is all straightforward stuff, but the point is that you should 'stand back' from your finished essay and look at it almost as an aesthetic object. Does it look inviting to read? It is surprising how many first essays seem to have words crammed on to every square centimetre of paper. Be generous with space and 'page-proud'. Unless your essay looks as though *you* care about it, it is hard for your reader to care.

Spelling, punctuation and grammar: These contribute enormously to ease of reading. The whole point of *punctuation* is to help the reader to approach your words in the right way, and the rules of *grammar* are what enable the reader to construct the sense intended by the writer. Mistakes in either make the reader stop in order to puzzle out what is being said. Poor spelling also causes frequent interruptions to work out what the mistake is. None of these technical abilities is particularly easy to improve quickly, and all fall beyond the scope of this book, but if you think you are particularly weak on these matters you should seek help. However, important though these technical accomplishments are, you may take heart in the knowledge that tutors will often battle gamely to 'read through' to your intended meaning, and will also attempt to help you improve.

Language

Your language should be direct rather than fancy. Always go for short and simple sentences where you can. This is especially the case at the stage where you are building up a basic essay-writing style. (You can always play with more elaborate words and grammatical structures later, when you have established a good basic technique.) Don't beat about the bush reciting formalities; pitch straight into answering the question in a simple and purposeful way.

Fluency

Try to make your essay flow from one sentence to the next. As we have seen, this is partly a matter of *structure* and partly of *signposting*. It is vital to think of your essay in terms of its overall structure — to move points around, to cut and trim and so on, in search of a clear simple sequence for your ideas. Then, having arrived at a structure, you have to 'talk' the reader through it, emphasizing the key turning points in the essay, summarizing where you have got to, showing how each new point follows from the last, and finally bringing it all to a conclusion.

Explaining

You need to be able to think of things from your reader's point of view. The reader cannot see into your head, so you have to explain your points quite fully and carefully. You need to give examples to illustrate what you are talking about. You don't want the reader to be wondering, 'What's this all about?' With a well written essay it should be obvious.

4   Conclusion

Let me highlight a few key messages to take from this discussion. One is that there is no great mystery about *what* good writing is. We can spot it just by reading it. The mystery is how to produce it. (That is what the next chapter is about.) However, since there are different facets to writing well, you will find it useful to return to the *criteria of good essay writing* on page 148 from time to time and to consider how your writing is developing. When you are about to submit an essay to a tutor, or after you get it back with comments on it, you can check through the list and see what progress you are making.

Another point to think over is that, in the process of reading the sample essays in this chapter, you have had a glimpse of the role your tutor plays. As you saw, it isn't easy to read other people's writing and make sense of it. Nor is it easy to pinpoint what the strengths and weaknesses are and to work out how to give appropriate advice. This carries two lessons:

1 Be sympathetic to your tutor and present your work as clearly as you can.

2 Don't be too upset or too irritated if your tutor misses your point or if he or she offers advice you don't think is appropriate or fair. It is almost impossible to get these things right all the time.

You should also have gained some useful insights into what a tutor is likely to be looking for.

Finally, take note that *you don't have to worry about getting your writing 'perfect' before submitting it*. None of the essays we looked at was anywhere near 'perfect', but they were all fine as first essays. These students were doing exactly the right thing in 'getting stuck in' and having a go. You just have to assume that your first attempts will not be particularly wonderful and get on with it. It is a sign of a good learner in any field to be prepared to make mistakes. In the next chapter we look at how to set about developing your skill as a writer.

CHAPTER **6**

How to write essays

1 Introduction

After looking, in Chapter 5, at *what* you are trying to produce when you write an essay, we turn in this chapter to the vital question of *how* to do it. Most people find writing hard. The adult students who wrote the short essays you saw in the last chapter all said that they took a lot longer to write than the two hours I had suggested. They also said they found it difficult. I don't tell you this to depress you, but to cheer you up when *you* find writing difficult. You are *not* alone if you find writing takes a long time and never seems to run smoothly. If you get stuck, it is *not* a sign that you are a poor writer, or that you are going about it the wrong way. And it is certainly not at all unusual to find that you hate what you have written.

To turn to the positive side, *writing can also be an extremely satisfying activity*. So many of our interesting thoughts drift away from us without our ever really formulating them properly, and at a later date it can seem almost as though those thoughts never existed. Consequently it can be very satisfying to preserve at least some of the products of our thinking on paper. What is more, the discipline of writing often has the effect of shaping thoughts into a clearer and more coherent form. This is also a source of great satisfaction. The fact that you have persevered so far into this book suggests that you are interested in the realm of ideas. I would deduce therefore that the rewards offered by writing ideas down are likely to appeal to you.

To strike another positive note, since you now know for certain that writing essays is always a challenging and demanding activity, you can *forearm* yourself by working out a sensible strategy. In this way you can enjoy the satisfactions of writing without feeling overwhelmed by the challenges. It is only too easy to run into the kind of doubts and frustrations that beset Sandy in Chapter 1, but *you* don't have to be as helpless as she was in the face of them. There are many ways of taking a more active and constructive approach, so that you can drive through to the end of the task. To explore these is the purpose of this chapter.

Incidentally, I should make clear at the outset that there is no single approach to writing which suits every writer, or every kind of

156

writing task. However, it would make a long and tedious chapter if I tried to cover all the options. Instead, I shall follow a particular line of thinking and present a basic writing strategy, which I assume you will modify to suit your own studying style and your own purposes. Even the process of rejecting some of my suggestions will help you to firm up your own approach.

Reading guide As with Chapter 5, there is a lot in this chapter, and you may want to approach it in stages, taking a rest between each. I suggest studying it in three chunks:

1 Sections 2 and 3
2 Section 4
3 Sections 5 and 6.

2 The craft of writing

How do you picture really experienced writers setting about the job of writing? Do you imagine them sitting down with a blank sheet of paper, or a blank word-processor screen and just spilling out words? Do you picture them being visited by *inspiration* and immediately starting to pour out beautiful and compelling sentences, which are ready to be sent off for publication? It is almost never like that — certainly not with the kind of 'expository'* writing you do as a student, where you are trying to develop a carefully constructed argument. Putting well-formed sentences on to paper ready for sending to your tutor is only the last of a series of stages in the process of putting together an essay. Before that a great deal of thinking and preparatory work has to be undertaken.

It is helpful to think of writing as a *craft*. Picture, for example, the furniture maker setting out to make a table. First he or she has to conceive of a design for the table, then choose the wood, prepare it, measure it, mark it, cut it, shape it, make the joints, and finally put it together. And even then it still has to be smoothed, waxed and polished. Writing essays may not be quite as elaborate a process (or you may not have time to let it be), but it does have some of that quality — requiring you to work methodically through a whole series of closely linked activities. If you simply sit down when you have finished reading the course texts and try to write a whole essay in a

---

* 'Expository' writing explains, describes objectively, analyses and argues — in contrast with 'expressive' writing (e.g. poetry) which attempts to express feelings and emotions, and 'narrative' writing which tells stories. Another term used is 'discursive' writing. This means much the same thing as expository writing.

single sweep, you will get nowhere. The job is too big. You *have* to break it down into stages. Then you can take it stage by stage and work your way to a finished product.

Learning the 'craft' of writing

Each of the stages in the craft of essay writing is important in its own right. And each requires you to develop your own techniques.

If you are to fulfil your potential as a writer you need to give careful thought to each stage, experimenting with different approaches and looking back over your successes and failures to refine your strategy.

Of course, you can't expect to master every aspect of writing straight away. At first you just have to get on and do some without worrying too much. However, you *will* find it very useful to be able to think about the separate stages whenever your writing is not going as well as you would like. The main stages of essay writing are:

▶ thinking about the essay title

▶ gathering together material for the essay

▶ getting some ideas on to paper

▶ organizing the material

▶ writing a first draft

▶ reviewing your work in the light of the essay title

▶ writing a final draft.

2.1 Thinking about the essay title

When you know you have an essay to write, you should take a good look at the title a few days before you intend to get down to serious work. This is useful in two ways:

▶ It helps you to make sure that you cover all the necessary ground with your reading.

▶ You will find that having the title floating about at the back of your mind for a few days helps you to clarify what the question is asking and to shape a strategy for approaching it.

Either at that preliminary examination of the title, or later when you start serious work on the essay, you will need to take a very detailed look at the wording of the title. One extremely useful technique is to highlight or underline what you think are the key words or phrases in the title.

ACTIVITY BREAK   Underline the words you think are particularly important in the essay title we worked with in Chapter 5:

Is the rapid growth of new 'high-tech' shopping centres a bad thing? Discuss in the light of Carl Gardner's article.

I would be inclined to underline as follows: 'Is the <u>rapid growth</u> of new <u>'high-tech' shopping centres</u> a <u>bad thing</u>? <u>Discuss</u> in the light of Carl <u>Gardner's article</u>.'

Having done this, I can now focus more sharply on some of the things my essay would need to give attention to. The underlining draws the following points to my attention:

▶ It is not just 'shopping centres in general' I am writing about, but the new 'high-tech' ones in particular.

▶ I am not being asked to write in detail about the centres themselves, but to examine the fact that their *numbers* have been *growing rapidly*.

▶ I am not asked to explore *why* the centres have been springing up (though I might decide to say something about that in passing). The main focus is to be upon whether their growth is a 'bad thing'.

▶ The word 'discuss' suggests that there are arguments *for* and *against* and it indicates that my essay should look at *both* sides.

▶ Finally, I must remember that I am not simply to discuss my own views on the matter. I am to pay particular attention to the arguments which are discussed in the *Gardner article*. I might want to bring in some additional material of my own, but I must be certain to give the arguments in the Gardner article pride of place.

I can see now that the words in the question put quite a tight frame around what is to be in the essay. I am certainly not being asked to write everything I know about shopping centres, nor being given free rein to follow up any pet themes I might be interested in.

KEY POINTS

▶ Thinking carefully about the title is a vital part of producing a good essay.

▶ It is very important to look carefully at *each* of the words, or phrases, in turn. Otherwise you can easily waste a lot of time writing about things for which you will get very little credit.

2.2   Gathering together material for the essay

When you start to work in earnest on the essay, your first task is to go back over what you have recently been studying to check what might be relevant to the essay. One reason why it is useful to have read the essay title some time in advance is that you can hold it in the back of your mind as you work on the course. Then, when you come across something which might be useful, you can make a note of it.

Whether or not you *have* already made notes as you studied, you will need to go back over relevant parts of the course making notes specifically for the purposes of the essay.

Figure 6.1 shows some notes I made for the purpose of answering the essay question. They are fuller than I would normally make, since they have to make sense to you, my reader. However, you will see that they are more *selective* than the notes I made in Chapter 2 (see Figure 2.5), because this time I *only* needed what would be relevant to the essay title.

Evidence of rapid growth
- 1988 – 89   – 35 new shpg. cntrs.
- 1980 – 87   – retail space +50% – sales +76%
- £1.7b retail design business
- shopping hours up – now no. 3 leisure activity

Arguments for

Socialist   – consumption = bad – capitalist commodities cannot truly satisfy
theory   – manipulation – new shpg. cntrs. – part of a capitalist con trick to sell more
                                                        – feed delusion of pleasure
                        – (shopping – a form of disease – shoppers as victims)

Worpole   – shpg. cntrs.   – destroy urban fabric
                             – highlight division of rich and poor
                             – promote crime

Labour   – focus on poor pay & working hours
& TU's

Arguments against

Gardner   – high st. has not died – must beware 'romanticising' city centres
            – shpg. cntrs. – 'reclaim' medieval market place – social meeting places –
            protected from British climate
            – family & leisure orientation – has led to longer time spent shpg.
            – new s.c's creates pressure to improve public environment – set better standards
            – s.c's offer experience of being pandered to – as compared with dreary housing,
            civic architecture and city centres
            – manipulation theory shows contempt for way most people live
            – we need a better understanding than that of why people find shopping in these
            new centres gratifying
            – left should recognise that pleasure through 'consuming' is legitimate in our
            kind of society

Figure 6.1 *Notes from the Gardner article taken specifically for the essay*

The importance of note taking

The stage where you are taking notes for an essay makes a very important contribution to your studies in general. While you are searching through course material to pick out what is useful for your essay, you are forced into thinking about the content very hard and very purposefully. *Choosing* what is relevant and what is not makes you focus very sharply on *what a text is about*. This process of selecting produces some of your most intensive 'learning'.

You need to allow plenty of time for this part of the task of essay making.

One of the most basic mistakes that Sandy had made, when we came across her in deep despair in Chapter 1, was to attempt to start writing without a set of notes around her, which already contained a lot of the material she needed for the essay.

KEY POINTS

Don't try to start writing an essay until you have collected together plenty of notes drawn from the course.

2.3 Getting ideas on to paper

By writing notes for your essay, you have already begun the process of getting ideas on to paper. However, up to this point your main emphasis has been on getting hold of what *other* writers have to say. Once you have completed the gathering together of material, you have to switch to thinking in terms of what *you* are going to say. You certainly *don't* want to be 'copying out' what you have taken from others. That would be far too boring and would gain you very little credit. Worse, it would contribute nothing to your understanding of the subject, or your ability to express ideas. Instead, at this point, you need to put your notes on the texts to one side for a while and set to work developing your *own* thoughts on how to approach the question you have been set.

Sitting with clenched fist pressed against your brow is not the best position in which to do this. You need a pen in your hand, and some scrappy bits of paper which you *know* will not be part of the final essay. This means you won't worry about what you write on them. If you have only clean sheets handy, mess them up with a few scribbles. You need to be *quite* sure that what you are about to write is *not important* — that you will quite happily change it, scribble all over it and eventually throw it away.

Then just *jot down lots of thoughts relating to the title,* without worrying about what comes out. Write down points *for* and *against* the title — perhaps a whole sentence if one comes to you in a nicely rounded form — and any *extra questions* that the essay title throws up. My own jottings in Figure 6.2 are a sample of 'off the cuff' ideas I might possibly want to explore in writing the essay on the Gardner article. I just wrote them out as they came to me. They may not make a lot of sense to you, but that hardly matters. *I* would only use them for a day or two as I worked on the essay, so it is perfectly all right if they are bitty and undeveloped.

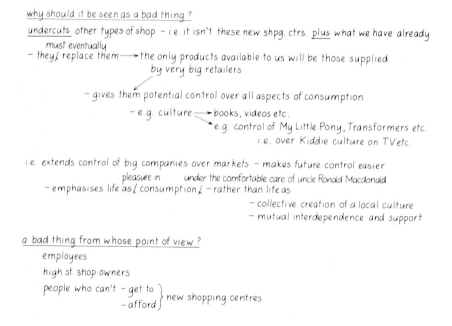

Figure 6.2 *Sample of jottings related to the essay title*

Basically what you are doing is trying to *trap* some of the ideas floating around in your mind. As you study the course all kinds of thoughts are set in motion. These will be churning away in your mind in an unresolved form. Now you need to convert some of them into a more *fixed* form, and you want them *outside* your head where you can look at them and work on them. You do this by *very quick and rough jotting.* Be prepared to flit from point to point, so that you don't risk losing some thoughts while you are in the process of writing other ones out. Once a few thoughts are out there on paper, you can move them around, draw arrows linking one with another, cross bits out, tidy them up, think of a better word here and there, and so on. But you need to get quite a lot of words on paper before you start too much 'organized thinking'. Taking a more critical and analytical approach may dry up your flow of ideas.*

This process of jotting down ideas for an essay is very similar to a technique known as 'brainstorming', in which you simply write down fragments of thoughts as quickly as possible, to provide a rich source of ideas. The notion is that you will get access to ideas you would never reach by more logical thought-processes. After the brainstorming session, you then sift through ideas, throwing most of them away, but holding on to the few which show promise. You will not, however, want to work at quite the frenetic pace of a 'true' brainstorming session, since you are *not* producing random ideas. You are working out ideas connected with the reading you have been doing and you will almost certainly need to stop to think as you jot.

A very significant point about this jotting activity is that it helps you overcome the problem of 'the clean, white, blank page'. It so often happens that your mind seizes up as you take the plunge and try to write the first sentence, that it may be best not to try to begin by writing the first sentence, nor even to begin with sentences at all. When you are busy jotting down odd notes, with your thoughts in full flow, you will sometimes find that whole sentences come out fully formed, or even a paragraph, that you can set aside to be used later, but don't force it — wait for it to happen.

Once you have a lot of words jotted down you have something to work on at the next stage, instead of sitting wondering where on earth to start. It is much easier to produce a basic supply of sound and interesting ideas in this informal way than to achieve inspiration on the run while you are writing out a full draft. It is advisable to generate a lot more ideas than you will eventually need, so that you can throw some away and be left with just the best.

---

* This sketching-out process is so useful that special computer programs called 'outliners' have been developed for people who use word processors. These programs enable you to type out odd words and phrases under numbered subheadings. You can type in a new subheading any time you think of one, or a sub-subheading, or a sub-sub-subheading. And you can later move all these categories and subcategories around and link them together in new ways. If you use a word processor, it is certainly worth exploring the uses of an outliner, even though in the end you may find it also helps to do some rough jotting on scraps of paper, to free your thoughts. I used a computer outliner for this book. The outlines amounted to about twenty-five pages.

2.4 Organizing the material

When you have 'externalized' enough of your ideas (by giving them
an existence on paper, outside your mind), you need to start sifting
through them, getting them into some sort of organized shape. *Any*
kind of crude dividing up will be useful to begin with. For example,
you can begin by separating your jotted notes into points *for* and
points *against* the proposition in the title. If it helps, cut your notes
into strips and sort them into piles. Then you can look at one of
these groups and begin to work out the order in which to take the
points within it, perhaps separating them into sub-groups. After that,
you can sort through the points in the other group. Then you will be
in a position to sketch a rough outline plan of how the essay might
be organized.

Simpler is generally better as far as essay plans are concerned. You
will see that in my notes in Figure 6.3 I have gone for the classic
structure for a short essay:

▶ introduction

▶ points against the shopping centres

▶ points for the shopping centres

▶ conclusion.

Unlike the students whose essays you have read, I decided to argue
against the growth of the shopping centres before looking at the
points in favour. I felt that, given the way that the Gardner article
conducts the debate, it would be easier to write a punchy essay by
covering the *worries* about the shopping centres first and then
coming back to Gardner's *counter-arguments*. Until you have pointed
out the strength of the opposition, his points seem rather bland and
obvious and his enthusiasm about the shopping centres somewhat
odd. Equally, it is difficult to comment effectively on the arguments
against the centres if you have put them second, because you have
already used the ammunition. I think that is why the conclusion to
Ann's essay was weak. The basic structure of the essay didn't lead to
a sharp conclusion.

KEY POINTS

It is important to think in broad strategic terms in sketching your essay plan. You should try to work out a sequence which will enable you to arrive at a conclusion you would like to draw.

ESSAY PLAN

paragraph no.

1. <u>intro</u> – the pace of growth – quote figures

2. <u>against the shopping centres</u>
   - trad left theory – con trick – delusory desires
   - Worpole   – destruction of urban life
   - Labour/TU's   – jobs with poor pay & conditns.
   - (my note)   – worry abt. domination by commercial culture
                    – dependence on corporate giants –
                      undercutting indpndnt cultr.

3. <u>for the shopping centres</u>
   - Gardner – objections to Worpole's account – and trad. left
     - the 'new market place' – a public space for family & leisure
     - raising standards of the built envirnmnt.
     - the need to accept pleasure in 'consuming' as legit. part of life

4. <u>conclusion</u>
   - need to ask 'bad for whom' – some will gain some lose
   - summarize arguments against and arguments for
   - draw out conclusion which answers question in the title

Figure 6.3 *Sample essay plan*

Notice, incidentally, that I have found a place in my essay outline to put some thoughts of my own, as well as making sure I draw out important points from the article. I would have worked in a few more of my own thoughts, but I didn't want to make the plan look too fearsome.

When you have a longer essay to write and more texts to work from, you may find you want a more elaborate structure than this one. However, there is *no virtue in complexity* for its own sake. You will find your essay *easier to write* if it has a simple structure. Equally important, your reader will find it *easier to read*.

Groping towards an essay plan

Often the point at which you are groping towards a suitable plan for your essay is quite uncomfortable and unsettling. Because your thoughts are slowly resolving themselves, the shape may take quite a time to emerge. When it does, it may be so simple as to make you wonder why it took so long. However, the simplicity is a sign that your thoughts *have* reached a stage of resolution.

Once you have sketched out a simple essay plan, you can go back through your various notes, labelling each point according to the section of the plan in which you think you will use it, or ruthlessly throwing it out because it doesn't fit.

KEY POINTS

▶ The planning stage is of crucial importance, since it is at this point that your argument acquires its central coherence.

▶ If you tend to write *too much*, it is at the organizing stage that you need to make tough decisions. You *must* limit your essay plan to what can be managed in the space you have.

2.5 Writing a first draft

When you have your notes roughly sorted and organized according to your sketched plan, you are ready to begin the writing. You have decided *what* you are going to try to say. Now you have to concentrate on *how* to say it in a way that your reader will be able to understand.

It might seem that this ought, in principle, to be a fairly straightforward stage, since it is simply the writing out of all that you have planned in note form. However, it is more than that. Writing is, as I said in Chapter 5, a very specialized kind of *conversation*. You are *talking* to someone — *your reader*. You have to take the scraps of ideas set out in your notes and *speak* them as whole sentences. You have to give examples to *illustrate* to your reader what you are talking about. And you have to take your reader carefully step by step *from* the question in the title *through* the points you want to make, *showing* how they follow one from another.

KEY POINTS

If you are a person who tends to write *too little* in your essays, you may not be giving enough attention to how much *explaining* you have to do to get your points across to someone else. You probably need to discuss more examples and show more carefully how your points link up with each other.

To be able to write fluently and convincingly you need to be able to give all your attention to 'talking' to your reader. This is why you need to have done so much preparatory work in the previous stages. If you are trying to 'think up' the *content* at the same time as you are *addressing* yourself to your reader, you will usually do one or other job badly. Either your points will be weak and disconnected, or your language will be insufficiently clear and expressive. Worst of all, you will run out of ideas and hit that dreaded 'writer's block' where you can't think of anything worth saying.

KEY POINTS

'Talking' in writing takes all your powers of concentration. Because of this you need to have the *substance* of the essay *already worked out*.

Finding your 'voice'

Writing is a very formal activity compared with speaking. As I said in the last chapter, *you* have to make all the decisions about *what* the topic is, *how* it is going to be treated, *what* big issues are at stake and, most importantly, *what* kind of *relationship* is to be assumed between you and your reader. In a conversation, by contrast, all these decisions are taken collectively. They emerge as the discussion progresses.

You also have to take responsibility for making sure that the reader is continually kept in touch with what this one-sided conversation is about.

Unfortunately, the strain of taking all that responsibility tends to cramp your style. Often you find it difficult to get meanings over to your reader with the clarity and force that you can achieve in conversation. You sense what you *want* to say but, when the words come out on paper and you read them over, it is clear that you have not conveyed what you intended. The words are there to be read but they come across in a way that seems dull and dead. There seems to be no 'voice' speaking them.

Most of us have had far more practice in establishing 'spoken' relationships than 'written' ones. One approach is simply to do much more writing on a regular basis, to build up practice in occupying the role of writer. A particular technique along these lines is called 'freewriting'.* Here the idea is that you simply write *continuously*, for say ten minutes, about anything that comes into your head (a bit like brainstorming except that you write in sentences), and without concern about quality or about being read by others. When you have finished the writing you put it away and on subsequent days you do some more. Some days later you come back and read over the first day's work with the specific aim of trying to find bits where you feel that your 'voice' breaks through — where your writing achieves some force — possibly a phrase, a sentence, or even a whole paragraph. (You might exchange samples of freewriting with another student so each of you can search the other's text.) In this way, over a period of time, a number of changes should come about:

▶ Sheer accumulation of practice at 'being in the writing situation' takes some of the awkwardness and formality out of your writing style.

▶ The freedom to write 'anything' releases you from the constraints which normally crab your writing.

▶ The repeated hunting for your 'voice' sharpens your perceptions of when you are writing powerfully and when you are not.

▶ You become more aware of what kind of orientation towards your writing helps you to break through to an authentic writing voice.

* Peter Elbow introduces freewriting like this. 'To do a freewriting exercise, simply force yourself to write without stopping for ten minutes. Sometimes you will produce good writing, but that's not the goal. Sometimes you will produce garbage, but that's not the goal either. You may stay on one topic, you may flip repeatedly from one to another: it doesn't matter . . . Speed is not the goal, though sometimes the process revs you up. If you can't think of anything to write, write about how that feels or repeat over and over "I have nothing to write" . . . If you get stuck in the middle of a sentence or thought, just repeat the last word or phrase till something comes along. The only point is to keep writing . . . There are lots of goals of freewriting, but they are best served if, while you are doing it, you accept this single, simple, mechanical goal of simply not stopping.'

You can read a lot more about freewriting and many other very interesting ideas about writing in Elbow, P. (1981) *Writing with Power: Techniques for Mastering the Writing Process*, Galaxy Books, Oxford University Press (New York).

It's not necessary to start your drafting with the introduction to the essay and then work steadily through to the end. You may find it easier to start somewhere else. It might, for instance, be safer to get some of the main sections down on paper to get a clearer sense of what it is that you have to introduce and how much space you have left for introducing and concluding. (It is awfully easy to spend far too long beating about the bush with your introduction, and lead your reader off the track of your main argument.) If you find a section going badly, it may be as well to break off and write another part, or else to start the section again, approaching it in a different way. But don't throw the old version away. You may end up preferring it, or being able to combine bits of both.

Once you have started writing, try to maintain your momentum and keep yourself writing. It is not helpful, for instance, to spend ages going back over and over each sentence as you write it — changing this word and then that and eventually changing them back again. It is better to press on to the end of the first draft, coming back to the whole thing at the end to see how it reads. While you are writing you are too close to the words to make reliable judgements about them, and it is easy to waste time fiddling about with small changes when a fresh run at the piece might show a useful way of recasting a whole sentence or paragraph. There is no right and perfect way of making your points. One way will work well for one reader and another for another. You need to develop an open attitude to your prose, so that you can be both *critical* in examining what has worked and what has not and, at the same time, *relaxed* in the knowledge that, although there are other ways of saying what you have said, it is not worth tinkering for very long, because there are so many other interesting things for you to move on to write about.

An 'experimental' approach to writing

I once took an art class. Drawing my first picture, I put the main subject right in the middle, taking up most of the space. The art teacher pointed out that this was dull to look at. Since I didn't seem to get his point, he drew a small oblong box in which he asked me to sketch the figure and background quickly in a different relation to each other. Then he told me to draw another dozen oblongs and do a new version in each. When I had finished we went over them and I began to see that some of them were much more effective as compositions than others and would give me a much better basis for an interesting picture. What surprised me most was that *I* had been able to do them when at the outset I had only been able to see one way of drawing the picture. Afterwards, I began to notice that many well-known painters have had the habit of doing numerous

sketches of the same scene, each with its own special qualities.
In other words, having spent hours working intensively on
creating a representation of some subject, they would see
nothing wrong with starting all over again and producing a new
and quite different version. No particular one of these would
necessarily be the 'correct' version. Each would achieve a
different effect.

Writing is like this. Every piece you compose in words could
potentially be written in many different ways — some
interesting and clear, others confusing, or dull. Yet, when you
start to write, your imagination may be restricted to seeing only
one way ahead. It might be a very good exercise to have to
write every essay in three completely different versions — quite
exhausting of course, but it would help one develop a greater
repertoire of writing techniques. This is too idealistic perhaps.
However, you *can* sketch several different outline plans (the
equivalent of the oblongs I had to fill for the art teacher) and
you *can* try two or more completely different versions of a
particular paragraph, or several ways of opening or closing the
essay. Working in this open and 'experimental' way helps to
make you feel less imprisoned inside a particular style of
writing. It emphasizes your powers of expression and the wealth
of possibilities that lie in front of you. Paradoxically, it also
makes it easier to be content with what you produce, because
you know it is only one of many versions you could have
produced, none of which would be the 'correct' one.

2.6 Reviewing your draft

When you have finished your first draft it is extremely important to
force yourself to read through it again. This is an uncomfortable but
necessary process, since you are bound to have made mistakes and
left things out. When you have your face pressed right against them
you cannot tell how the sentences and paragraphs work, nor how the
overall sense of the essay works. If you have the time, leave the
reviewing to another day, when you can view it from a greater
distance and therefore more as your reader will view it.

As you read through, check the following:

▶ Do the sentences 'work'; that is, does the 'sense' move along
reasonably smoothly? A good check is to read aloud. If you find
you stumble, or have to pause to snatch at the meaning, then
probably you have a sentence which is too long, or has something
important missing (such as a verb, or a link to the previous
sentence).

▶ Do the divisions into paragraphs work? Do the breaks feel as though they come at the right place — when the focus of the discussion shifts?

▶ Have you given enough explanation and illustration to enable the 'intelligent person in the street' to understand what the discussion is all about?

▶ Does the argument follow? Does it make sense as you move from point to point? Have you signalled the main moves clearly to your reader?

▶ And perhaps the most important check of all, *have you answered the question in the title*?

Reading aloud

Since writing is a form of speaking (though a very constrained and lop-sided one), it is often helpful to hear what a written piece sounds like when read out loud. It gives you a new angle on how well the sense flows through the sentences. What is more, if you know someone (a fellow-student, a friend, or a member of your family) who is prepared to listen, reading to another person can help with the problem of establishing a *sense of audience* and a *voice*. It hardly matters whether or not the listener comments on what you have written, because in the process of speaking the words to someone you will *hear for yourself* which passages work best and which don't come across as you intended.

Most people feel rather shy about exposing their written work to other people, particularly if they are operating in unfamiliar territory. However, you are writing in order to be read by some-body, somewhere. If you can summon up the nerve to 'be there' as the message is received by someone, it gives you fresh insight into the process of communication that you are engaged with.

You may well find, as a result of the reviewing process, that you discover some major restructuring you can achieve without too much disruption to the various parts of the essay. But it is more likely that you will put in a few extra words here and there, change the punctuation, correct the spelling, and perhaps alter some paragraph divisions. You will rarely have time to consider any large-scale changes, and it is unlikely to be appropriate to do so, since you have other calls on your study time. That is not the point of reviewing. At this stage you have to 'go with it', as they say. The review is essentially a tidying up process and usually a very necessary one.

2.7 Writing the final draft

At last you come to the point where you write the words your tutor will see. In principle this is straightforward, since the final draft is simply a neat and tidy version of your corrected first draft. With all other pressures off, you can now concentrate on keeping handwriting legible and your page layout neat. You write your name and the title at the top of the first page, allow generous margins, and then set out to produce the polished end-product of all your labour.

Why bother doing more than one draft?

Since the last stage of 'copying out' a neat draft is rather mechanical, you might wonder whether it is really a sensible investment of your study time. Could you not hand in a carefully corrected first draft? There are two reasons why I would argue that you should not.

First, since you invest a lot of time in any case in your writing, you might as well see the process through and produce something which *looks* as good as it is. It is important to the spirit in which you undertake the whole essay-writing venture that you feel committed to taking some pride in what you produce (like the craft worker). A well-presented essay is good for your own sense of satisfaction. What is more, your tutor is bound to be more kindly disposed if your essay is not full of illegibilities, mistakes and inconsistencies.

Secondly, and more fundamentally, the *intention* of writing a final draft has a powerful impact on the process of producing the *first draft*. The fact that you know your first draft is *not* your final word takes a lot of the pressure off at that crucial stage, when you are trying to turn your notes and your plans into intelligible sentences and paragraphs. You will write much more fluently and creatively knowing that you can come back and change it later. Not only will you write better essays in the short term, you will also develop your writing style more effectively in the longer term, because you will have more scope for experimentation in the writing process.

So although it *is* a slog writing out a neat final draft, it is far from being a fancy extra. It is part of the process of approaching essay writing as a 'craft'. If you are serious about becoming a better writer, you cannot really avoid thinking in terms of writing more than one draft of your essays. And in the end I doubt whether it takes very much longer. Trying to write your finished version straight-off cranks up the pressure, stifles your creativity, and leads directly to problems of drying up. Those mental blocks use up time far less productively than writing out a final draft. It may even be *quicker* to write more than one draft than to attempt the whole thing in a single sweep.

Having said this, we all work differently, so don't let the thought of writing out more than one draft put you off writing altogether. Think seriously about it, and then do what fits your purposes and your circumstances.

3   The advantages of treating essay writing as a craft

As anyone who has tried knows, it is very easy to get stuck when you are writing essays — to sit wondering what you are trying to say and how you can get yourself moving again. It is enormously helpful to be able to break the job down into smaller more manageable tasks, which you can take on one at a time. It helps to dispel some of the mystique of writing to think of it as a fairly ordinary activity of making a finished product through a series of practical processes: to see yourself as a craft worker going through a series of closely-linked stages. It also gives you a chance to think *strategically* about your writing. You can *plan* a sequence of activities which makes sensible use of the time you have available. And since you have a set of identifiable tasks to work at, if you *do* become stuck it is perfectly possible to move on to a different task. If you find, for instance, that you have run dry as you are 'getting your ideas on to paper', then you can move on to thinking about your plan.

KEY POINTS

Awareness of the distinct stages of essay writing greatly increases the options open to you and gives you more control over the writing process.

Now that we have been over the stages in detail, let us summarize them again:

173

The stages of essay writing

Taking in the title: Underlining the key words in the essay title and thinking about it over a period of days.

Gathering material: Gathering together notes for the essay from various sources within the course.

Generating ideas: Getting ideas on to paper; quickly jotting down thoughts, sample sentences, etc.

Planning: Organizing your notes into a simple outline plan.

First draft: Writing a first draft; talking through your argument with your reader.

Reviewing: Reading over your work in the light of the essay title and correcting errors and omissions.

Final draft: Writing a final draft, paying attention to legibility and general presentation.

Although it is very helpful to be able to think about these stages separately, it would be a mistake to treat them as completely separate and rigidly sequenced. In fact, they overlap considerably and are best tackled flexibly. As you plan, you may suddenly think of another source book you ought to look at quickly, or some notes you made that you could, after all, use. When you are writing the first draft, you are quite likely to become aware that an aspect of your outline plan is not going to work out and that there is a much better solution — leading you to go back and rework the plan. And when you are reviewing your first draft, you may suddenly think of a question you wrote down in your jotted notes which could be recast and used as a good introduction to the essay. All the stages of essay production are bound up with each other and you often need to move back and forth between them. Obviously there is a certain logical sequencing to them. You can't *start* your reading of the source texts *after* you have written the first draft. On the other hand, you might well go back to *check* something. So no single process is entirely complete until the whole is complete.

This might raise doubts as to whether it is really worth making the distinctions between the stages. If you are moving back and forth between them all the time, can they really be regarded as separate stages? I think they *can* in terms of the specific contribution each makes to the end-product. That is to say, each stage constitutes a different function in the production process. The functions of the seven stages are as follows:

▶ Formulating the overall *purpose* of the essay.

▶ Working out what use you can make of the *course* you are studying.

▶ Getting hold of *your own* thoughts on the topic.

▶ Working out what *shape* to give to the *argument* of the essay.

▶ '*Speaking*' your ideas to your reader, *explaining* your argument (turning your plan and notes from your own 'private' language into 'public' language).

▶ *Quality* control.

▶ *Presenting* a polished end-product.

The functions cannot be separated neatly from each other in terms of the practical operations you have to perform in writing the essay. However, all these functions do have to be fulfilled if you want to produce as good a quality essay as you are capable of. So it is an advantage to be able to identify them and focus attention on each.

An attraction of drawing on the image of a craft worker is that it reminds you that you wouldn't expect to produce a perfect table at your first attempt. It isn't done by a blinding flash of inspiration. Everybody makes a mess to begin with. You have to learn through experience how to blend a complex sequence of activities together, how much time to give each, and where your own particular strengths lie. You should not be too despondent if your first efforts at essay writing turn out less well than you might have hoped. Becoming skilled in a craft involves accepting that there will be a period when your output is not particularly impressive. As you practise you will get steadily better. Seeing writing in these practical workaday terms helps you to 'get stuck in' and build up that practice, instead of worrying about whether you are a genius or an inarticulate dimwit.

Finally, in case this very practical listing of stages makes essay writing sound a rather technical operation, with much less scope for *originality* and *creativity* than you had imagined, I must stress that this is far from the case. It is a misleading idea of creativity which presents the image of an unfettered spirit wandering wheresoever inspiration takes it. Creative work is nearly always achieved within well-defined constraints. It is out of the struggle with constraints that creative solutions are born. If you *strive* to be original, you will often find that other people are unimpressed. By contrast, you may find you are commended for the originality of your ideas when you have done no more than say what seemed perfectly obvious to you. Originality is something you are likely to stumble across, rather than achieve by deliberate effort. What you need is a framework within which you can see a way of taking the next step forward. Viewing your writing as a craft involving a series of stages will enable you to do that.

KEY POINTS

A 'craft' view of essay writing implies that:

▶ You should treat essay writing as a *practical* task not as a mysterious search for inspiration.

▶ It is not, ideally, a *one-session* job, but should be spread over several days.

▶ You do not simply sit down with a blank sheet of paper and start to write.

▶ In fact, you do the bulk of your work *before* you write the 'real thing'.

▶ You break the task into *stages*, so that you can tackle it *a bit at a time* rather than facing the whole thing at once.

▶ You think *strategically* about how to approach the writing assignment in all its stages.

▶ You work *flexibly*, moving back and forth between the stages as necessary.

▶ If you get stuck you move to a different stage.

▶ Your level of essay-writing performance is dependent on a range of separate skills, not one monolithic 'ability to write'.

▶ You can work at developing your strategies and skills within each separate stage.

4   Making your essay flow

In Chapter 5 we took a close look at some samples of writing by students who were new to essay writing. Now I want to switch to considering how experienced writers approach their work. One obvious source of ideas on this is to look at the article by Carl Gardner again; this time specifically from the point of view of writing style. How did he organize his argument?; what devices has he used to make it flow?; and so on. I am not suggesting that we treat him as a model writer (although I myself found his style engaging). I am simply taking the article as an available example. *Again, you will find it very useful to have a clean photocopy of the article to work from.*

4.1 Link words

The first thing I want to focus on is how the line of argument in the article is 'carried along'. Look at the start of paragraph 2. The first words are '*Though* varied'. Clearly we are being referred *back* to the new centres (i.e. '*what* vary?' — answer 'the shopping centres'). Note that the 'though' sets up the expectation of something counterposed against 'varied' ('though X, also Y' is the form of construction being used). This is quite a neat way of handling point Y when you know that, if you say it on its own, readers are likely to think, 'but what about X?' You get X out of the way by quickly conceding it. Then you get to your real point, which is Y. There are several forms of words which can do this little trick for you, such as 'while X, on the other hand Y', or 'clearly X, but we must not overlook Y'.

Paragraph 3 starts with 'All this investment'. 'This' is a very useful word for doing linking jobs. It tells you that the subject of the new sentence is whatever was being discussed in the last sentence. By saying '*all* this' the range is extended to the whole of the preceding paragraph. And by adding 'investment' the subject of the preceding paragraph is *converted* from a topic to do with *architecture* to a topic to do with *economics*. Suddenly we are being asked to think of these flashy new centres in a different way. Somebody has decided to invest a lot of money — why?

In three words Gardner has turned an important strategic corner in his argument. Having in paragraph 2 aroused our interest with a passage of *description,* he now achieves a smooth and rapid shift to a more *analytical* discussion, at the same time maintaining the thread of meaning. Writing an essay is a bit like a relay race, in that each paragraph has to hand the baton of meaning on to the next.

Try examining the opening words of the other paragraphs to see how this is achieved. It is a challenging task, but I hope you will find it an intriguing piece of detective work. You are interested in building up your *own* writing style, so the more time you spend exploring how other people's styles work, and the more attuned you become to the various effects which can be achieved, the greater will be your awareness of the range of options open to you and the greater the breadth of your verbal imagination.

ACTIVITY BREAK   Starting with paragraph 4, underline the first *word* or *phrase* of each paragraph.

Then work out how the words underlined help to achieve the transfer of meaning from one paragraph to the next.

(You may feel you have seen enough of the Gardner article by now. However, since you know it so well, it will be easier to look past the 'message' and concentrate on the style. Also, I shall be able to express points more succinctly, knowing that you know what the article is about.)

How did your 'link word' analysis go? In paragraphs 4 to 7 I underlined:

'Then . . .'

'But . . .'

'At the same time . . .'

'This . . .'

Paragraph 4 begins with a nice straightforward 'Then'. Gardner uses this simple but very useful word for signalling that he is extending the theme of paragraph 3 by moving to a new aspect of it.

Then, at the start of paragraph 5, we see the first of four instances of 'But' as the opening word.

Breaking 'rules'

When I was at school we were told never to start a sentence with 'and' or 'but', let alone a paragraph. Is Gardner breaking the rules? In fact, the rule *is* a useful one when you are not very confident about sentence structures. You may be tempted into leaving scraps of half-formed sentences lying around in the hope that an 'and' or a 'but' will connect them up to something. In formal grammatical terms the words are 'conjunctions', which are placed between two equal items within a sentence, to link them together. Strictly, they should not be used at the boundaries of a sentence. On the other hand, they are so handy as economical devices for carrying meaning over from one sentence to another that it is often worth breaking the formal rule, provided you know what you are doing.

'But' is particularly useful because it is such a quick way of saying 'I am now going to balance something against what I have just been saying'. Also it can be used in combination with other words to achieve subtle variations. Gardner has 'but . . . not just'; 'but . . . first'; and 'but . . . perhaps'.

Paragraph 6 starts with 'At the same time' — a phrase which enables you to signal that you are moving on to a parallel theme. Then paragraph 7 uses 'This' again, but in a more specific way than the earlier 'All this'. Here it is focusing on the *leisure* element in what has gone before.

Now we come to a special case. Paragraph 8 does *not* begin with an obvious link word. However, if you recall, this is the point at which the whole article shifts from a discussion of recent social *trends* to a discussion of *theories* which explain those trends. *Instead* of linking back directly to the previous paragraph, Gardner does two things:

▶ First he *summarizes* all that he has outlined in the previous seven paragraphs, under the term 'retailisation'.

▶ Then he makes a *link* right *back to the title* of the article, by quoting it: 'spend, spend spend'.

So in starting paragraph 8 Gardner rounds off what he has said thus far and reminds us what the article is about. This sets us up to be ready for the main discussion.

Having reached the section of the article which 'explains' and 'debates', we find a different kind of linking phrase. Between paragraphs 9 and 13 we have:

'To understand . . .'

'But first we have to dispense with . . .'

'A more coherent line of attack . . .'

'There are several problems with . . .'

'At one level it is possible to see . . .'

These phrases all have the function of launching us into new aspects of the debate. Gardner is moving swiftly between a series of points of view, ending in paragraph 13 with his own view. The link phrases help us to see how each new step in the debate follows on from the previous one, so that we can keep in touch with the line of argument.

Then, having arrived at his *own* position, he proceeds to expand and consolidate it in paragraphs 14 to 17. Here the link phrases become shorter and more direct. We find:

'Certainly . . .'

'Of course . . .'

'In fact . . .'

'Perhaps . . .'

Link phrases for 'arguing'

Notice that these opening phrases between paragraph 9 and paragraph 17 all use words you might use in an *argument*. They are words which enable you to 'set up' the *relationship* between two parts of an argument. They tell you that the next point is an extension of the previous point, or a contradiction of it, or a qualification of it, and so on. In other words, instead of leaving all the points in the text just lying around separate from each other, they are woven together in an intricate set of relationships with each other.

This sounds a bit grand and formal. But it is what we do without noticing in ordinary speech. It's just that when we come to writing — in the effort of getting the sentences written, and in the absence of a live audience to say 'What do you mean?' — it is easy to forget to put in the words necessary to make clear to the reader the connections we intend between the ideas we present. It is no accident that Gardner uses so many of these 'logical relationship'-type link words in this particular passage, because that is where the main *debate* or *argument* is carried on in the article.

In the last four paragraphs the pace quickens and we get a fairly brisk sketching of some broader issues. With the heavy argument over, Gardner is doing some quick tidying up of loose ends before finishing. Now the phrases become looser and more generalized:

'But there are perhaps other factors . . .'

'At the same time . . .'

'None of this is to deny . . .'

'But, perhaps . . .'

In fact, the link phrases here echo those used in the first part of the article.

KEY POINTS

A writer carries a *thread of meaning* through a piece of writing by using linking phrases which take you on from one sentence to the next. These show you how to approach each new sentence, given what has just been said in the last one.

We could go on to look at other link words used *within* the paragraphs, but we have done enough.

4.2 Signposting

Some of the links we have looked at serve a signposting function as well. For instance, 'But we're not just talking numbers here', at the start of paragraph 5, serves the function of sharpening our focus on *what we have just been talking about* and at the same time signals a *new* direction to the argument. Similarly, 'But first we have to dispense with', in paragraph 10, is telling us that we are going to make a brief attack on a specific target before moving to the key issue just raised. At other times, Gardner uses a signposting phrase to draw things together, as for instance at the end of paragraph 11, when he says 'in short'. This signals that he is about to summarize what he has just said.

Another place where we see Gardner using signposting is in the handling of lists. It often happens, when you are writing, that you need to present what is in effect a 'list' of similar points. This can be awkward to handle, since lists often read rather inelegantly and it is easy to lose the reader's interest. Gardner shows us one way of varying the texture of a list in paragraph 2. He signposts some of the items, giving them priority over others, saying 'most importantly' before the first and 'more importantly' before the last. Another way is to 'guide' your readers through the list as you proceed. In paragraph 7, Gardner uses 'firstly . . .', 'Then . . .', and 'And . . .' as signposts showing how the list is progressing, and in paragraph 12 he uses 'Many . . .', 'And . . .', and 'Yet . . .'. On the other hand, where a list is fairly long, it is sometimes best just to get on with it, holding the list together simply by maintaining the same rhythm of sentence structure to help the reader move through it quickly.* To some extent this is how paragraph 6 works, in that there are eight fairly short points to be made in quick succession and no signpost words are used, apart from a 'but' early on. (The paragraph is, in fact, also structured by a thread of argument running through it, so it isn't a pure list.) In other words, it isn't the case that you need to place a dutiful 'signpost' on *everything* you do. It can become boring and overdone. You have, in the end, to make judgements about how much signposting your reader will find helpful. When in doubt though, it is best to err on the generous side. It is seldom as obvious to your reader as it is to you where your arguments are leading.

---

* On a technical note, when you are listing things, you separate items in the list with a comma, and you put the word 'and' before the last item, as in 'bacon, egg, tomato, and chips'.

> ## *The need for signposts*
>
> When you are writing an essay you are talking your reader through an argument. In order to follow your train of thought the reader has to know what questions and issues to hold in mind; what direction you are heading in and why. Readers have their *own* trains of thought which they are likely to follow in preference to yours unless you keep them in close touch with what you are doing. To maintain the thread of argument for the reader you have to pay attention to *signalling* what is going on. One essential means of doing this is to use *linking* phrases whose function is to pass the meaning across from one sentence to another, and *signposting* phrases which tell you where you are in the development of the argument. Some phrases perform both these functions at the same time.
>
> One important aspect of being skilled in the craft of writing is to have a good repertoire of handy words and phrases which you can call on to do this job for you.

Because he is writing a magazine article rather than a formal essay, Gardner sticks to 'local' level signposting. However, in an essay you will also need to indicate progress on the broader front, using words such as, 'Before discussing X we must ask question Y', or 'having considered the arguments against, we now . . .', or 'a final set of issues we must take into account concern . . .'. To see some more examples, you could look back at Chapter 5 to see the signposting devices I used when I rewrote Sam's and Ann's essays; signalling, for example, that I was moving from arguments on one side to arguments on the other.

KEY POINTS

Signposting is *reminding your reader* from time to time *where you have reached* in the argument and *pointing the way you are going*.

4.3 Paragraphing

One way a writer signals the unfolding of an argument is, as we have seen, through the use of *linking* and *signposting* phrases. Another is in the way the words are actually set out on the page; the way they are grouped together in sentences and the sentences grouped into paragraphs. When we examined the essays in Chapter 5, I pointed out the advantages of aiming for short sentences wherever possible. However, there are also advantages in *varying* sentence length in order to shift the rhythm of an essay. Similarly, you can vary the number of sentences per paragraph to alter the texture of the writing. Again, we can get useful insights by examining what Gardner has done.

ACTIVITY BREAK I want to suggest a very simple exercise I devised for myself as I was looking at this article.

1   Take a red pen and mark the end of every sentence in the Gardner article by putting a bold slash: '/'.

Now look at the overall pattern of red marks. You will get a fair impression of how many sentences per paragraph Gardner tends to use and in which parts of the article they tend to be longer or shorter.

2   (a) Underline in red all sentences with twelve or fewer words. (I found eight.)

(b) Using a different colour, draw a box round all sentences with forty of more words. (I found ten.)

You should now be able to see some broad patterns in the way sentences and paragraphs are used in the article.

3   Look *where* the short sentences come and see if you can work out *why*. Then do the same for the long sentences. (This is rather more tricky to work out.) What is your understanding of the overall shifts in the way sentences and paragraphs are used in the article?

4   While you are looking in such detail at the sentences in the article, here are a couple of other small things to look out for:

(a) There is a 'sentence' in the first paragraph which is not a proper sentence. What is missing?

(b) There is a grammatical error in the second sentence of paragraph 8. What is it?

I did some extra analysis in the form of some calculations, revealing the following:

▶ The lengths of sentences vary from seven words to fifty-five words; the average length of sentence is twenty-three words.

▶ The lengths of paragraphs vary from one sentence to eight sentences.

▶ The average length of paragraph is four sentences.

▶ Paragraph 6 has the shortest sentences, with an average of eighteen words per sentence, followed closely by paragraphs 1 and 19.

▶ Paragraphs 9 and 13 have the longest sentences, with averages of forty-six and fifty words per sentence respectively.

What can we draw out of all this detailed analysis? To begin at the beginning, we see that Gardner starts with a paragraph of short sentences. In fact, the very first sentence is a short one. It is also a very *simple* one; a direct statement of a fact. Why do you think he started in this way? I suggest it is to make an immediate impact; to grab our attention. This opening presents us with a small bite of meaning to take in. A new shopping centre has opened. He is starting his train of thought from a very safe, uncomplicated point. He then continues with short, simple, descriptive sentences and closes the paragraph with a particularly short and simple sentence. Thus, his opening paragraph aims to achieve a punchy impact; to get us hooked; to focus our thoughts on his subject matter.

Paragraph 2 continues to use short, simple sentences, largely of a descriptive nature. Essentially it is plying us with basic information about the nature of these new shopping centres. As he has a lot of information to get across (it is the second longest paragraph), he sketches quickly, using visual images and attempting to be entertaining on the way. This paragraph is doing a 'bread and butter' job of telling us what we need to know before launching into the main discussion, so it is trimmed down to a very economical style.

Paragraph 3 is where he shifts to a more analytical approach, suggesting that this trend in the building of shopping centres is part of a general shift in the nature of the British economy. Immediately the texture of sentences and the paragraph structure changes. This is one of the *shortest* paragraphs in the article, having only two sentences, but the sentences are long. So we have moved from a paragraph with many, short, descriptive sentences, to a paragraph with few but longer and more analytical sentences. Having raced us through the background information, we are suddenly slowed down to ponder over the implications. After this, paragraph 4 gives us a rest by returning to description, using average length sentences to pump more information into us.

Paragraph 5, however, has a big job to do in introducing a new theme. Gardner starts the paragraph with *a sentence containing only seven words*, which has no other job to do than to tell us that we are switching to a new angle. This immediately alerts us to the fact that something is going on here. The following sentence then introduces the new theme. Then the rest of the sentences in the paragraph ply us with more information to bolster the theme. After the dramatic opening, it is an average length paragraph with average length sentences.

Paragraph 6 is like paragraph 2, only more so. It has the shortest sentences but the most of them. In fact, its job, like that of paragraph 2, is description; quickly sketching out the cultural changes we are witnessing in connection with shopping. The snappy final sentence economically summarizes the general nature of the cultural shift.

Description does not however *have* to involve short sentences, as we see in paragraph 7. Gardner begins with another of those punchy, short sentences, to announce the theme of the paragraph. But then we get a change of texture, with longer, more relaxed, descriptive sentences. Our imaginations are allowed space to wander around the 'exotic' themes of the new centres. This is in fact the last moment of leisure we are allowed, because we are about to plunge into the difficult part of the article.

When we look at paragraphs 8 to 17, where the main debate of the article unfolds, we find a general tendency towards longer sentences but fewer per paragraph. However, the pattern is uneven. Where Gardner is attacking the opposition he can be quite brief and snappy, as in paragraphs 8 and 10; delivering a series of short to middling sentences; firing off one point after another. Where he is developing his own theme, on the other hand, he expands into longer sentences. Paragraph 9, for example, is making a rather tricky case about the general position he is taking. Here he uses two fairly weighty sentences which make up a whole paragraph. The most extreme example is paragraph 13. It deals with perhaps the most startling claim that Gardner wants to make; namely that these new centres are actually reviving the functions of the medieval market-place. This paragraph has only a single, very long sentence. In other words, Gardner spells out his own arguments at some length, but softens the impact of the added complexity by using short paragraphs. Indeed, eight of the last nine paragraphs are three sentences long or shorter. Instead of leisurely description, there is a relentless to and fro between various debating positions, each with its own paragraph.

This trend is even more marked in the last four paragraphs. They have few sentences and mostly short ones, which has the effect of creating a tight and forceful conclusion. In fact, by the last paragraph, the style is similar in some respects to the opening, with a series of direct propositions relating to everyday life. The article, having taken us deep into some quite abstract discussion, leads us back out to the world it plucked us from.

We have seen here that there is a clear and direct interplay between the way the *argument* of the article is introduced and developed and the *style* of sentence and paragraph structuring. What is 'going on' in the article in terms of its content is reflected in the way the words are put together. The writer makes *choices*, whether consciously or not, about the length of sentences and about the way they are grouped into paragraphs. These choices are made so as to help to get across the shifting purposes of the argument.

Playing with sentences and paragraphs

The way sentences and paragraphs are put together can do a lot to lead readers through an argument and to bring out its force. Each paragraph does its own job within the argument of the essay and each sentence makes a specific contribution to its paragraph. As a writer you have a great deal of scope in choosing *how* to make them achieve those functions. For instance, you can make sentences or paragraphs long, *or* you can make them short, *or* you can vary them deliberately. Developing an effective writing style is partly to do with playing around with the effects that can be achieved, so that you know how to ring the changes and keep the focus of your reader's attention where you want it.

I hope that, having done this analysis of Gardner's writing, you will now be in a position to make further explorations of your own. If you are interested in finding out more of the 'tricks of the trade' of writing, choose a writer you like and do the same kind of close study of the moves made and the devices employed to achieve particular effects.

Did you spot the mistakes?

The 'non-sentence' in paragraph 1 is the one beginning with 'Liverpool'. It doesn't have a verb. Gardner could easily have slipped one in but presumably, in the general cause of brevity in the opening paragraph, calculated that we could grasp the sense without.

In paragraph 8, the verb in the second sentence should be 'finds' not 'find'. The subject of the sentence is 'socialist theory', which is singular, whereas 'find' is the plural form: 'it' *finds*; 'they' *find*.

4.4 Summary of practical tips

Basically we have been looking at how you guide your readers through your essay; how in your introduction you pick up your readers 'from where they are', by getting hold of their attention and starting a train of thought. Then, in the main body of the essay, you divide what you want to say into segments and lead your reader from section to section. Finally, you draw together the ideas you have been developing and try to show the reader what has been accomplished.

KEY POINTS

Linking
Use *link* words and phrases to *carry the meaning forward* from one paragraph to the next — words like:

however	not only . . . but also
on the other hand	whereas
nevertheless	conversely.

Signposting
Periodically *remind your reader where you have got to.* Use words and phrases like:
  in short
  as we have seen
or more directly:
  to summarize
  having dealt with X we must now consider Y.

Sentences
Sentences can vary a great deal in length. If you need a punchy opening or conclusion, use a short sentence. If you have a lot of items of information, a series of simple, shortish sentences can be effective. You will tend to need longer sentences when you are explaining and developing your argument. Sometimes you may want to change the sentence length simply to vary the texture of your writing and maintain your reader's interest.

Paragraphs
Paragraphs are clusters of sentences. You should have *one* main theme per paragraph. In other words, the paragraphs mark the natural breaks in your argument, when the focus of attention shifts. Each paragraph should have its own job of work to do for your essay. Avoid excessively long paragraphs. Paragraphing is part of the signposting which shows the way through the essay; readers will get lost if the signs are too far apart.

5   Making a convincing case

As you know, an essay should have an argument, but how do you persuade your reader to take your argument seriously. The fact that *you* hold a particular view means nothing to your reader unless you can show *why* you hold it. You have three basic weapons available to you in this cause. One is to show that you have drawn your ideas from an *authority* on the subject. The second is to offer *evidence* to support your case. And the third is to use *logic*. However, each requires a certain amount of know-how to be used effectively.

5.1   Using ideas drawn from other writers

Since one of the purposes of an essay is to show your grasp of the course you are studying, you are bound to draw heavily on other writers' ideas. In effect, the *point* of an essay is to provide a brief guided tour around the established debates on the topic defined in the title. But as well as introducing a selection of relevant ideas from those debates, you have to give details of where they come from.

Listing references

Whenever you draw on another writer's ideas you should give the *reference*. That is, you should say *which* particular piece of writing you are working from (as Gardner did, for example, when drawing on Ken Worpole's ideas). Ideally, you should give the *page* number and the *date* of publication so that, if necessary, your reader can find the particular edition of the work and look up the page to check whether you have represented the author's views fairly and accurately. You can give the details of the reference at the foot of the page, but the more usual way in an essay is to have a list of references at the end. In the text itself, you simply refer to the author by name and put the year and the page number in brackets; the reader can then turn to the end to find out the details, if he or she wishes.

In most essays you are likely to be using a small number of basic source texts over and over. If so, you don't need to go through the full rigmarole every time. After the first reference to Patel, you can say 'as Patel argues', assuming the same source as quoted the first time, until you say differently (though if you are making a very specific point, it would still be useful to put the page number in brackets).

Your reference list should give details of the author's name, the year or date of publication, the title of the book or article, and the publisher — like this:

GARDNER, C. (1988) 'Spend, spend, spend', *New Statesman and Society*, 16 Dec.

WORPOLE, K. et al. (1987) *Trade Winds: The Changing Face of Retailing and Retail Employment in the South East*, Stevenage, South East Economic Development Strategy.

KEY POINTS

In an essay you often have to discuss *other people's ideas*. When you do, you are expected to *acknowledge* where the ideas come from — to say 'as Smith argues', or 'according to Georgiades' account', and give the *reference*.

Quoting

At some points you may want to use an author's exact words, in order to convey the precise point he or she makes, or to provide evidence that the author did indeed say such a thing. In this case, *it is essential that you use quotation marks*. For example, you might write:

In Gardner's view the eating facilities at shopping centres offer 'a vantage point from which [customers] can see and be seen, an . . . element of the unashamedly voyeuristic . . . culture.'

Notice here that I have inserted the word 'customers', to allow the sense of the sentence to be read properly. To signal that this is *my* addition, I have put it in square brackets. I have also left out a few words which I didn't need. By using three dots, I have again signalled this change.

This exactness in the use of other people's words is extremely important. You may *think* you have done a pretty good job of capturing the essence of the author's ideas. But it is vital that, if you are going to attribute words to somebody, you attribute *completely accurately*, or signal clearly if you have made any changes. I have frequently, when marking an essay, found myself thinking, for example, 'Surely Freud wouldn't say *that*?' On going back to check, I have found that a vital word has been left out which completely changes the meaning of the quotation.

In most essays you shouldn't need to use quotation marks very often, since the essential point is to learn to write in your own words, not to copy other people's. But when you do quote you *must* be accurate.

KEY POINTS

Everything between quotation marks, including punctuation, should be *exactly* as in the original text. If you deliberately add or omit something, you should *signal* the changes with square brackets or with dots.

Avoiding plagiarism

While we are on the topic of working with other people's ideas, I must reaffirm an important point made in Chapter 5. The emphasis has to be on 'working with' other people's ideas, rather than 'reproducing' their words. If you rely on 'copying' your material directly from a text, you will be accused by your tutor of *plagiarism*. That is, in effect, 'stealing' other people's ideas. In the world of writing, plagiarism is pretty close to rustling cattle in the Wild West — just about a hanging offence.

Seriously though, you have quite a fine line to tread between being accused, on the one hand, of *not making enough use* of the writers you have been reading in the course, and, on the other, of *having followed them too slavishly*, to the point of plagiarizing them. (See Chapter 5, Section 3.3 for an illustration of sticking too closely to the text.) One of your early tasks as a student is to get a feel for how to strike the right balance.

KEY POINTS

If you rely heavily on another writer's words, and if you fail to use quotation marks to acknowledge your borrowings, you will be accused of plagiarizing.

Avoiding idiosyncrasy

If using other people's ideas is a delicate matter, so is using your own. Again, I made reference to this in Chapter 5. (Remember George's essay which was entirely off on its own orbit.) You will find that the same tutor who criticizes you for staying too close to the course texts, will also criticize you for being *idiosyncratic* — that is, going off into a discussion of your own pet themes. You may find you are encouraged to bring your own thoughts and ideas into your writing, but then are admonished when your tutor does not find them relevant. If you take off on a line of your own without showing how your thoughts link to the main stream of ideas in the course, you will be told your ideas are idiosyncratic. Until you get into the swing of this kind of writing you will find that it is safest to go for large doses of the ideas in the course and small doses of your own. In fact, your own ideas often emerge most clearly and convincingly when you are discussing the ideas of others.

KEY POINTS

You cannot assume that your ideas hold any interest for your reader unless you can show clearly how they connect with other debates on the subject.

5.2 Using evidence

What if you want to support your arguments with evidence? What counts as evidence? This is a tricky question because simply 'telling stories' drawn from your own experience, or what someone told you, does not count as convincing evidence. *You* are not a reliable witness as far as your reader is concerned. Your account will be seen as a 'subjective' one (i.e. slanted in line with your own biases). Your experience cannot be used to 'prove' a case. You need to draw your evidence from elsewhere.

Essentially this means drawing on research that other people have done. Gardner did this in his article. He drew on survey findings about current attitudes to shopping, on evidence about the growth of the design industry, on figures for growth in retail sales, and so on. (However, as this was a weekly magazine article rather than a more formal academic article, he didn't give full details of all the sources.)

In essays you will often draw your evidence from figures, tables and diagrams in the *same* course texts from which you are drawing your basic arguments and ideas. Nevertheless, you need to get into the habit of quoting the specific evidence on which you are basing the point you are making, even where this has already been done in the course text. It is important that *you* show how to draw appropriate conclusions from the evidence. The fact that the author of the text has already drawn conclusions is not going to convince the reader. *You* have to show how the evidence works. As with any material drawn from other writers, don't forget to give details of references.

KEY POINTS

When you make a claim about the way things are in the world, you must offer the reader *evidence* and say where it comes from.

Illustrating

Something which is often confused with giving 'evidence' is 'illustrating' your points. When you are presenting an argument, you often have to use words and ideas which are open to a range of interpretations. To help to fix what you are saying more precisely in your reader's mind, it can be very helpful to give an example to 'illustrate' the point.

You can, if you want, use the same illustrations as appear in the original text. However, it is much more impressive to think up illustrations of your own. *This* is where you show your tutor that you really know how to *use* the ideas for yourself. It is also a chance to bring your own life and experience to bear. It is very helpful, in learning new ideas, to think through and explain to somebody else how they apply in a context that is 'real life' for you. It is also a way of livening up the essay for your reader.

On the other hand, there are dangers. Your reader does not want to read story after story about your life. In any case, he or she will be suspicious as to whether you are a reliable reporter of events you have taken part in. You must always use your own experience carefully and in small doses. Remember that the purpose is to *illustrate* what you mean when you make a particular point, *not* to *prove your case*. Your own experience is *never* reliable *evidence* on which to rest your argument. Furthermore, if you sprinkle your essay with little excerpts from your life without showing how they illustrate specific points, you will be told your style is too *anecdotal* (i.e. it relies too heavily on 'stories').

> **KEY POINTS**
>
> One of the most effective devices for fixing your reader's mind on what you are talking about is to use an example to *illustrate* how the argument works.

5.3 Arguing logically

The third way of convincing your reader is by logical argument; in other words, by showing how the case you want the reader to accept follows *by force of 'reason'* from things the reader might already be expected to accept. In everyday speech, people can be quite careless about saying that something follows from something else. Often they simply mean that *most people accept that it does*. However, when you *write* an argument down it becomes much easier to examine where the weak or sloppy bits are and your reader is quite likely to stop and say, 'Hold on — that doesn't follow'. So you have to give more attention to what you claim follows from what.

We do not need to go into the technical details of logic, which make a course of study in their own right. However, I can *illustrate* the form of a logical argument by taking an example from the opening of this chapter. At the end of the second paragraph in the Introduction I said:

> The fact that you have persevered so far into this book suggests that you are interested in the realm of ideas. I would deduce therefore that the rewards offered by writing ideas down are likely to appeal to you.

How well does this work as a logical argument?

1 I have taken as a 'premise'* that you *are* reading the book.

2 I have gone on to deduce from it that you are interested in ideas.

3 Then I have gone on to make a second deduction from the first — to the effect that you will find writing satisfying.

This gives a tightly linked sequence: A leads to B; B leads to C. I am arguing that, if you accept A, you should also accept that B and C follow.

However, *you* might point out that the initial premise does not hold in your case, because you are *not* reading — only 'dipping in'. *The rest of the argument does not, therefore, apply.* Or, even if you conceded this premise, you might challenge my *first* deduction, saying, 'No, I'm just looking for a few tips for my essay'. Or you might object to the *second* deduction, saying that it is perfectly possible to be interested in reading and thinking about ideas without wanting to write them down. So what I have argued may be weak on several fronts.

However, by setting the argument out as a sequence of logically linked points, I have made it easier for you, the reader, to work out whether or not you agree. What is more, you can identify exactly the point, or points, at which you disagree. That is the reason for setting out arguments logically: not necessarily because you think they are perfectly watertight (very few interesting arguments that relate to 'real life' are watertight), but so that they provide a worthwhile basis for discussion and debate.

---

* A premise is a starting point in a sequence of logic — a proposition which is assumed to be true (i.e. which the argument will take for granted).

Incidentally, since you are trying to be precise in analytical writing, you have to be careful not to claim *more* than you are entitled to. And because *very little* can be said with absolute certainty, you have to develop a style in which you say things in a cautious, tentative way. We see this when Gardner uses the phrase 'At one level . . .', to limit the range of what he is about to claim. It actually *strengthens* your argument to put it more *cautiously*. If you claim a great deal (for example, that 'All schoolchildren are lazy. Therefore they need perpetual goading.'), then your opponent only has to find one instance to disprove you (one example of a hardworking schoolchild) and your whole argument falls down. By couching your argument more tentatively, with 'conditions' attached, it is harder for your opponent to knock it down. For example, 'All schoolchildren *tend* to be lazy' (weaker claim); or 'All schoolchildren *tend* to be as lazy as they are allowed to be' (weaker and 'qualified'); or 'All schoolchildren are lazy in subjects they don't like' (conditions attached); or 'All schoolchildren *feel* lazy on Friday afternoons' (weak and with conditions). Initially, it may seem somewhat precious to be so careful. However, you can, in the end, mount much more powerful arguments if you learn how to lay the groundwork carefully.

Don't be too concerned about the formal rules of logic. It will cramp your style if you worry a lot. It is more important that you try to sort out your points so that they follow in a sensible sequence. Give time to the jotting and planning stages, where you can try grouping your points in different ways and presenting them in different sequences, until you have a nice tight line of argument.

KEY POINTS

▶ You should try to say exactly what you mean and then check that your points really do follow logically.

▶ Don't worry if you find this difficult. It is. It takes practice.

6 The experience of writing

Writing is not an activity most people feel blasé about. Writing a carefully composed piece is often an intense experience, though not one people talk freely about. Why should writing evoke strong feelings? And why do we tend to avoid discussing those feelings with others who also experience them?

6.1 Revealing yourself

As skills go, writing is a special case. It isn't like, say, conjuring or ice-dancing, which are take-it-or-leave-it skills. By contrast, communicating with others is absolutely fundamental to your life. What is more, the ability to communicate well tends to be associated with perceptions of how intelligent you are. Revealing a lack of prowess at conjuring, in public, is not too much of a threat, whereas revealing a lack of ability to express yourself in writing is a much more 'personal' thing.

But *do* you lack writing ability?

6.2 By what standards are you to judge yourself?

We are surrounded in modern life by the printed word. One gets the impression that the world is full of people who find writing easy. It seems almost shameful to be inept at it, just as one feels dreadfully inadequate the first time one has a driving lesson. All those other drivers speed confidently about, passing each other by a cat's-whisker, parking on a postage-stamp. And driving is such a 'public' performance — how shameful to be crunching through the gears in the middle of the road with a queue of people behind, waiting to overtake. One can scarcely imagine all those people going through the same humiliation themselves once upon a time.

With writing the situation is worse, because what we see in print is 'public' writing. In fact, most of what we read is written by *experienced* writers *selected* for their talent in writing. We never see the writing of all the ordinary plodders who muddle along as best they can. Instead, we see the output of writers who are the equivalent of rally drivers. So when, as beginners, we look at our own written work, what are we comparing it with? Almost inevitably our writing looks weak in the light of comparisons we are in a position to make. This must be at least one reason why we are often very shy about our writing and are so ready to believe that we are chronically poor writers. Having compared ourselves only with the seasoned professionals, we live with this private 'problem'. Nobody knows the secret that we are — oh horrors! — inarticulate in writing.

6.3 The private–public ambiguity

Although many of us feel impelled to treat writing as a very private activity, it is paradoxically also intrinsically a public activity. It is private in that we do it by ourselves, locked in our own thoughts and according to our own habits and perceptions, with very little idea of how other people cope with the challenges it presents. But it is also public in that what we are producing is intended to be read by others, perhaps strangers. Indeed, writing can become a kind of public property which is discussed by all and sundry, with very little reference back to the author. Critics feel able to pronounce on what the words 'really' mean, without needing to ask the writer, who spent hours struggling alone with the words, trying out saying things this way and then that. In fact, there is a large gulf between the private world of writing and the public world of reading and discussing.

The thoughts which float in your mind are potential gems, whose possibilities all lie ahead. The act of putting them on paper immediately 'fixes' a particular formation of those thoughts and destroys all the other possibilities. It is a fateful act. One immediately has the urge to take the words back and recreate all that 'potential' — the great book inside waiting to be written one far-off day. Can the real words on the page ever live up to those hopes? And what of the further barbarity of showing these written words to others, who care nothing for the great possibilities, only for what they can see? Surely this is a violence too hard to bear? And yet you *do* want the words to be read. This is the great contradiction in your impulses. You *want* 'the world' to read what you write, because that is the purpose of writing, but at the same time you don't want *anyone at all* to read it *yet* because it is so personal, and might not be understood as you meant it.

Obviously you do not write an essay with the public at large in mind as your audience. Nevertheless, these contradictory impulses arise: a desire to 'speak' in writing, immediately followed by a desire to retract; a feeling of vulnerability, and yet an urge to go on. In this, as in other respects, writing is a process which gives rise to intensely ambivalent feelings; surges of enthusiasm and satisfaction, accompanied by waves of doubt and self-criticism.

6.4 Taking advantage of criticism

One particularly ambivalent moment is when you get your essay back with comments written on it by your tutor. From talking to people about this experience, I gather that it is quite common to take a quick look at the *grade* and then put the essay aside to 'look at later'. In fact, it seems that some students find it quite difficult *ever* to get round to a close reading of the tutor's remarks. The comments which the tutor has patiently thought about and written out are set aside as too intense and penetrating to face. This, all too rare, offering of 'feedback' is put off to some future day that may never arrive. Why?

It is easy to take comments made on your writing very 'personally', as though you are being told that you are stupid, that your ideas are no good and that you are inarticulate. It is very difficult to 'stand back' and see essay writing as a process of 'skill development', in which you benefit from doing quite tightly defined exercises and receiving very direct comments on your peformance. Each piece you write 'feels' like a personal statement on the issue in question, a contribution to the wealth of knowledge in the world, rather than simply a process of going through your paces in front of a 'coach'. However, from the tutor's point of view, there are probably some very specific things he or she is looking for, and you will be told quite directly how well you measure up. The relationship set up between you and your tutor breaks the usual conventions of politeness between adults. But by taking off the constraints and allowing very direct comment you are being given the chance to try out new ideas and new techniques and find out whether they work. Your tutor may 'sound' very critical, even rude, in the frankness of his or her comments, but that is just the convention adopted in this particular type of relationship. It allows the tutor to tell you 'straight' when the point you want to make just doesn't come across, where the sequence of ideas is confusing, where the logic is unconvincing, and so on. This gives you the chance to try to remedy the problems, so that eventually, when you write 'for real', for readers who will see your errors without ever telling you, you can avoid making mistakes.

Having direct and detailed comments on your writing is, then, a great opportunity, but not an easy one to respond to, because of the very personal feelings you have about your writing and because of the unusually direct nature of the relationship you have with a tutor. It is important to be able to put the relationship into an appropriate perspective; to be able to 'ride out' the irritation of criticisms which seem to miss your point; to be glad of the detailed crossing out of your words and substitution of others; to be able to pay close attention to the subtle nuances of the alterations suggested.

Wouldn't it be wonderful to have a tutor who was like an indulgent parent, admiring everything you wrote. But to learn how to cope with the 'big world' you have to leave parent figures behind and go to 'school'. You have to be able to brace yourself for whatever comes from your tutor, recognizing the specialized nature of this relationship. Most tutors will do their best to be civilized and considerate in their remarks, but that will not prevent you from feeling annoyed and misunderstood. These are feelings you have to come to terms with in a teaching–learning relationship.

197

6.5   Routine hardships

One major reason why writing is an intense experience is not at all deep and 'psychological'. Writing is just plain difficult.

Open-endedness

For one thing, writing is a task in which *the product you are aiming for is very ill-defined*. When you paint a door, you know roughly what you are aiming to achieve and how to set about it. When you are writing an essay the only thing you can be certain of is that the end-product will be quite different from anything you had in mind. This means that you have to think very hard at the outset, as you set about establishing a 'frame of reference' within which to set your remarks. And you have to continue to think hard as you develop your line of argument within that frame. This *struggle to forge the way ahead* gives rise to a mixture of feelings from frustration and exhaustion at one end of the scale to satisfaction and elation at the other, so that your mood may swing quite sharply as you write.

At the same time, the quality of open-endedness in the task of writing creates a more general feeling of uncertainty, aimlessness and an absence of solid 'meanings' to hold on to. As creatures dependent on being able to make sense of our surroundings, we find it intensely uncomfortable to be faced with sustained uncertainty, so the experience of writing tends to have a restless quality about it. You want to keep getting up to do something else — something more solid and routine. In fact, it *may* be useful to switch back and forth between writing and various routine chores, to give yourself a break from the pressures of uncertainty.

An uncertain 'relationship'

Writing is also uncomfortable because of the uncertainty of your relationship with your reader. On *your* side, this relationship is a very personal thing, because it involves the way you project yourself. But the other side of the relationship is shrouded in mystery. Your 'audience' is a mythical entity, in that the tutor who *actually* reads your essay will take on the role of the 'intelligent person in the street' in order to read it. This hypothetical audience is one you can never meet, to check whether you are adopting the right tone of voice. You can only guess, from the remarks your tutor chooses to make, whether you are anywhere near the mark. Consequently you can go through great self-doubt as you re-read what you have written. Thinking of your audience in *one* way, it reads like a nursery book; but then thinking of them in *another* way, it reads like over-condensed gobbledegook.

Being too close to see

When you are in the thick of wrestling with a line of argument and trying to construct intelligible sentences, your attention is so highly focused that is is almost impossible for you to judge what the words you write will mean to someone coming to them fresh and without any emotional involvement. All you can do is press on and hope for the best. It is probably only after a period of several weeks, even months, that you can come back and look at your work with a reasonable feel for what its impact on others would be. Again, this adds a layer of mystery and uncertainty to the writing process.

Keeping going

Finally, essay writing is a rather long-drawn-out process. With so many different stages to it, you have to develop a certain stamina to write regularly. It can be tedious at some times and disappointing at others. Consequently it draws on your inner resources of will power and determination, as well as your courage in facing possible disappointment. It is great when it 'comes right' in the end, but that moment can be a long time coming.

7   Conclusion

Putting the whole picture together we see that writing essays is a very challenging task. In the course of it you may feel:

▶ frustration when you are stuck

▶ uncertainty when you can't see where you are heading

▶ boredom when it goes on and on

▶ despair when you are overwhelmed by the time it takes

▶ distaste when you read what you have written*

▶ gloom when you see the limitations of your own abilities

▶ annoyance when you read your tutor's comments.

But don't let any of this put you off! I am simply working on the principle that these experiences and feelings *will* come to you at some time or other and that, since writing is so private, you need to

---

* According to Peter Elbow (see footnote on page 168), 'nausea' will always hit you at some point in your writing. It may come right at the start as the words leave your pen, or some time later when you come back to re-read your work, or at any time in between. Basically, he says, it is a reaction endemic to the process of writing. So if you escape it earlier expect it later.

be told in advance that *you are not alone* in having such reactions. You need to be *prepared* for a struggle so that you do not give up when the going gets tough. If you are ready to cope with the hardships, you will still be around for the good times which will come eventually.

Why do sane adults bother writing essays at all? For the same reason people choose to do many other somewhat gruelling things: because it is also *intensely rewarding*. No other experience in your studies is likely to be more satisfying than that of having completed an essay and handed it in, nor more elating than finding that you have done better than you expected when your essay is returned.

KEY POINTS

Some basic principles

▶ Your ability to express yourself is a fundamental aspect of your existence in a human society. Developing that ability is one of the most profoundly worthwhile activities you can undertake.

▶ You cannot learn formal *rules* of writing. Essentially you are learning to *communicate* ideas to a reader. Your style will only develop through practice at explaining things to a reader in your own words.

▶ Think of writing as a craft in which you are an apprentice. You learn by practising a range of different skills, and you get this practice by regularly turning out one piece after another and getting comments from a skilled craftsperson.

Some useful thoughts

▶ Don't worry too much about writing beautifully straight away. Just pitch in and write. You have to be prepared to write badly in order to learn how to write well.

▶ Remember that most of what you read is written by 'professionals'. If you are a beginner, then compare yourself with other beginners.

▶ You cannot be a good judge of your own writing until some time after the event.

▶ You have to learn to 'let go' and allow others to see your writing, however far it falls short of your ideals.

▶ Think of your tutor as a 'coach' who is working on your technique. You won't *agree* with everything he or she says, but you *will* make more *progress* with the coaching than without.

Practical hints and tips for essay writing

▶ Work to the question in the title at all times.

▶ Use material drawn from the course.

▶ Work at 'constructing' an argument — i.e. putting points together in groups, organized around a simple essay plan, with a beginning, a middle and an end.

▶ Write clearly and simply.

▶ Write for the intelligent 'person in the street'.

▶ Read your work aloud to yourself (or to someone else, if you can) so that you can 'listen' for sentences that don't work.

▶ When you get an essay back from a tutor, read any suggested corrections out loud and then read your original to 'hear' the differences.

▶ Keep practising. Write short pieces regularly (get comments from a fellow student if you can't get them from a tutor). This will:

- help you to establish a 'writing voice'

- help you to adapt your writing style to the conventions of detailed analysis and objectivity

- extend your repertoire of phrases which help to make your writing flow

- increase your sensitivity to the processes of structuring and signposting.

CHAPTER 7

Preparing for examinations

1 Why exams?

Are you looking forward with eager anticipation to the examination at the end of your course? Perhaps not. Exams are not a favourite pastime for most people. In fact, they can cause a fair amount of stress and disruption in students' lives. So why have they not been abolished? Is it just mean-mindedness on the part of teachers? Come to that, why are you, as an adult student, presumably of your own free will, putting yourself through a course which has an exam? Masochism?

Of course you *might* say that you simply take exams out of necessity, because that is the way qualifications are acquired. And certainly exams *are* used for 'testing' purposes, to check whether people have learned sufficient to be regarded as knowledgeable on particular subjects. However, it is far too narrow and negative a view of exams to see them *simply* as an unpleasant but necessary means of certifying people's competences. After all, some people actually take certain kinds of exams entirely for the sake of it, without any expectation of practical benefit from passing. For instance, lots of people with no professional ambitions take tests and exams in piano playing, ballet dancing, swimming, and so on. They do it as a way of setting targets and notching up achievements. An examination sets up a framework within which you expend exceptional amounts of effort on developing skills and knowledge which you would otherwise never take the trouble to master. So being examined is not a wholly negative process. It presents a challenge which puts you under pressure, and which thereby produces very positive effects.

In fact, *pressure* has interesting effects when it comes to complicated mental activities. We are often able to think very efficiently in a crisis. In our daily lives, our minds churn away doing the work that has to be done — thinking through various issues that crop up, weighing things up, organizing our actions, and so on. But when we hit a *crisis* the whole mode of operation shifts. Our attention narrows down instantly to the matter in hand and we sift rapidly through the main options, cutting corners and ignoring lots of little questions that might normally catch our thoughts. We go straight, as they say, 'to the bottom line'. We find ways of formulating difficult issues much more simply, and we draw conclusions that we would never be able to reach under normal circumstances. When we have time on our hands, there is always another day for thinking through the *really* difficult issues, but when it's 'now or never' we launch ourselves into thoughts we would usually put off, and we drive on until we reach a conclusion, regardless of doubts which may arise on the way.

Pulling the whole course together

In a way an exam is a device for creating a 'mini-crisis', which enables you to find the resources of will power and energy to take matters in hand and finally pull the ideas of the course together, into the best shape you can manage. Studying is challenging work at the best of times, so one is always inclined simply to get on with the next task and to put off the bigger job of standing back and asking 'What is this all about?' Essays, of course, also have the effect of creating mini-crises in your life. And they too help you pull the course together. But they usually operate at a more localized level, drawing just one section of the course into a more coherent shape in your mind. Exams have a larger job to do and they create a correspondingly larger disturbance in your equilibrium.

The way exams create this pressure is through bringing a *performance* element into the task. Whereas in an essay you can write *when* you choose and for *as long as* you choose, until you are ready to submit your work to your *own* tutor, in an exam you have to *perform* at a specified time and place, to the satisfaction of an audience you don't know. You have to 'think on your feet', so to speak, and you have to get it right first time. This brings considerably more pressure to bear on you, but the pressure is potentially a very creative force. In effect, the exam is a 'ritual' which creates the conditions of a public performance, so that you can draw a peak performance out of yourself.

Preparing for 'performances'

There are many people who *regularly* perform in public, such as actors, public speakers, sports stars and politicians. They too experience the pressures of the long-term preparations for their performances and the intense build-up of tension in the period immediately beforehand. Indeed, some of the most famous of public performers have reported feeling tense to the point of nausea immediately before big occasions, and yet have gone on to give outstanding performances, whether singing, or playing a sport, or debating with intense eloquence — performances way beyond the everyday run of human activity and beyond their *own* normal standards. It takes the big occasion to bring out that performance. In the dress-rehearsal, or the warm-up rallies, the performances may be good, but it is on the public occasion that good turns into brilliant. To be successful, a public performer has to know how to make creative use of pressure and stress:

▶ how to channel it into an *obsessive drive* in the *period of preparation*, so that the impending performance is put above everything else going on in life around

▶ how to use it to *'wind-up' for the occasion itself*, so as to reach performance pitch at the right time.

Stress, then, is powerful fuel. However, like many fuels it is also dangerous to handle. It has adverse side effects, which need to be controlled. If you don't have strategies for channelling the tension and putting it to productive use, then the side effects begin to override the benefits. At worst, a performance can 'go to pieces' if the effects of stress get out of hand. The sign of the old trouper is being able to remain in control whatever happens — keeping the tension working positively and ensuring that the show goes on. The same applies to taking exams. There is much examinees can learn from taking notice of and thinking about what professional performers do to get a consistently high standard of performance out of themselves, under taxing circumstances. What you are out to achieve in your approach to exams is not total freedom from stress, but techniques for successfully *managing* it and *using* it, just as many people learn to do in other walks of life.

I have started our discussion of exams with the issue of stress, because I think it permeates all aspects of the examination process and cannot sensibly be ignored; but also and more importantly because I want to establish from the outset that it is not an entirely regrettable and unhelpful phenomenon. Stress in connection with exams, as in other aspects of life, is a powerful but double-edged weapon with which much can be accomplished if handled properly. You should treat exams and the stresses they create as a positive opportunity to achieve a great deal. You have set out to study because you want to learn. Properly approached, exams will help you enormously in achieving an overall grasp of what you have been studying.

KEY POINTS

▶ The stress created by exams is a positive force which you can harness to help you pull the course together and consolidate your grasp on it.

▶ Your aim is to find ways to 'manage' exam stress and put it to good use.

2 Cutting through some myths about exams

One side effect of the tensions associated with exams is that our *perceptions* of them become warped. We develop distorted images of the processes involved in being examined and we become unrealistic in our strategies for tackling the problems ahead of us. Worse still, the *collective* effect of generations of students experiencing these warped perceptions and anticipations is that a good many unhelpful myths have grown up around exams. It will be helpful to begin our discussion by disposing of some of these myths.

2.1 Failure would ruin your life

One of the most valuable aspects of the stress of 'performing' is that it helps you to become obsessively concerned with doing well. This is excellent in that it focuses your energies very intensively on the task in hand. But the reverse of that particular coin is that you may begin to think that failure to do well is the worst thing that could happen to you. You begin to get the whole enterprise out of proportion and start to worry at a level that is quite inappropriate. Of course, it *is* unpleasant to do less well than you hoped, after you have put a lot of time and energy into something. But exams are *not* a life-and-death matter. Most people don't do too badly, but if you *were* to fail — so what? If you have tried your best, why worry? Taking a course of study is a noble and challenging undertaking, from which you are almost certain to gain a great deal, whether you pass the exam or not. Life will go on. In many cases you can have a second attempt at the exam. Sometimes people go on to great success in their studies in spite of such setbacks. In fact, some very eminent scholars failed exams during certain stages of studenthood. So while you obviously don't want to approach the exam with the intention, or expectation, of doing any less than your best, it certainly is not worth turning your life into a nightmare over it. If you recognize the fact that you can survive the worst the exam can throw at you — namely failure — it will help you to keep things in proportion.

> **KEY POINTS**
>
> Failing an exam is not the end of the world, so keep your anxieties in proper proportion.

2.2   The exam could expose you as a fool and a fraud

It is not at all uncommon to have a lurking anxiety that an exam will suddenly reveal you as an imposter; that the hoax you have been carrying off all through the course, pretending to understand as much as everyone else, will finally be exposed; that the examiners will sternly probe for signs of weakness and mercilessly cast aside those who show less than a watertight and comprehensive knowledge of the course. (Incidentally, it is quite common to have recurring dreams along these lines years after taking an exam. This indicates the intensity of the hopes and fears that exams arouse.) But of course exams are not at all like that. The examiners are delighted to have students pass and they usually go out of their way to seek out what is good in the answers they read. Nobody will think you are stupid, or that you have been wasting their time, if you don't do well. They will just be sorry and hope that you do better next time. If you have made a genuine effort to understand the course, and if you have made progress with your assignments during the course, then there is something wrong with the exam if you fail.

> **KEY POINTS**
>
> Everyone *wants* you to pass, including the examiner.

2.3   You should have read everything in the course before attempting the exam

Most students, and especially part-time adult students, have to miss out some sections of any course. Even the best students tend to specialize in those areas which interest them. You have done well if you make it as far as the exam. It's no use, at that stage, worrying about what you have left out. It is far better to consolidate what you *have* done rather than to attempt any desperate catching up on what you haven't. An exam is where you gather together the products of your months of study and make use of them in achieving a peak performance. It is too late for studying from first principles.

To put things in perspective, just think about the practical constraints that apply to exams. How much can you write in a three-hour exam? Not very much! So you are not aiming to know everything there is to know. If you have to answer four questions, you need to know enough to produce, say, three or four sides of discussion on each question you tackle. Equally significant — the person who marks your script isn't going to be checking over it in fine detail to see whether it is worth a Nobel prize. He or she will spend between five and ten minutes on each answer, going quickly through it to see whether the general gist seems right, whether a reasonable number of the key points are there, and whether the argument flows tolerably well. That is what exams are like. Your essays during a course are your chance to put together detailed and carefully thought out arguments for close reading by a tutor. The exam is a much more rough and ready exercise, both in the writing and in the marking. So you *don't* have to worry about having left things out, so long as you can pull together enough from what you *have* studied to write for thirty to forty minutes on chosen topics.

KEY POINTS

Don't worry about what you *haven't* done during the course.
Work out how to make the best use of what you *have* done.

2.4 If you have not understood what you have read it isn't worth taking the exam

It is quite normal to feel confused as you reach the later stages of a course. You can be sure that many other students will be experiencing the same doubts. A course which is any good will have set all kinds of ideas whirling around in your mind, some of which you will still be sorting out a year or two later. Indeed, it is hard to imagine what a 'final' and 'complete' understanding of a topic of any significance would be like. If you *have* understood everything you have read, then you are studying a course which is too easy for you.

Naturally, in any course, there will be certain central ideas you will be expected to have made progress with. And if you have *tried* to make sense as you studied, you probably have developed more of an understanding than you realize. But if the course is at all challenging you could hardly expect to arrive at a resolution of every issue it raises by the time of the exam. In fact, the exam may be just what you need to spur you on to sort out some of these central issues. The point is to use your preparation for the exam to pull things together; to make *the best sense you can.*

KEY POINTS

No one understands 'everything'. There are bound to be areas where you feel underprepared and confused.

2.5 Exam papers are unreadable

Your first look at a past exam paper for the course you are studying may give you a bit of a fright. Exam questions often look tremendously broad and demanding on first sight. They also tend to be rather abstract in form and may seem somewhat oblique in their wording. However, the obliqueness is not accidental or malicious. It is usually because the examiners want to *point* you towards a *specific topic* in the course *without* answering the question *for* you. In other words, they are trying to be helpful, without giving the game away. You need to remember at all times that the exam is a test of your understanding of the course you have been studying, not your general knowledge. So *somewhere* within what you have been studying lies the answer to each question on the paper. Don't panic at the sight of the paper. Instead, carefully match what you know of the *course* against what the *questions* seem to be asking, until you find the specific part of the course each is pointing you to. There is no mystery. The examiners want you to display an understanding of some specific parts of the course. It's just a matter of working out *which* bits.

KEY POINTS

Don't panic when you read exam questions. Almost every exam question is linked quite directly with something you have covered on the course. You just have to work out the link.

2.6 Exams are for people with a good memory

Everybody has a good memory. It is a matter of how you use it. However, that is not the key point. Most of the exams adults take are *not* intended as 'memory' tests. The purpose of the course you study is to develop your *ideas*. And the purpose of the exam is to provide you with the chance to show how well you have grasped the ideas in the course. You will be asked to *use* the ideas in *arguing a case*. If you revise constructively before the exams, the role of 'pure memory' will be relatively small. If you have an organized *understanding* of what is in the course, and if you can see the *relationship* between the course material and the question, you will have the core of an answer. On this basis you will find it fairly easy to remember sufficient details of examples, names, and so on from the course. So don't even think about your memory. Concentrate on *organizing* your notes during your revision. Let your memory take care of itself.

KEY POINTS

Exams tend to be about what you *understand* rather than what you can *remember*. Getting your course notes organized will sort your memory out.

2.7 The exam will show up all the gaps in your education

Some people feel anxious in a vague generalized way before an exam — feeling that their whole educational background is somehow inadequate to the task ahead, and that failings and omissions in the distant past will at last come home to roost in the exam. This is a misleading trick that anxiety plays upon us. An exam is *not* a test of general knowledge. (It would be impossible to mark in a standardized way if it were.) It is a test of your grasp of the course. If you have studied the course effectively, you can perform well in the exam, regardless of your previous education. In fact, it is a grave mistake to read a question on an exam paper and then try to answer 'off the top of your head', using your 'general knowledge'. The person marking your paper is not likely to be impressed. The examiners' marking guide will indicate some quite specific points from the course for which marks can be given. Going off on your own tack — however well-informed you may be — is a very risky strategy. If general knowledge and educational background do come through, it is in the 'roundedness' of answers to questions, and in refinements of writing style, which might push a 'good' answer up to 'excellent'. In other words, educational background may help to put a finishing gloss on a performance, but it is not part of the basics of getting the job done.

KEY POINTS

Don't worry about what you didn't learn *before* the course.
Consolidate on what you have learned *during* the course.

2.8   Exams are just for 'speed merchants'

Can you think quickly enough and write quickly enough to pass an
exam? Probably! As far as the *thinking* is concerned, you need to
make sure you have done most of that in advance of the exam itself,
as we shall see in Section 4. So the extent to which sheer speed of
thinking matters is very limited. What *will* matter is how well you
have *organized* your ideas and how well you have *planned* your
exam strategy. If you are working to a good plan you can be
extremely efficient in your use of the time in the exam.

As far as your speed of *handwriting* is concerned this *may* have an
effect if it seriously restricts the amount you can get down. If you
can get down, say, 500–700 words in forty minutes, that should be
sufficient to get a high mark, although it is impossible to give hard
and fast rules on this. Some students write short pithy answers
which are very good, while others write pages without saying much.
The fact that you have a lot of adrenalin pumping in an exam will
help you to write much more quickly than usual. But if you have
doubts, then give yourself some practice in writing at speed to limber
your hand up. If you suffer from a physical disability which makes
you a slow writer, then you should get advice on whether you can
be given special support in the exam, or extra time. In general,
however, it is far more important to focus on the quality of what
you write than the speed at which you can produce it. In any case,
your speed of progress is as likely to be affected by the rate at which
you can work out the next point in the argument as by the purely
technical process of putting the words on the page and, as we shall
see, this has a great deal to do with how you prepare yourself in
advance of the exam.

KEY POINTS

Speed in an exam is to do with having a very clear plan as to
how you intend to use your time.

2.9 You have to revise till you drop before an exam

The folklore of exams is full of stories of amazing last-minute spurts of work, deep into the night. There may be some truth in them, in that we *are* capable of extraordinary feats when the pressure is on. But the telling of the stories is as much to do with the feelings that frenetic preparations for exams produce, and the intensity of people's hopes and fears, as to do with accurately describing reality. It is *not* the case that all preparations can effectively be done at the very last moment, particularly as you get older, and especially if you are studying part-time and have to keep another life going at the same time.

Our minds function somewhat differently under pressure, and you need to understand the differences if you are to 'manage' yourself well in building up to the big performance. In the days immediately before the exam the tension builds up and you become highly charged. This means that you have plenty of nervous energy and can get lots done, but it is harder to keep yourself under control, so as to channel the energy in the best directions. Being highly charged makes you very good at focusing attention on *concrete* matters in hand, but conversely it makes you less good at sorting out *broad, abstract* issues. The obvious answer is to do your broad planning well in advance so that, by the final stages of revision (and in the exam itself), you have clear-cut strategies already worked out — strategies for tackling the revision, for allocating time in the exam, for taking the exam questions apart, for structuring your answers, and so on. You need to become like an efficient exam-crunching machine. If you have a well-developed sense of purpose and a framework within which to work, you may find you can think surprisingly clearly once the exam has started. But none of this is likely to happen if you leave all thoughts of exam preparations to the last couple of days and nights before the exam.

KEY POINTS

You probably *will* do a lot of work just before the exam. But you need to do it in a planned way, using your time efficiently and conserving your energies. You don't want to turn your life into a complete misery just because of an exam.

These then are some of the myths about exams — that they are gigantic obstacles, which can be surmounted only by people of extraordinary capabilities; that they are devised and marked by sadists to expose the weaknesses of ordinary mortals; that they threaten one with life-shattering consequences, and so on — myths with a nightmare quality. But, as we have seen, the reality is much more mundane. Exams are just another part of the education process — admittedly a part which presents a greater challenge and in consequence creates greater stress. The essential secret of achieving the results that you deserve in exams, and also of experiencing the least pain and discomfort, is to take a 'practical' approach to them; to be *realistic* about *yourself* and about *what is required of you* by the exam, so that you can prepare yourself carefully and sensibly to give a 'peak performance'. The last thing you want is to waste your energies dithering about in a panic, or spend all your time on useless activities because you can't let yourself stop to think clearly about the task in hand.

3   What the examiners do not like

Having disposed of some of the myths, let us look in more detail at the reality. One way of getting a sharp focus on what *is* wanted in exams is to consider what boards of examiners have to say in their reports after marking exams. Since you are not likely to be in a position to do that yourself, I will summarize for you the comments made in some Open University examiners' reports for social science courses. Often these reports stress *how well* many students answer questions. However, here I think it is useful for us to highlight the *faults* examiners find.

3.1   Failing to answer the question

In answering exam questions, it isn't just *what* you know that counts but *how* you say it. A great deal of emphasis is placed on being able to *use* what you know to *argue a case* which relates directly to the *specific question*. If you don't do this, your script marker sighs and writes 'Doesn't answer the question' below your answer. According to the examiners' reports, there are several ways in which you can miss the mark:

▶ Failing to recognize what one of the *key terms* in the question means (answering a question, say, on the *'retail* boom' of the 1980s as though it meant the same as a *production* boom). In other words, you have to think carefully about what each of the words in the question means. If there is a term in the question you don't know, avoid the question. You will get very few marks if you guess and get it wrong.

▶ Failing to realize *which issues* from the course are being raised. Every question is intended to direct you towards particular questions and concerns which have been discussed in the course. You have to spot which ones.

▶ Failing to offer *critical analysis* and *argument* relating to the question. However the question is posed, it is generally expected that you will be presenting arguments *for* and *against* a particular *point of view* (or points of view) implied in the question. Your first job, as you read a question closely, is to *identify the point of view* it presents. Your next job is to remind yourself of some *other point(s) of view* from which you can criticize the first position. Your answer can then be constructed as a *debate* between two or more sides.

▶ Failing to take an *objective* enough stance in relation to the question. You cannot get away with 'haranguing' your reader with your opinions dressed up in lots of committed rhetoric. You have to observe the same principles of objectivity as in your essays (see Chapter 5, Section 3.5).

▶ Failing to end the answer with any *conclusions* regarding the question. You greatly increase the impression of purposefulness and relevance in your answer if you make a point of *coming back* quite specifically *to the question* at the *end* of your answer and briefly showing how what you have said helps to answer it. You don't necessarily have to come down on one side or another, but at least you should point out what is at stake.

These of course are all familiar enough points. We have come across them all in connection with essay writing in Chapter 5. So there is nothing particularly new for you to think about here; you should simply note that exam answers, though much shorter and more scrappy, are judged along roughly the same lines as essays (but to much lower levels of expectation, in recognition of the constraints).

3.2 Failing to draw on material from the course

Examiners complain that it is hard to tell whether some students have actually *studied the course*. In other words, these students completely forget one of the basic principles of any end-of-course exam; namely that it is set up as an opportunity to *demonstrate* that you have worked on and thought about the content of the course. It is essential that you treat each question as an excuse to bring in *terms* and *ideas* presented in the course. And when you are arguing a point you must back up your case by using *evidence* and *examples* from the course. For example, if you say, 'The traditional High Street is being eroded by the new style out-of-town shopping centre', it sounds like a personal opinion of yours. If you add 'according to Worpole', it shows firstly that it isn't simply your opinion, but a case argued by an authority on the subject, and secondly that you recognize that it would be possible to argue against this conclusion. You don't need to have dozens of names or 'facts and figures' scattered through your answers, but putting in a few important ones shows that you are not just making your answer up as you go along.

Some students give the impression that they are trying to answer the exam questions simply by rummaging around in the rag-bag of their general knowledge for something vaguely relevant and then attempting to work out an argument from first principles, on the spot. In fact, it is very difficult, even in an essay (when you have time on your side), to make significant progress on any issue without drawing on the accumulated wisdom of those who have already studied it and written about it in depth. The chances of doing so in an exam are slim indeed. You cannot expect to impress the exam marker without showing that you know what others have said on the subject. Equally, you cannot base your answers entirely on your own experiences or those of people you happen to know. You have to be able to bring in some more generally recognized *evidence*, as appropriate. Don't rely solely on anecdotes or on-the-spot analysis, even when you are desperate. Use material from the course.

3.3   Stuffing your answers full of names and facts

You should use the course material discriminatingly. You are *never* asked, 'Write all you know about . . .'. The exam marker is not interested in whether you can *memorize* a section of a book and *repeat* it. He or she wants to know whether you can *put* the ideas and information in the book *to work*: whether you can *select* useful material from all that you have come across in the course and *use* it to answer a specific question. If you cram your answer full of facts and names without *selecting* them for their relevance, or without placing them in the context of an argument, the marker will suspect that you don't understand the subject and are hoping that sheer memory for items of information will do as a substitute. It won't.

3.4   Using your time badly

A very common failing is to produce a very long first answer, followed by a somewhat short second one, a very short third, and finally a fourth which is just a paragraph and some scrappy notes.

This is an unfortunate practice, since the allocation of exam marks is usually very straightforward. Each question carries a certain number of marks and good work on one question cannot be carried over in any general way to your overall score. It is very difficult to push your mark up beyond 90 per cent for your best answer. However, if you did manage a 90 per cent on your first answer, but followed it with 45 per cent, 30 per cent, and 15 per cent, your overall score would be 45 per cent. On the other hand, if you spent less time pushing the first answer into the highest ranges and got, say, 75 per cent, but used the time gained to do the considerably easier job of pulling the other questions up the lower ranges, you might end up with, say, 60 per cent, 55 per cent, and 50 per cent. This would give you an overall score of 60 per cent which, as you can see, is a much better result. It is much easier to accumulate marks at the lower end of the scale than at the upper end, so it *always* makes sense to spend roughly the same amount of time on each question, however weak you feel on some of them.

3.5 Poor presentation

Finally, examiners also complain about answers which are:

▶ unstructured (i.e. lacking a beginning, a middle, and an end)
▶ lacking any division into paragraphs
▶ written in note form rather than sentences
▶ in illegible handwriting.

Again, these requirements are familiar enough from your essay writing. Obviously, it is harder for you to pay attention to presentation under exam pressures. But equally the exam marker's job is harder than your tutor's, as he or she has to work through a mountain of scripts. With the best will in the world, it is hard to do justice to judging an argument which is very difficult to read. And, unlike your tutor, the script marker doesn't know you and can't so easily guess what you might be intending to say, so it is all the more important to provide coherent and legible answers. You cannot help the relative scrappiness and untidiness of your exam answers as compared with your essays. But neither can the exam marker help being influenced to some extent by the relative difficulty of working out what you are trying to say.

These then are the things examiners complain about in their examiners' reports (alongside the very pleasant and encouraging things they also say). Let us now turn to considering how you can make sure that they say nice things about *your* answers. There are three areas in which you can tune up your performance, by careful planning and sensible application. These are:

▶ the revision process

▶ 'gearing yourself up' during the last day or two

▶ sitting the exam itself.

4 Revising for exams

4.1 What is the point of revision?

The most important purpose of revision, as I have already said, is to pull together all the work you have done in studying the course. Revision is *not* primarily a massive *memorizing* task, as people sometimes think. It is a much more *constructive* activity than memorizing. It serves the function of rounding off the course. While you are studying the units you are constantly challenging your existing ideas and throwing them into disarray. Revision is the process of tidying up the mess and getting your ideas back into a useable shape. Without this period of revision the course would just drift away from you. Revising provides you with the opportunity to *reconstruct* the course for yourself so that the ideas you have developed as you studied are rendered more coherent and put in 'working' order.

The consequence of this is that revision has to be made into an *active* process — not just a mechanical 'scanning through pages hoping something will stick'. It needs to be planned in a *purposeful* way and to be designed around *activities* which are meaningful, engaging and thought-provoking, not repetitive, tedious and mind-numbing. Revision is a substantial and time-consuming part of the course which *you* have chosen to study, so you should make sure *you* get some pleasure and value out of it. Don't just do it for the sake of the examiners.

What kinds of things, then, are worth doing, given the strictly limited time you have available and the importance of making all your efforts count? We shall now consider some of the key strategic questions.

4.2 When should you start your revision for the exam?

There is no 'correct' answer to this question. Basically it is something you have to work out for yourself. Some students leave it to the last fortnight, while others make a start two months before the exam. The right time for you depends on:

▶ your personal commitments in addition to studying, and the time you can spare for the revision process

▶ your personal style of studying — whether you are more capable of short intensive bursts of effort, or longer sustained periods

▶ what you are trying to get out of the course.

It would be a shame if you panicked too early and spoiled the latter parts of the course by being obsessed with revision. On the other hand, it is a grave mistake to avoid all thinking about the exam until the very last moment and then just hope for the best. You will get far less out of the course and you will suffer in the exam itself, if you leave yourself no time for revision. It is a good idea to begin to have some thoughts about revising a couple of months before the exam, even if you don't actually start the revision itself until later. If you were just to jot down a first attempt at a plan of the last weeks of the course, sketching out how you might try to fit in some blocks of revision time alongside the normal course work, it would be a useful start. It doesn't matter if you have to scrap the plan and draw up a new one (or have to keep scrapping plans and drawing up new ones). The effort of making a tentative start on a revision plan on the back of an envelope will set in process the necessary shift in orientation as you move towards the final stages of the course.

4.3 Getting hold of old exam papers

This is an excellent idea, although, as I have said, your first look at an exam paper may make you gulp. Until you have done some serious revision, you may not be able to imagine how you will ever be able to tackle such broad questions. Nevertheless, it is much better to get the fright over with long enough before the exam to be able to do something about it. You certainly don't want to have that experience for the first time in the exam itself.*

It is sensible to be suspicious of exams, particularly if you haven't done one for a long time. You need to find out as much as you can about them in advance. There may be printed notes to guide you as to the nature of the exam and what is expected of you. And your

---

* Can you get hold of past exam papers? If it is the first year of your course, clearly you cannot. However, in such circumstances, you may be supplied with a specimen paper instead. If it isn't the first year, make a point of finding out how to get hold of old papers. Ask you tutor, or experienced fellow students, or write to the examining body.

tutor, or more experienced fellow-students, will be able to give you a lot of tips and clues as to how the exam process works in practice. But in order to focus your mind on the task at hand, there is no substitute for looking at past exam papers. You will be able to see exactly how the questions are set out on the page; how many there are; whether there are separate sections from which you have to choose questions; what kinds of questions are set; how the questions 'map' on to the content of the course; what sort of language they employ; and so on. For example, a typical format for a three-hour exam paper might be to have a dozen questions from which you have to select four, one of which has to come from the second part of the paper.

Note:
Exams vary in length and in the number of questions you have to answer. To avoid unnecessary complications, I am going to write throughout in terms of a three-hour exam in which you answer four questions, each of which requires an essay-type answer, and each of which carries 25 per cent of the marks. When you have found out the details of *your* exam, you will have to make the necessary adjustments to any figures I give for time per question, length of answers, etc.

You will need to check whether there is an obvious relationship between the structure of the exam paper and the structure of the course; for example, whether a question is set on each major section of the course. This information is crucial in guiding your *revision strategy*. Your revision time will be limited and you need to be sure you are using it wisely.

By the time you sit down to take the real exam you need to be very familiar with what the paper is going to look like and to have a pretty good idea as to what questions you are looking for on it. You cannot be guaranteed to get the *specific* questions you want, but you should be able to form a reasonable idea of the *general* areas the questions are likely to cover. You cannot afford to waste time in an exam dithering or changing your mind halfway through a question. One of the most important projects before an exam is to form a clear *plan of attack on the paper*. Both for your general revision strategy and for detailed planning for the exam itself, you need to make yourself very familiar with the way the exam paper is likely to look.

4.4 Should you re-read the whole course?

This is the sort of fantasy that floats across your mind in moments of remorse at past failings and steely resolve to set things to rights. It is hopelessly idealistic. It would take far too long, but more importantly it would be dreadfully tedious. Your mind would be numbed. You would learn little except a distaste for the course and for revision. You need to take a much more selective and more active approach as you return to your earlier weeks of study. You need to make a careful judgement, based on your study of past papers and on any advice you can get from your tutor, about *how* selective you can afford to be. Then decide exactly which parts of the course you are going to focus your efforts on.

Many exams are deliberately designed in such a way as to allow you to be selective in your preparation. Provided that you have made a point of carefully checking the logic of the choices open to you, you can be quite ruthless about setting aside whole sections of the course and ignoring them. It is not 'cheating' to do this. The most successful students are often those with the confidence to be extremely businesslike in selecting precisely as much of the course as they need (taking account of the need to have some cover if a question does not come up in quite the form expected). They then give their full attention to revising the chosen areas very thoroughly.

4.5 Drawing up a detailed timetable for your revision

As I have said, exam folklore is full of legends of people leaving things to the last few days and then 'studying around the clock'. However, if you are a part-time student, possibly with several years of exams ahead of you, a more temperate approach is likely to serve you far better. You have to retain a balance between the exam and the rest of your life. You need to make out a timetable of the last weeks of the course and see how many hours, in total, you can reasonably hope to set aside. Allow a proportion of your time for studying the last part of the course. Set aside some time for practising exam questions, and for the final stages of polishing up your act. Then divide the remaining time into equal parts for each of the areas of the course you have decided to revise. It is tempting to allow more time for sections of the course where you feel particularly strong and to try to squeeze the weak areas in at the end. However, it is best to assume equal time for each area since, as we have seen, each question carries the same number of marks. It is only too easy to end up with too little time for the topics which most need sorting out, or conversely to leave no time for brushing up the very topics you had hoped to do best in. Fill in your timetable with a rough schedule showing how you hope to spend the time. Although you won't be able to stick to it, having some kind of plan will help you to focus on the nature and the size of the task. You can then keep readjusting your sights to take account of reality.

4.6 Sorting out your course material

One of the central features of revising is getting yourself organized. Unless you have a superbly efficient filing system, you will have accumulated mounds of assorted bits of paper, notes, handouts, photocopies of articles, and half-read books. Setting aside an evening to do nothing other than sort everything out is more than just 'housekeeping'. The act of putting all the material into new tidier mounds reminds you of what material you have and pushes you into thinking about the overall shape of the course and how things can be grouped together. When you can look around you and see *what* you have got and *where*, you will be in a much better position to get a clear run at a spell of revision.

4.7 Should you try to memorize your course notes?

No — it would be a complete waste of time and effort. If you set out to do routine, boring things like dutifully scanning over old notes until you can recite them, your mind will switch off in protest. You need to be able to *think* in the exam, not *recite* back your notes. So you need *ideas* in your head, not strings of words. You need to do something much more constructive as you read your course notes, such as picking out key points, or trying to work out what questions you might be asked. Any 'memorizing' of the course material should come in the last day or two and should be based on 'summary' notes (see Section 4.9 of this chapter).

4.8 Identify the central questions at the heart of each section of the course

This is a very powerful strategy. Try to identify one or two central questions in each section of the course that you are revising, and try to write notes that answer those questions. In other words, what is this part of the course all about? What is the *point* of it? Sometimes an author will have identified the key questions for you. At other times you will have to tease them out and pose them for yourself.

Similarly, the author will sometimes have made a point of drawing conclusions on the main issues for you, while at other times you will have to summarize and draw conclusions for yourself. The process of seeking out key questions and answers to them gets your mind working in the way in which it needs to be working during the exam. It will alert you to the kinds of questions that *could* be asked on the course content you have been studying. It will also help you to think in terms of the broad sweeps needed for putting together answers based on the course material.

4.9 Is it worth writing new notes at this late stage in the course

Yes it is an excellent idea to work with a pen in your hand, actually *creating* something as you work! This gives a much more constructive feel to the task of revision and will engage your mind more effectively for long spells of work. One very good way of working is as follows:

1 Make *very condensed notes* from various books, notes, etc., that you have gathered together for revision on a particular topic.

2 Then extract the main points from these condensed notes to produce a single *summary sheet* of headings with key points, names, etc. for that *topic*.

3 Finally, having done this for the topics within a given section of the course, take the main headings from all the topic summary sheets and produce a single *master summary sheet* which outlines the main subject matter for that whole *section* of the course.

Figure 7.1 shows this method of working in the form of a diagram.

The effort to 'boil' the course down in this way, so as to extract its concentrated essence, is extremely valuable because it converts the broad themes and the detailed discussions of the course into a form which is much more manageable for the purposes of answering questions in exams. As you know, you do not have time to write at tremendous length in exams, so you don't want to wade through mounds of detail in your mind trying to sift out an answer. This condensed version of the main points of the course is much closer to what you will have time to think through and write about.

What is more, when you come to answering a question on a particular section of the course in the exam, you can remind yourself of the 'master summary sheet', to identify what main topics lie within the section. You then work out which of the topics are relevant to the question and remind yourself of the 'topic summary

221

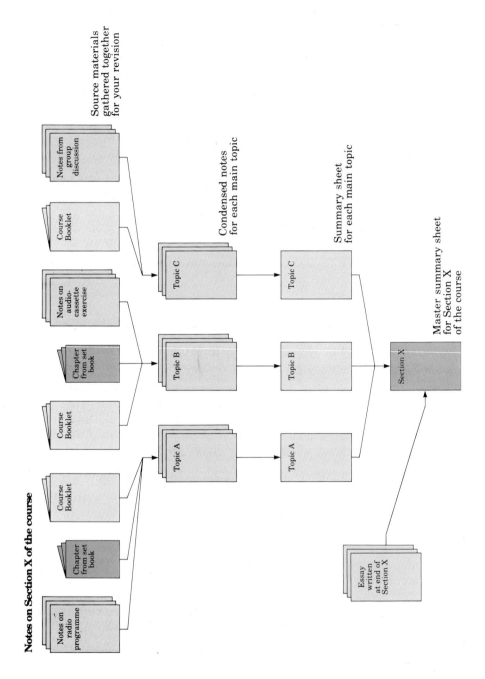

Figure 7.1 *Illustration of the process of condensing notes from a range of sources on to a single sheet*

sheets' concerned. You scan mentally through the main items on any given topic summary sheet and select whichever are relevant. This then leads you back towards the condensed notes which 'lie behind' those items on the topic summary sheet. In other words, having, in your revision, constructed pathways *down* from the basic source materials through condensed notes and topic summary sheets to a master summary sheet, you can then, in the exam, quickly trace your way back *up* those pathways, to locate exactly the material that is relevant to the question. Perhaps the practice is rarely quite as neat as that, but at least this 'note-condensing' approach gives you the basis for a systematic overviewing and retrieval system.

Furthermore, a strategy such as this gives you a well-focused and absorbing task to be getting on with, rather than the aimless scanning back over old material which sends you to sleep and dulls your spirits. And finally, condensed notes will supply you with just the kind of 'pulled together' version of the course which will be invaluable in the future, when you want to remind yourself of what the course was about.

4.10 Should you try answering past exam questions?

Probably the single most useful revision activity of all is to attempt old exam questions. You don't need to write out a full answer every time, though the occasional practice at that would probably be useful. A quicker exercise which you can do much more frequently (and which you should try to do over and over during the final stages of revision) is to rehearse the vital first few minutes of working on a question; in other words, the minutes when you examine the question carefully and sketch out rough notes for an answer. Give yourself, say, ten minutes to produce an outline answer to a question you haven't looked at before, then look back at the course material to see what you have left out.

As you tackle each question, go through the routine of answering the following points:

▶ What is the question getting at? (Underline the key words in the same way as for essays. See Chapter 6, Section 2.1.)

▶ Which section of the course does the question relate most directly to and which topic(s) within that section?

▶ What themes, examples, evidence, ideas can you draw on from the course?

▶ What would be a good order in which to take the points? (i.e. a sketched outline of the content)

The reason this is worth doing many times is that it helps you develop the intellectual agility to do what examiners so clearly want you to do, which is to answer questions precisely and to draw on relevant parts of the course in doing so. It helps you organize your knowledge in the right sort of way for the job in hand. You get used to going very quickly through the processes of:

▶ *sifting* through what you know of the course material

▶ *selecting* the most relevant items for the question, and

▶ *arranging* them in a suitable order for a coherent answer.

You don't need practice at writing out full answers quite so urgently because, once you have an outline, the writing itself is pretty much the same as writing an essay, except that you have less time. In other words, you have already practised that area of skill in your essay writing during the course. What you have not had practice at is 'thinking on your feet' and fixing very quickly on a line to take. Our normal modes of thinking about essay questions are too reflective and lumbering for an exam. You need to practise a much more nimble style to get yourself into fighting trim for the exam.

If you run out of questions from sample papers, you can always make up some more of your own (see Section 4.11) or, better still, exchange made up questions with another student. One of the greatest benefits of this exercise of regularly sketching out quick outlines for answers is that you soon begin to discover that the ground you covered early in the course, which had seemed no more than vague shapes in a haze, soon comes back into sharp focus, and you find that you have learned much more than you had realized.

4.11 Try to think up exam questions for yourself

It is an excellent exercise to try to think up questions you could be asked. Apart from stretching your mind, it makes you step over to the examiners' side of the fence, which helps you develop insight into the way they think. It helps you to take a broad view of the course, looking for the big issues and the underlying themes. On the other hand, you *might* guess badly, so don't pin *all* your hopes on your own hunches.

4.12 Should you set yourself a full-scale 'mock exam'?

If you haven't taken exams for a long time, it is obviously useful to get some practice at working on exam questions 'against the clock'. On the other hand, you might find it hard to make the time, or find the stamina, for a full-length practice. It depends on your own abilities and inclinations as to how useful it is to spend time this way. It might be just as useful and more practical to set yourself to write a single timed answer every now and then. After all, you will have the benefit of a lot more nervous energy to help you perform great feats on the exam day, so you may underestimate your powers in an informal try-out. A further word of warning — don't be discouraged if the answers you produce look unimpressive compared with your essays. Answers produced under exam conditions are always pretty flawed.

4.13 Have you time to attend tutorials during the revision period?

Make time! It is easy to develop a distorted perspective on exams during revision. You begin to think your problems are much worse than they really are, or you bias your revision too sharply in one particular direction. The best way to keep a sense of proportion is to talk to other people about what you are doing. This is probably the time when attending tutorials is *most* useful. I don't want to imply that, if you are obliged to study on your own, your chances are necessarily poor. It's just that if you *can* get to classes you will make your revision a lot easier and more pleasant. It is a mistake to think that time spent at a tutorial is simply time lost from revising at home. Group revision can be extremely efficient. It throws up all sorts of insights into problems and misperceptions which might otherwise remain hidden. It helps to sort out your ideas and offers many valuable clues and tips.

4.14 Should you team up with other students for your revision?

It can be very valuable, particularly if you are new to exams, to meet fairly regularly with other students, to compare your revision strategies and your progress, to set each other questions, to comment on and criticize each other's outline answers, and to provide mutual support in general. Since exams have a tendency to draw out our anxieties and to foster myths, it is extremely useful to be able to make contact with other people's ideas of reality, which helps to keep your own perceptions and plans within reasonable bounds.

4.15 Summary of hints on revising

KEY POINTS

Strategies for revising for an exam

▶ Study *old exam papers* and specimen papers thoroughly.

▶ Carefully *select* the parts of the course you intend to revise.

▶ Make a *timetable* for revising.

▶ Seek out the central *questions* in each of the parts of the course you have chosen to revise.

▶ *Condense* the content of your chosen sections into very brief summarizing notes.

▶ Think up *questions* you might be asked.

▶ Practise jotting down *outlines* for answers to questions.

▶ Practise *writing* out one or two answers in full against the clock.

▶ *Keep in touch* with other students and with your tutor to broaden your ideas and maintain contact with reality.

5 Getting yourself 'geared-up' in the last day or two

Is it a good idea to relax and get plenty of sleep and outdoor exercise in the day or two immediately before the exam? Perhaps you ought to get away for a short holiday? Sounds great doesn't it — but is it realistic? Probably for part-time students it isn't even within the bounds of possibility, given all the other demands of daily life. More importantly, it is not at all obvious that it would be good for your exam performance anyway. That last day or so is when you should be gradually building yourself up to a peak of preparation. You can concentrate wonderfully when it's too late to worry about the frills. You can forget your plans for re-reading that book, or the thorough going over you were going to give to that theory you never really understood. With all those possibilities left behind, you are in a position to concentrate all your energies on making the best job you can of marshalling what you do know. 'Relaxed' is the last thing you want to be when you enter the exam. Calm and unruffled — possibly (if you can manage it) — but you should be keyed-up like a tennis star at a tournament, or a stage performer on the first-night, ready to give your big performance of the year, transcending your normal limits by force of all that nervous energy and your single-minded concentration.

5.1 Get your thinking in before the exam

How will you do justice to everything you have learned in months of study, when you only have three hours in the exam. How long do you spend on an essay? Six hours — ten hours — a week? How on earth can you condense all those writing processes into four forty-five-minute bursts? Clearly you can't. Consequently exam answers don't look like essays. They are shorter, more fragmented, and much less polished than ordinary essays. You can be sure that most students are glad that their work is thrown away when the marking is over. On the other hand, it is surprising how much you *can* get into an exam answer in spite of the time constraints. What you can't do is gradually work out a carefully considered response, as you do for your essays. You have to be able to pitch in after spending only a few minutes deciding on what line to take. This means that you have to have done a lot of your thinking *prior* to the exam itself. You need to have decided *which parts of the course* you are going to choose to answer on. You need to have the *central issues* of the sections of the course you have revised clearly held in the forefront of your mind. You need to have practised *setting up arguments* between the main points of view in the course. And you need to have decided exactly how you are going to use your *time* in the exam. Then, in the exam:

▶ you pick your question

▶ you settle after a few minutes on a particular way of using what you know to answer it, and

▶ you stick to it, for better or worse.

In other words, you have to get yourself into a very particular frame of mind for the exam. A highly organized, efficient and pragmatic one. One in which, having stopped worrying and wondering, you have focused on making the best of the immediate tasks in hand, cutting every corner you can and generally using your native cunning.

5.2 Changes to your mental powers

The last couple of days, then, are about loading your plans and strategies into your head, going over your summary note sheets and generally winding yourself up for action. Because the pressures build up in these final days, your mental powers will change. You will probably be *less good* at *deep thinking* tasks, such as sorting out the underlying meaning of a difficult chapter of a set book. But you will be *better* at working at *routine* things like checking over your notes, practising answering questions, or reminding yourself of your strategy for the exam. So don't leave *basic revision* to the last few days — you'll only depress yourself and get into a panic. Plan to switch you mode of work. Use these days as your 'polishing-up' period for the big performance. As with the actor at the dress rehearsal, it's too late to learn new lines or decide on a different interpretation. You just have to 'go with it' the way it is, and keep running over your lines in your head, to make sure everything is in place.

5.3 Anxiety

It is possible that, as the exam draws closer, you will begin to find the tension gets on top of you. There are several varieties and levels of anxiousness which can develop at exam time. As I have already said, you may experience a general uneasiness about the task ahead that builds up gradually over a long period until (very usefully) it provides the spur to getting down to a really intensive burst of work. This is a normal precursor to any kind of performance. What you need to do is to make sure you *use* this tension productively. Set yourself practical tasks in preparation for the exam so as to keep yourself busy. Remind yourself from time to time that this is *your* exam; you are doing it because *you* have chosen to, and because the tension it creates is a very *productive* force which will *help* you with some difficult learning. In other words, the ideal situation is that you learn to live with the pressures and to use them to achieve things for yourself.

Your anxiousness may, however, develop into a pall of gloom which spoils the last part of the course. You may find that all your thoughts become centred on the exam. In this case, you will find it useful to keep talking to other students and to your tutor. You need to share your thoughts about the exam and about your plans for tackling it. Talking to others will release tension and will help you to keep things in a realistic perspective.

For a few students though, this is not enough. Their anxiety in the period immediately before the exam builds up to a point where sleep is difficult and their health begins to suffer, or where work or family and friends begin to be affected. If you find this happening to you, then go to your doctor for advice. Some people find breathing exercises helpful, or meditation, or some other way of focusing intensively on reducing the physical manifestations of tension. If you feel bad, don't suffer in isolation. Look for help.

5.4 Checking the arrangements

In fact, because you need to get so 'geared-up' in the last day or two, you may become rather inattentive to the ordinary details of life. People sometimes make quite odd mistakes, like turning up for the exam on the wrong day or at the wrong place. So it is a good idea to get all the details of the exam sorted out well in advance. You don't want to be worrying about anything trivial on the day. Mark the time very clearly on your calendar. You might even consider making a practice journey to the exam centre and finding the room, so that you don't have any last-minute panics about which bus to catch, or where you left the address of the exam centre, or where the entrance to the building is.

5.5 On the great day

On the day itself, try to approach the exam calmly. Go about the normal business of getting up and starting the day in an unhurried way. Take a short stroll perhaps, or do a few exercises, to get yourself tuned up and functioning properly. Don't attempt any last-minute revision or even glance over your notes. It will only disturb your carefully stored ideas. Get to the exam in good time and keep walking around if you have to wait to get into the exam centre. Don't let the other candidates disturb you. Remain aloof if you need to. When you are in the exam room, find your desk and calmly settle yourself in your seat. Set out whatever you have with you on the desk and check that you have everything you need. The exam room always seems a strange place, full of people you don't know, all locked obsessively in their own thoughts — but don't let the strangeness distract you. Just keep your mind 'ticking over in neutral', ready to slip into gear when the lights change. If you have prepared yourself sensibly there is no point in worrying. In fact, once the exam has started you may find it surprisingly exhilarating and challenging. It's astonishing how much you can do in only three hours when you have keyed yourself up to a peak of mental fitness.

6 Working out your tactical plan for the exam

We need finally to consider in detail what you are going to attempt to achieve in the examination itself. You don't want to let yourself drift towards the exam like a leaf caught in a whirlpool, circling round passively for ages until you are sucked down the hole in a rush. You can't afford to leave everything to chance. You need to work out exactly what has to be done and exactly how you think you will tackle it. If you do you will improve your performance enormously.

6.1   The nature of the task ahead of you

When you enter the exam you have to be ready to work at peak efficiency. You have three hours to make the best show you can of all the work you have done during the course and during the final revision stages. You cannot afford to waste time dithering, moping, or staring at the ceiling. You have to have a clear plan of attack on the task in front of you. You may not be able to stick to it, and in the end that may not matter. What is important is that you are clear at all times about what you intend to do next.

In order to give a very practical flavour to the discussion, I shall assume as I said earlier, a three-hour exam in which you are asked to answer four questions, selected from, say, twelve; the questions being similar in style to essay questions and all carrying equal marks. I will assume also that you can take them in any order you like, that you can write any notes and jottings in the exam book, so long as you cross them out afterwards, and that you are allowed to have only a dictionary in the way of books.* If your exam is different, you need to find out *how* it differs and make the necessary adjustments to what I suggest below.

6.2   Reading the question paper

The signal that the exam has started is when the invigilator tells you that you can turn the exam paper over. The general appearance of the paper should not be a surprise to you, if you have done your work on the sample paper or past papers. However, you may find it difficult to take in the words at first because you are so keyed up. So, although it might seem sensible to read carefully through the

---

* Some exams allow you to take in course books or even notes, though this is a very doubtful privilege. It is scarcely consistent with the style of high speed work you are doing in an exam to be thumbing through books and notes and reading them. In some subjects it may be reassuring to know that if you need a particular formula you can look it up. However, in essay-based exams you need the ideas in your *head*, where you can think with them, not scattered around you in books. You might imagine it would be reassuring to have your books with you. However, it is just as likely that, if you are the nervous type, you will spend far too much time desperately trying to find things to be sure you have them right. Far better to take the plunge and say to yourself: 'This is it! I have to press on with what is in my head — and hope for the best. If I get some things wrong, so what! It's the *argument* that's important *not* the details from the books.'

whole paper first, you may not be able to do that effectively. It may be better to do something more active to get you moving.

Certainly it is no bad idea to scan quickly through the questions, putting ticks against possible ones and crosses against ones you definitely won't attempt. This will give you a first impression of what is on offer. But don't ponder over every question in detail. Search out the questions you have prepared yourself for. It is a desperate gamble to allow yourself to be deflected from a prepared subject on to an unprepared one, just because of the wording of the questions. Your chosen topic may look more difficult to you simply *because* you know so much about the topic. Other questions may look easier *because* you aren't clued-up enough to realize their full implications. Don't attempt to 'flannel' your way through an unrevised area. You are much more likely to produce a solid answer on one of your prepared topics, even if you feel unhappy with the question.

6.3 How soon to start writing

It may be a good idea to find a question you *know* you are going to attempt and pitch straight into it. If you are inclined to 'freeze up' under pressure, or if your mind tends to 'go blank', then starting some writing can be a good way to get yourself past those opening moments and into action. There is no reason to worry about starting your first question before reading the rest of the paper, if you are sure it is on one of your chosen topics. Many people prefer to scan through the whole paper first, but if it suits you better to jump straight into the swim of things, do it. However, you *will* need to think a bit about the wording of the question and to jot down some notes before starting to write the answer proper.

6.4 The order in which to take the questions

You are allowed to tackle the questions in any order you like, so you may as well follow your own best interests. Some people recommend starting on your very best question, so as to build up your confidence. Others say take your best question second, when you are nicely warmed up and when you are not so likely to be tempted to run wildly over your time allowance for it. In any case, it is a good idea to take your best questions earlier rather than later, to make sure that you have enough time to score well with them, to give you confidence, and to allow you to relax into your stride.

6.5   Examining a question

As with essays, it is an excellent idea to underline the key words in the questions you intend to do. It makes you take a positive approach from the outset, and it focuses your attention on developing an answer to the precise question set, rather than producing a string of vaguely relevant information. The words you underline are the ones you will have to think about carefully in deciding what material you can use and how to organize it (see Chapter 6, Section 2.1 for an illustration of key-word underlining). If you rush into the question and make mistakes about the issues it addresses, you will seriously damage your marks.

6.6   Drawing together material to put into your answer

As soon as you have underlined the key words in the question, the next thing is just to jot down very quickly those sections of the course and topics you think are intended to be used in answering it. Don't worry at first about *how* to use them. Just write words down to reassure yourself that you have enough material to work on. You need whatever concepts, theories, examples and names you can conjure up. (This is where you think back to the summary sheets you produced from your condensed notes.) When you have a brief preliminary list (it may contain only five to ten words), you can begin to sort out what to use and what to leave out. The point to hold in mind is that exam questions are *always* asking for material from the course, so you need to write down a few headings and names from the course *before* you start taxing your mind with working out your plan of attack on the question. Once you are grappling with the challenge of constructing an effective answer to the question, your mind will be fully occupied. You will then be in danger of suddenly discovering that an important aspect of the argument has completely slipped from your mind. A single word is usually enough to trigger your memory and enable you to retrieve the point. Work fast and uncritically to get your list of potential material and don't hesitate to make a mess of your exam booklet. You can cross out all your jottings later.

6.7   Strike a balance between what you know and what the question asks for

As you answer a question, you have to steer a course between two equally dangerous traps. One is that you will become so mesmerized by the abstract and challenging nature of the question that you will lose confidence in the fact that the answer to it lies in the course material. The danger here is that you will stop believing that if you search properly you will find the material you need amongst all that you have stored in your head; that you will feel drawn instead to blustering your way through, trying to answer 'off the top of your head'. The opposite danger is that your mind will become so fixed upon all the material you have recently stored in it that you will not be able to resist the urge to spill your knowledge out all over the pages of the exam booklet, regardless of the specific question you are answering. Both these are very easy traps to fall into. The approach to tackling the questions which I have set out here is deliberately designed to try to play these two temptations off against each other.

What I propose is that you move back and forth between the question and the knowledge stored in your mind. In this way you can make sure that each has due influence upon the other. In other words, you choose the question and do a quick 'first take' on what it is about. Then you leave the question and go to your knowledge of the course to jot down some possible content. Then you return to the question to get it more sharply focused in your mind. Then you go back to the preliminary list of course material to knock it into the shape you need. And finally, with a quick look back at the question, you start answering it in a way which brings the two together (see Figure 7.2).

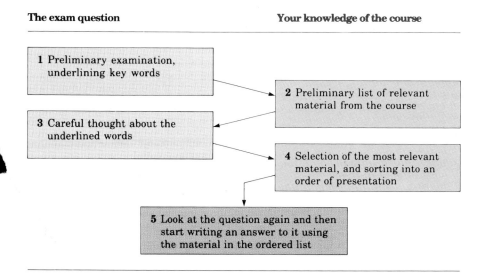

The exam question   **Your knowledge of the course**

1 Preliminary examination, underlining key words

2 Preliminary list of relevant material from the course

3 Careful thought about the underlined words

4 Selection of the most relevant material, and sorting into an order of presentation

5 Look at the question again and then start writing an answer to it using the material in the ordered list

Figure 7.2 Five steps in preparing an answer to an exam question

233

6.8   Taking time to plan your answer

These preparations for your answers sound very well — but will you have time to spare for such refinements. It takes a lot of nerve to spend precious time in the exam preparing your answers. But bearing in mind the comments of examiners on 'undisciplined' answers, it is time very well spent. Of course, you will have to carry out your preparatory activities at high speed. So how long should you spend? In the end this is something you will have to judge for yourself, but between five and ten minutes is a reasonable target. If you don't sketch out a plan, you will run the risk of 'going blank' in the middle of an answer.* Expressing your arguments in writing tends to absorb the whole of your attention. Then, when you get to the end of a paragraph and reach for the next point, it's gone. The argument jerks to a halt and you are too keyed up to retrace your plans. At this point you will waste far more time than writing a plan would have done, scratching about desperately for scraps to flesh out the rest of your answer.

6.9   Sticking to the point

In your enthusiasm to show your knowledge of the course, don't forget the importance of keeping to the question. It irritates exam markers, who are searching for points which relate directly to the question, to have to wade through paragraphs of unsorted and uncensored material. You begin to *lose* marks rather than *gain* them if you give the impression that you are uncritically throwing course material before the examiners' eyes in the hope that you will fool them into thinking you know what you are talking about. Similarly, you need to be a little careful about 'name-dropping'. Of course, you must make sure to draw in plenty of material, including names and so on, from the course, but you must always do it with a clear purpose, so as to avoid appearing to be 'padding-out' your answers, or flannelling to conceal your ignorance. Everything you write should have a clear relevance to the question. Anything else is just wasting your time.

---

* I thought of showing a sample of a sketched outline, such as you might produce in an exam, so that you could see just how very brief and scrappy they can be. But I found it impossible to construct anything that would be meaningful without knowing the course you are studying. You will need to work with your tutor and fellow-students to form an idea of what you should be aiming for.

6.10 When to plan your later questions

When you have your first question under your belt, it is a good idea to 'rough out' plans for all of your other three answers, before writing out your second answer. The reason for this is that you need time on your side when you are planning. It is very hard to think straight in the final stages of the exam, as you become aware of the approaching deadline. All too often a last answer represents the desperate casting about of a mind which has long passed beyond the stage of thinking in a coherent way about such broad issues as the relationship of a question to the course content. *You will probably be able to write at your fastest during the last hour of the exam* provided you know what you intend to say. So do the thinking which requires calmer analysis in the second quarter of the exam, when you have passed through the initial tension and have settled into a steady working mode. Then you will be in a position to take advantage of your 'manic' energy in the later stages to get reams of useful material down.

6.11 Drawing up a 'time plan'

With time at a premium, it is important to be realistic and think clearly about how you are going to use it. To assist with this you can draw up a plan of how, ideally, you would hope to use the time in the exam. Figure 7.3 shows one possible version.

Time

10:00   Turn over the paper and glance through it, marking the questions you
        think you might attempt. (5 mins)

10:05   Start planning your first answer. Underline key words in the question.
        Jot down relevant course material. Return to the question and work
        out a plan. (10 mins)

10:15   Start writing out your first answer. (35 mins)

10:50   Finish the first answer and plan out the other three. (25 mins, i.e. 3 x 8.3 mins)

11:15   Write out the second answer. (35 mins)

11:50   Write out the third answer. (35 mins)

12:25   Write out the fourth answer. (35 mins)

13:00   Finish

Figure 7.3 *Sample time plan for a three-hour exam*

This is, of course, a very idealized plan. You wouldn't be able to stick to it exactly. In fact you would certainly have to modify it as you went along in the exam. Moreover, other people might suggest different allocations of time.* But it is not important whether *this* is the 'best' possible plan. What *is* important is that *you* draw up your *own* plan, so that you have a clear idea of how you intend to use the time.

If you find that you are falling behind schedule as you answer a question, draw the answer to a close as quickly as you can. Don't leave the question half finished in the hope that you will have time to come back to it. Most likely you won't, since you are running late. But, more importantly, by then you will have lost the train of thought. Make the best of a bad job and write out whatever conclusions you can manage to draw while the question is still hot in your mind.

6.12   What to do if your time runs out

If, in spite of all your plans, you do end up with too little time for your last question, it will help to write out some notes showing how your answer would have developed if you had time. If you present an answer *entirely* in note form, you are unlikely to scrape a pass. However, if you have *part* of an answer already written out, then some clearly written notes indicating where you intended to go might convince the marker that you are worthy of a reasonable mark. But it would scarcely be fair on the other candidates to allow you the benefit of the extra time you spent on the earlier questions *and* a generous benefit of the doubt on an uncompleted question. The marker will probably give you *some* credit for good notes, but basically you need to write out an answer in full to be safely in the running for a reasonable mark. So make sure you *don't* run out of time!

6.13   Presentation

Most people write less tidily and legibly than their best in an exam. But do try to do the best you can to make your work legible. Start each question on a new page and number the questions clearly. Draw a line across the page between your jottings and the essay itself. If

---

* For example, some would advocate leaving time for checking through at the end (though, in my own experience, given the high-energy state I am in as I complete the frantic scribbling out of my final answer, I find it very hard to read with close concentration — and in any case I have little stomach for looking back over what I am afraid might turn out to be nonsense if I looked closely).

your handwriting or your command of written English are poor, it is too late to worry. You can't do much to change your basic style of expression or your handwriting at short notice. You can only work to improve them gradually over your years of study. On the other hand, try to remember your reader a little as you write and avoid being so overwhelmed by the need for speed that your writing descends to a desperate scrawl.

KEY POINTS

Practical tips for the exam itself

▶ Scan through the paper finding the questions you have prepared for.

▶ Start writing soon, if it helps to 'unfreeze' you.

▶ Take your best question first (or second).

▶ As you tackle a question:
  - examine the wording carefully
  - very quickly list some relevant points from the course
  - move back and forth between the question and your list as you sketch an outline plan for your answer
  - take the time to plan your answer before you start writing
  - everything you write should be relevant to the specific question asked.

▶ Consider planning later questions in advance.

▶ Draw up a time plan for the exam.

▶ Don't run wildly over your deadlines.

▶ Do your best to write legibly.

---

7 Will you do as well as you ought in the exam?

Of *course* you ought to pass the exam (assuming you have been getting on all right with the course itself). Really you should do about as well in the exam as you have been doing with the course itself. In principle, the exam is just another way of confirming what your work during the course has already shown. But although this is more or less how things turn out for many people, it is not so in all cases. After all, there are at least four possibilities:

1 Some people do *better* in exams than in their course work. Exams actually bring out the best in some people. Perhaps *you* are one of

237

these (or could become one with the right approach to exams).

2 Many people do just about *as well* in the exam as in their course work. This is obviously fine and as it should be.

3 Some people tend to perform *somewhat less well* than their course work suggests they should (scoring say 10 to 20 per cent lower). They pass, but at a lower level than they had reasonably hoped. *If you are one of these people, then this chapter is especially for you.* Read it regularly every year as you start the revision period and remind yourself of all the very practical things you can do to get a better performance out of yourself.

4 A very few people have a tendency to come crashing down way below their potential in exams. If you are one of them, then I hope this chapter has been helpful, but I would strongly recommend that you also try to *talk* to someone about exams and get direct support and advice. There is no point in struggling on your own if you persistently ruin your good work when it comes to exams.

Whichever of these categories you think you fall into, however, you have nothing to lose by thinking positively. *Of course* you deserve to pass. You will leave things out in the exam, but so will everyone else. Your exam answers won't look as impressive as your essays, but the same is true for all the others. Your four scrambled forty minutes' worth of answers are only going to be compared with other scrappy efforts. So don't let the exam intimidate you. *Be realistic!* You are *likely* to pass. Yes it *is* a chore. Yes you *will* have to focus a lot of attention and energy on it. But you *will* also learn a lot in the process. And if you follow all the suggestions in this chapter, you *can* make yourself into a superbly efficient exam *performer*, achieving feats way beyond your normal everyday powers. Who knows, perhaps the exam might turn out to be the highlight of your course after all.

Postscript

You have reached the end of the book. But of course you have not reached the end of the process of becoming a better student. That process will never end. Indeed, there will be times when you slip backwards. Just when you think you have your note-taking technique sorted out into a smoothly functioning routine you will find that it has become too mechanical; that you are taking too many notes, or not the right notes; or you will run into a book that defeats your routine. Just when you are beginning to think that you have 'cracked it' with writing, you will come to an essay that somehow won't come right, or a tutor who criticizes the very things you thought you were good at. At all these times when your studies take an unexpected turn and knock you back, you will find it useful to be able to come back to this book and return to basic principles. What is more, many things which you have taken in at one level will acquire a different significance as you proceed further into your studies. When you then come back to the book afresh you will find you can extract another range of meanings built upon your new levels of experience as a student. So don't set this book aside for ever. Keep it where you will be able to find it, when you need it again. Learning to study is a lifelong process.

Spend, spend, spend

Carl Gardner on the life of a "shopping junkie"

1 A new upmarket shopping centre has just opened in London's Kings
Road. It is done out in angular, 'raw tech' , neo-constructivist style by
Crighton Design, with a giant 'drawbridge' spanning the central space. It is
only the latest — and as befits Chelsea, the most sophisticated — of a
clutch of new or refurbished shopping centres which opened across the
country in October and November. Liverpool, Bath, Nottingham,
Rotherhithe and Guildford — five distinctive new centres for five widely
divergent markets. Over 30 more are in the pipeline for 1989 and 1990.

2 Though varied in size and style, nearly all centres offer the same basic
features. Most importantly, there are spectacularly engineered glass atria or
glazed barrel-vaults to flood the shops and walkways with natural light.
Plants and trees by the forestfull are being used too, and many of the
shopping centres are finished in polished steel with mirrored walls and
marble or terrazzo flooring. For winter and night-time use, they bristle
with the latest in high-tech lighting — massive heating and air-conditioning
systems provide perfect environmental control. Those on several floors
generally have opened-sided escalators, or glass-sided, wall-rising lifts to
give customers a short scenic ride. And many have incorporated centrally
located 'food courts', offering a range of 'eating experiences' where
customers can sit and eat. More importantly, it's a vantage-point from
which they can see and be seen, an essential element of the unashamedly
voyeuristic shopping centre culture.

3 All this investment reflects one central fact — that the retail sector of
the British economy is its most dynamic component, and has been growing
at an enormous rate during the eighties. Retail space alone increased by 50
per cent between 1980 and 1987 and investment in new palatial shopping-
centres and stylish retail-chains to fill them — such as Next, Tie Rack,
Body Shop and hosts of others — has been ever-upward.

4 Then there are the numerous refurbishments and rebuilds underway,
both of existing, slab-like sixties' and seventies' city-centre malls, as well as
the ageing departmental dinosaurs of the business. We've already seen
Debenhams and BHS completely remodelled, at the hands of Ralph
Halpern and Terence Conran respectively — now more famous, traditional
department stores are getting in on the act. Barkers of Kensington, for
example, completes its overhaul this month and Whiteleys in Queensway
will be born afresh next spring.

5 But we're not just talking numbers here. The eighties has also seen an
enormous growth in sophistication in both marketing techniques and retail
design. One recent estimate of the value of the burgeoning British design
business posited a figure of £1.7 billion, the largest part of which —
graphics and interior design — is undoubtedly retail-related. Design giants

like Fitch & Co, McColl, Michael Peters and Conran Design, now have staffs of hundreds, and turnovers in the millions. They have been mainly responsible for the rapid and restless turnover of new images and interior styles which the retail business now demands.

6 At the same time as the increase in the retail floor area, spending has followed suit with a 76 per cent rise in retail sales in the years 1980–87. But as well as spending money, the British are spending much more time shopping. Retail growth has restructured leisure-patterns — shopping centres, in particular, have become new sites of pleasure. Warm, clean, colourful and fashionable, they offer a range of satisfactions for adults and children alike. The cold, windy, dangerous football terrace can hardly compete. Weekend shopping trips are now likely to fill a whole Saturday, rather than half a day, as was customary 10 or 15 years ago. According to recent surveys, the British now regard shopping as their favourite leisure activity, after holidays and television. What once was seen as a domestic chore, is now a pleasure.

7 This 'leisure' element has been reflected in several ways. Firstly, in the growth of themed interior designs, such as those at the country's largest centre, the Metro on Tyneside, which has a section done out as an ersatz Roman Forum, complete with statuary pediments, columns, mosaic floors and period murals. Trading on the British penchant for the package holiday, a fake 'Mediterranean village' is to follow in 1989 (pity about the Newcastle weather!). Then there's an increasing tendency to combine retail facilities with sports and cultural venues (such as the Coppergate Centre in York, next to the Jorvik Viking Museum). And if that doesn't work, there's the integration of leisure features proper within retail schemes, from street-theatre à la Covent Garden, through to restaurants and cinema complexes or even small covered 'pleasure parks', as with the Metro Centre's Metroland feature.

8 The 'retailisation' of Britain, the evident desire of the British to 'spend, spend, spend', presents several problems, and not just for Nigel Lawson. Socialist theory, fixated as it has been on production as the 'progressive' moment in the capitalist cycle, find shopping difficult to handle. For 150 years it's been a case of production = good, consumption = bad. According to the theory, commodities produced under 'alienated' capitalist labour conditions can't possibly offer satisfaction, only further misery.

9 To understand the cultural, social and psychic shifts that are taking place, it's not sufficient simply to denounce the retail boom as a cultural deviation or an economic time-bomb; nor to trot out some broad all-embracing truism about post-industrial culture. It's far more important to draw up a balance-sheet of both the positive and negative features of the boom — and to begin to come to grips with the underlying processes, the shifting web of desires and needs that make people look 'to the retail experience' as a major site of gratification.

10 But first, we have to dispense with the theoretical cornerstone of most left analysis of popular consumption, particularly that of a post-Frankfurt variety — the notion of 'manipulation'. Using this model, marketing and retail designs are seen as one giant conspiratorial con-trick on the part of capital, to sell more commodities and keep the system ticking over. The desire to consume is seen as an erroneous need offering delusory pleasures and satisfactions. This is shopping as a form of disease, with shoppers reduced to mere helpless victims. It's an argument which shows a sinister contempt for the way most people live.

11 A more coherent line of attack on the retail boom (though he stresses his position is not anti-shopping *per se*) is that mounted by Ken Worpole, co-author of *Trade Winds* (South East Economic Development strategy document). In a *Guardian* article last year (16 September 1987) he constructed a new demonology: both city centre and out-of-town retail schemes are, he argued, destroying our urban fabric, intensifying antagonisms between the haves and have-nots and catalysing crime. In short, retail developments of all kinds 'pose tremendous danger to the quality of civic life'.

12 There are several problems with Worpole's analysis. Many of his remarks on city centre schemes seemed curiously out of date and referred back to the old, monolithic malls of earlier decades. And the 'death of the high street', due to out-of-town schemes, has been predicted endlessly for the past decade or more. Yet most continue to thrive — Liverpool city centre, for example, with its two shopping centres and pedestrianised streets, is a vast improvement on the traffic-riddled hell of 10 years ago. One has to ask serious questions about the rather romantic evocation of 'civic life' pre-retail boom — in many cities and towns it's something which hasn't had any significant existence since the early fifties.

13 At one level it is possible to see many shopping-centres reclaim some of the functions of medieval market-places, or town squares and boulevards in southern Mediterranean cultures — in other words spaces not simply to buy and sell, but to promenade, meet, sit and enter into other forms of social exchange.

14 Certainly observation of the way people use shopping centres would seem to confirm such a role. This may not be their intended function, but in Britain's climate, their covered, weather-proof environment makes them eminently more suitable candidates for such an unofficial, informal role than open streets. The gradual tendency for longer shopping hours — and the inevitable arrival of Sunday trading — can only deepen this trend.

15 Of course, it should be mentioned that the retail boom has relied overwhelmingly on low-paid female labour often working long and anti-social hours. But it's unfortunate that the short-sightedness of both the Labour Party and the unions has resulted in a strategy to restrict opening hours and oppose Sunday trading. Once again sectional Labour interests are pitted against the legitimate rights and needs of the mass of consumers.

16 In fact, the experience of retail developments over the past decade has done much to improve the quality of the public environment. Out-of-town developments have forced councils and retailers to improve the facilities and condition of run-down city centre high streets — and many new city centre and edge-of-town schemes are both architecturally sensitive to the existing urban fabric, and possess environmentally pleasing interiors.

17 Perhaps one of the major attractions of the 'retail experience' is not so much the art of purchase itself, but the validation that modern retail institutions offer the customer, at least in environmental terms. For an urban populace brought up in mediocre housing located in dreary, poorly designed cities and towns, the quality of the environment, the use of 'luxurious' materials, the originality of design and the sense of space offered by today's shopping centres — and many individual shops within them — is a source of both excitement and gratification. Architectural excellence and attention to design are attractions that in general haven't been offered to most people either by home, school, hospital or any other civic institution.

18 But there are perhaps other factors helping to create Britain's retail culture. One was the experience of seventies inflation, which finally broke most people's conservative conviction that saving was better than spending. Then along came the easy availability of credit, and the final link was broken between money and commodities on the one hand, and wages and work on the other.

19 At the same time high unemployment in the early eighties shifted the stakes. Consumption became a defiant form of celebration, positive evidence that you were still part of the dominant culture, that you hadn't been marginalised — what mattered was not what you bought, only *that* you bought. Buying power itself became the real buzz.

20 None of this is to deny the real problems with the 'retail revolution' as it has currently developed. I agree with Worpole that, particularly as we reach 'saturation point' in retail developments, solutions must lie in more consultative planning and a careful social audit of the total effects of the new schemes together with an uplift in the status of retail work itself.

21 But, perhaps, long before then, Nigel Lawson's nemesis will have transformed the scene utterly. Even before the last trade figures were announced, forecasts pointed to a retail growth of only 1–1.5 per cent in the coming year. After the Christmas spree, higher interest rates could reduce retail spending still further, and many commentators see the eighties retail boom turning rapidly to slump. It may have been fun while it lasted, but the 'shopping junkies' amongst us could soon have to face a rather painful withdrawal.

16 December 1988

Index

Page references for discussion boxes are indicated by 'D', and those for footnotes by 'n'. Page references to illustrations are given in italic type.